THE ESSENTIAL SOCIAL CURRICULUM

MR. TOM W. GROVE

Copyright 2013 by Mr. Tom W. Grove

All rights reserved. Parts of this book may be reproduced or used with permission and citation given to and by the author, for the express use for training or other educational situations. Whole chapters may not be reproduced or used in any form or by any means, electronic, mechanical, photocopying, and recording or by any storage and retrieval system without permission from the publisher.

Internet addresses are intended as resources and do not constitute endorsement. The author and publisher are not responsible for the content or reliability of these sites.

Printed by Createspace.com

Library of Congress Card Catalog Number: Pending

ISBN: 0615778267

ISBN-13: 9780615778266

Library of Congress Control Number: 2013903978
tom grove llc, Champaign, IL

Printed in the United States

First Printing: March 2013

Contents

Introduction	v
The BIG Picture	1
Dancing with The Essential Questions	12
The Essential Questions	24
Precision in the Social Curriculum	54
Precision with Reinforcement: Olympic Training	62
Prelude to Management and Consequencing	76
Managing Problems versus Driving Values	80
Value-Driven Consequencing	87
Building a Reflective, Conscious Mind	110
The Value Driven Classroom	114
References and Resources	137

Introduction

All the glory for this work goes to God. He has blessed me with joy, much help, and many moments beyond coincidence. He routinely has put me in the right place at the right time. I have been there for teachers' worst and greatest moments, but always the right moments. I have several hundred children that care for me, and I for them. I have seen lives dramatically changed from destruction. The depth of wisdom and resiliency of students continues to delight me. Their immediate awareness of being loved and respected, of when they are being seen and heard as people with dignity renews me. They stop, listen, begin to trust, and to hope. I have several hundred children who love to write, read, do math, draw, sing, dance, and yak like crazy with friends. They, and I through their experiences, get discovery and amazement in practically everything all day. I watch them learn to love and be loved, to be generous, conscientious, compassionate, and wiser with life. I watch tremendously dedicated teachers change lives and instill never-to-be-forgotten moments into the course of a life that will touch many other lives for years and years. School is like having the greatest stories ever told lived out all at once day after day.

Although some students and staff come to school challenged by life and a lack of hope, I admire and value their willing spirit and tenacity to show up seeking greater life and hope. There are many teachers I know who are more than a soldier: they are warriors in life. Staff may be under so many demands and faced with so many personal and school problems that they are ready to walk out. The students may be hungry, barely parented, serially parented by substitute caregivers, uncertain, unattached, angry, hopeless, on edge, and living one moment to the next. Across the country, schools are seeing an increase in students needing social and mental health services. One district I work in has the highest rates of child abuse and neglect of any rural county in the state. Too many children do not recognize or trust the caring they receive at school.

What is school to these children—to any child? For what do they think they are coming? What do they need if they have to be there about seven hours daily? What do they tell us they want? I ask around, and what I hear back is uncomplicated yet something that schools can have a hard time delivering. Here are some of the things students tell me.

I want people to see me as a good person. I want to be greeted kindly and talked to calmly. I want teachers not to have an attitude toward me and see me as able to learn. I want to learn to stay focused, have an adult who believes in me, to feel my voice is heard, and to have fun at parties. I want help getting materials. I want to have a way to express regret and remorse. I want to have snacks. I want more help from teachers, more time to talk with my teachers, and to be safe from people giving me a hard time.

One student wrote, "I knew I wasn't going to make it in class today, so I just walked out." They need all the confidence and love we can give them. Some high school students said the counselors are only interested in the students going to college and the special education students. They also say they need more guidance and meaningful connection between school and life. "We get grades on tests. But we have little idea how we are doing in life." They do not feel they are being set up for success in the future or even what their future options are. How can school feel purposeful and relevant to them? How can school be something for them in which they can invest their best?

To create the best environment possible for students, staff, and the school in general has been my goal. What are the most effective, efficient, fruitful ways to have a school of peace, joy, learning, confidence, courage, and love? I have spent almost a decade in schools to find out, to make it happen, and to see what else is possible. With the help of some fantastic administrators, friends, teachers, and students, I have been able to test out, flesh out, and dream. I am fully convinced that what I offer here creates the school culture and climate students and staff need to attain peace, joy, aspiring learners, and confident, hopeful citizens. When it is all in place, it is not just phenomenal. It is supernatural, inspiring, deeply moving school. It is breathtaking. It is transmogrifying.

There are many people to thank, that I deeply appreciate and admire, that have seen the vision and helped it happen; Superintendent Dr. Judy Wiegand, Orlando Thomas, Dr. Susan Zola, Trudy Walters, Cheryl O'Leary, Jim Eastin, and the staff of Garden Hills Elementary in Champaign Unit Four. I am also grateful to Superintendent Mark Denman, Assistant Superintendent Dianna Kirk, Kimberly Pabst, Cindy Smith and the staff at Cannon Elementary, Tracy Cherry and The Kenneth E. Bailey Academy staff, Jason Bletzinger, Kim Norton, and many others in Danville 118 Schools.

I am grateful for all the administrators and many teachers in Champaign Unit 4, Danville 118, and Naperville 203 who had me in their classrooms and the tremendous daily devotion they show to students and their profession. I especially want to mention: Mi'Chelle Frazer, Betty Rowell, Abby Crull, Adrian Taylor, Mitzi Campbell, Priscilla Kennedy, Nancy Baird, Maria Burt, Dominique McCotter, LaQuanna Sparkman, Ellen Baranowski, Brian Rosten, Denise Pacey, Brian Allen, Kerrylynn Humphrey, Kristi Townsend, Brandon Rutherford, Juli Norcross, Carol Latina, Erin Olinger, Dominica Aguilera, Sean Morrison, Kendal Huffman, Leigh Ann Borkowski, and the ultimate power trio of Mr. Cravens, Ms. Golden, and Ms. Cosat. Many times you left me speechless as you brought light to the dark and troubled hearts of so many, and more brilliant light to those glowing already. You never stop, and no one is spared your unfailing love and joy.

CHAPTER ONE
The Big Picture

I want you and your students to have abundant joy and peace in all that you do within the constantly churning behemoth called school. That has become a bigger challenge over the past decade as more and more people within schools tell me the same thing. "I have no framework for these children." There have been significant changes in the daily practice of education. Who is coming to school has changed, who is teaching school has changed, the functions of school in society have changed, and demands upon schools have changed. There is not a lot new in the academic curriculum, but there have been massive shifts in the social curriculum. In other words, the "what" of education is pretty much the same—math, reading, writing, science, arts, physical education, and so on. The "how" of education screams for changes about how to run a classroom, create order, manage children, end disparity, reduce problems, and create zealous learners. In the main, I see the primary task of the classroom teacher not as shoving more information into students, but creating students that want to learn more and more.

I have spent almost a decade in schools studying and experimenting with the "how," the social curriculum, and have a framework that I see working across numerous schools at every level. Based on basic human neurology and psychology that has held true for decades, the fundamental needs of people, in general, and children, in particular, have not changed. Yet there are additional needs, more demands, and there are more students with intense needs. My life and yours probably attest to that. I do not think a canned behavior management program, a new chart, more punishments, more reminders to behave, more special parties (if I'm good or lucky), or even more rewards will solve my needs. What I need, have always needed, and will continue to need, is peace, joy, love, truth, integrity, devotion, connection, and value to or with someone else. I need to be so valuable and so worthy of dignity that I am redeemed and restored. I do not need some *thing* that is real. I need someone real and someone who is after my best. Positives are not enough, discipline strategies are not enough, and knowledge is not enough.

The social curriculum of education has to teach and instill love, truth, dignity, value, peace, and joy in every student. Anything less makes us bystanders to their life. We then become people that students cannot truly love or respect back. I have met thousands of students. Each one of them is looking for love, truth, integrity, peace, joy, and someone to be fully experienced by — to be emotionally attuned to or tuned in with. Not as a buddy or pal, not as a good cog in the wheel, not even understood, but as someone significant, enjoyable, meaningful, lovable, and felt within another human being. Some have given up actively looking. They are found in kindergarten classes, in high schools, teacher lounges, churches, and everywhere in between. The social curriculum of education is rarely teaching what matters most to our heart, our spirit, and our brains in a real way. If it is, it is often too weak and diluted to take most students beyond the level of emotional hunger and striving they bring to us. Achievement suffers and social problems persist as the spirit of students hungers for more and strives harder. Many students and staff remain unfilled with what they need in their spirit, despite implementing the latest behavior program or incentive package.

If we are not clearly communicating to students that they are inspiring to us, what should we expect in return? I think we should expect payback. We tell them education is vital and going to make them so happy in life. Then we teach them that they are not so thrilling. If we are always stopping for problems but not for their excellence as a person, what should we expect? I think we should expect them not to see our positive intentions or excellence either. We need to be so inspired by students that we just have to stop and talk about them in detail. In the majority of classrooms, I initially experience little that is inspiring. I sat for forty-five minutes in a classroom where the only encouraging words were " — "very nice" and those were said once. The teacher filled the rest of the time with lesson and procedure. I hear many statements like "I'm glad you remembered to raise your hand" or "Good job" that says little about students as people. How in the world can we raise up aspiring learners and citizens when that is all students are recognized for? The teacher is glad, what I did is a good job, but who am I? Can we expect students to be aspiring, inspired people and learners on such a paltry diet of teacher feedback? Can you sustain a dating relationship discussing how happy you are when he/she raises their hand to speak or walks safely in buildings? When your date asks if you feel like seeing more of each other, make their heart soar with "Sure, you did a good job." If that does not sweep them off their feet, tell them you have put their name on a list of possible winners, but they will not know if they have won a prize until Friday. Just pour the love and joy on them. The need for fulfilling connections and hope is enormous. If we are not inspired to actually stop and give love and dignity to students, who will?

In most kindergarten classes, there have been students who will tell me their teacher "Is the best mommy I ever had!" Other students cling to me and ask if I will be their daddy, even though we were in the same room for only twenty minutes. In these same classrooms, there are students who are two months into the year and still calling out, "Teacher lady." Neither does the student know the names of peers. They do not seek adult help when hurt and they wander about in anxious attempts to soothe themselves. These examples happen repeatedly wherever I travel.

There are many lost and angry fourth and fifth graders blowing up at the slightest threat that are far, far behind academically. They try but give up quickly. They have few skills to negotiate the social network they have to attend five days a week. So consumed with the social issues they rarely get to the academic issues. They are so far behind, and know it, that they avoid exposing themselves to further academic embarrassment with a variety of tactics.

In middle and high schools, I have watched students struggle to connect to anyone in any way possible or who have given up on any possible connections, and given up on trying to learn. I see teachers on their heels—afraid—while trying to engage and motivate a student as a pseudo friend, pseudo authority. I have met high school students who excel at academics and who, already accepted to a college, are afraid that their chosen profession will be obsolete by graduation and have little idea who they really are as a person. The teachers strive, the students strive, and many search.

Grounded in basic human nature, psychology, and physiology, *The Essential Social Curriculum* is a framework of hope for these students and everyone. Even if your class climate and culture are wonderful, you can use *The Essential Social Curriculum* to take it to greater heights of social and academic excellence because everyone has the framework in common.

The good news is that students still flock to the "good stuff." A high school teacher doubled her class enrollment because, in the words of her students, "She doesn't hold grudges over us, and really wants us to pass. She doesn't say if you need help let me know, she is there to help us." Students line up to hear about their good qualities from her. This teacher passionately engages with the students and extends hope to them, in contrast to others who decide students are "done." She holds a high bar on truth, love, and integrity. She is ruthlessly caring about what they need to keep, grow, and stop as people. Students need a lot of truth, a high bar, and sincere caring.

All my experience in schools by 2007 went into "*The Inner Wealth Initiative* which I wrote with Howard Glasser. However, I have been on a quest. Here is that quest six years later and continuing. I have rediscovered prior masters, found exciting new perspectives, and grounded what I am doing in research. Here, you will read about fundamental processes and characteristics of being human. We will focus on love, attachment, brain research, behaviorism, and communication as they shape all we do. My quest has taken me to ways of translating these forces into action for us to use immediately.

I have recently heard more administrators saying something like, "If you don't love teaching you need to reflect on why you keep teaching." That is certainly worth doing. Whether you love it or not, my thought is, "If you aren't teaching love, you are teaching something else." I know teachers fed up with all the demands of "teaching," teaching without contracts, working in ugly worn out buildings, but they are there to teach love to the students. This is the foundation of *The Essential Social Curriculum*.

Consider the words of prominent social researcher Kurt Lewin from 1943: "It is common knowledge that the success of the teacher of French depends as much on the social atmosphere he (or she) creates as on his (or her) mastering the French language or the laws of learning. Probably in no country have the schools been as much more aware of the importance of group management as in the United States." (Lewin, 1951)

Are we better off in 2013 than in 1943? We have the technology, we have hundreds of academic curriculums, and an army of teachers on the frontlines already. The struggle is with the social curriculum.

Jump ahead to 1991 and John Lounsbury's *As I See It* from National Middle School Association Press: "The school will have to concern itself even more with those social and psychological factors that largely control the ability or readiness to achieve academically. As middle school teachers, we cannot evade the responsibility that is inherent in our personal example and we should not try to. It is the hidden curriculum what occurs around the mandated curriculum that teaches them who they are and what life is like."

What is your personal example teaching your students? It is always teaching who we are, whom others are, what life is like, how you and I fit in, and what life can be. Do we look forward to joy or sarcasm? Who belongs and who is out? Who has value? Who doesn't? What is a problem? What isn't? Who cares and what is caring? How long before helping a student becomes a waste of time? Who will make it? In your mind, who has already failed and won't have a future worth living? There are many more beliefs, expectations, and decision points of which we need to be fully conscious and aware. They form our personal example, an example we can never turn off. It is always fully on. It teaches a lesson all day long. One person, you—can make all the difference. That is a research fact. Just one good secure attachment at any time of life can change a life. You are that life changer; this book provides your framework.

There are hundreds of social curriculums in canned formats. It is good to have a plan when you go to war. We are waging a war to save our schools. It seems a complicated war with many fronts, yet from the student perspective, it seems clear. Students tell us they are there to be loved, forgiven, redeemed, needed, wanted, sought after, believed in, worthy, connected, and are desperately striving to obtain any of these. Sometimes they tell us in ugly, harsh ways. Thank goodness they have not given up and still seek and ask. The solution does not come from a can. It comes from dynamic relationship with self and others. This is human nature.

In his 1969 book, *Schools Without Failure* William Glasser M.D. wrote many prophetic warnings, and this:

> Teachers are overwhelmed with students who need affection, but at present do not know how to react to the obvious need for love of many of their students. To say that helping to fulfill the need for love is not a school function is tantamount to saying that children who don't succeed in giving and receiving desperately needed affection at home or in their community (outside of school) will have little chance to do so. Having failed to learn love as a child, an adult is in a poor position to ever learn. I have offered some suggestion that I hope will return school to its original purpose: to produce a thoughtful, creative, emotionally alive, unafraid man, a man willing to try to solve the problems he faces in the world. Confident that he can build on his success, he may fail for a while, but he will know some success is possible. And when success does not come easily, he will not give up. If he can think, he can relate to his fellow man, if he can appreciate the beauty created by man and nature, he has a chance for happiness and a chance to feel worthwhile. Education can do no more for a man (69).

I assume he meant mankind, and certainly the central message applies to everyone in education. This was true in 1969, and even more so today. We already know that too many homes and communities are not doing well at loving. We must. I am not talking about the gushy permissive over-involved enabling some mistake as love. In this book, I refer to a love that wins wars we fight every day in the classrooms for meaning, hope, trust, joy, and emotional safety. Since it is impossible not to have a social curriculum and impossible not to be a personal example, it is only a matter of choice what your curriculum and personal example will be. If your social curriculum, your personal example, is not love, then it must be something else. Can it include more than love? Absolutely! It just cannot be without it. Am I talking about sappy, squishy, do whatever love? Absolutely not. I am referring to disciplined, agape love that is intentional and forgiving while encouraging others to reach toward higher values of humanity.

School has to teach love and hope. School is often a student's only hope. However, these same students are usually the hardest to reach, to like, and with which to connect. Research indicates that most people try to engage with sad and anxious children, yet generally will seek distance from chronically depressed or angry children. Educators need powerful tools for these children, as well as for themselves because classroom management issues are a significant reason teachers leave the field (Alliance For Education, 2005).

In his 1995 book, *Changing Theories and Practices of Discipline in Schools*, Roger Slee asserts schools must continually and democratically educate themselves and not become "institutions" of a closed society. They must be open systems and responsive to the changing needs of students and society. With this responsiveness, the goal of school is to produce good citizens who have an education, not just educate those already wanting to learn. This is not occurring with significant success. According to Carolyn Bacon Dickson's presentation at the 2006 US Department of Education's No Child Left Behind Summit, a million students drop out of high school each year. Indeed, the percentage of students who fail to complete high school is so high and the lack of true academic progress so low past the eighth grade, there is a consideration of eliminating the final two years of high school. Students are not the only ones dropping out. After three years, around a third of the new teachers have left the field. After five years, almost half of the new teachers have left. Inner city schools have even higher rates of students and teachers leaving (Dickson 2006). According to the Alliance for Excellent Education's "Teacher Attrition: A Costly Loss to the Nation and to the States," the cost of replacing teachers is in the millions of dollars per year. If education ran like a business, it would probably be out of business.

At this point, the greatest predictor of academic success in school is parental income. It used to be parent education, but that correlation has weakened. Minority students and/or students in poverty have the most difficulty succeeding behaviorally and academically at a national level. We know that failing to meet standards at the end of third grade in reading, writing, and math has a high correlation with prison later in life. Education is vital, as essential as food and water for living, yet the system of educating appears unable to get many students or teachers to sit at the table and eat and drink it in.

Still there are schools, high schools at that, producing thriving students with remarkable rates of graduation and academic achievement despite high minority percentages, high poverty, and low funding—all at the same time. Under dynamic leadership, some chronically failing schools thoroughly transform in as little as two years—and against all odds. These schools did not get a new building, megabucks of new technology or materials, or even a lot of new staff. They got a new social curriculum and infused the school with a vision in action. Building and infusing a powerful social curriculum into schools is the subject of this book. This book's objective is to help create schools and students full of peace and joy. It is about teachers being inspired by their students and inspiring students to aspire as learners and citizens. It is about inspiring students to want to be more as a person, and say "Give me more!" as a learner.

The leadership of the principal and the quality of staff makes an immense difference. Family support and approval of a school is helpful. It is crucial curriculum aligns with teaching methods and evaluation of student achievement. Foundational to the success of the school is the quality of instructional support—directly or indirectly—for the instructors, weeding out poor instruction, and propelling the achievement and reputation of the school. Yet the most significant factors are the mood and direction of the school, how clearly everyone feels connected and valued, and the values everyone manifests. My friend Dr. Susan Zola refers to this as the voice of the school. It speaks through everyone and everything all day every day. It constantly "teaches" the school climate and culture. It is the social curriculum of the school. This book articulates and operationalizes this voice so you can coherently send congruent loving and lasting messages that will literally change and guide the lives of everyone. As the elements of the book are so foundational to us as human beings, I call it *The Essential Social Curriculum*.

I derived *The Essential Social Curriculum* from working full time in public schools as a consultant to teachers and administrators. I have observed hundreds of teachers from pre-school on up, seen the ugly and the holy, seen schools break people, and seen others whose school saved their life from certain destruction. I have been in schools where teachers dislike students and do not believe the students can even learn. I have experienced abundantly financed as well as financially poor schools so full of love and joy that everyone can sense it within minutes after entering. My main experience has been with elementary and middle schools with little money and many poor-to-impoverished students. I must say that I am astounded by the dedication, courage, and beautiful love I have seen many teachers manifest day after day. The teachers and children I meet constantly renew and inspire me.

I have never met a child who did not want to be good, valued, loved, and to love others. I have never met a child who did not want to learn. I have met children temporarily blinded, confused, twisted, angry, and out of hope by the lives in which they were born. That does not stop me, or many of the teachers I know, from helping the students see clearly, experience truth, or find peace, joy, and abundant hope.

The primary lesson from school is how to live. Every day of school educators and everyone else in the building teach young minds how to live. You can live as a victim or a victor, in dread and pessimism or joy and hope, or like a robot going through the daily program. *The Essential Social Curriculum* is about dynamic living in schools.

The four main parts of *The Essential Social Curriculum* work together. The first is that of answering The Essential Questions. These questions underlie all the social interaction and relationships we have throughout our lives. They are listed on page 13. If you want a thriving climate and culture, this is the foundation. If you want academic progress, this is the foundation because brains do not learn well when stressed. The sending and receiving of answers to these questions determines the quality of the social curriculum, our learning, our emotional states, our attachments to our selves, to our future, to our life, and to others. We are able to grow, be happy, learn, love, and persevere when our questions have good answers. They form our attachments to self and others. They run through businesses, families, friends, neighborhoods, schools, and board members—all hearts, all minds, in all lives. They are the themes of the ongoing story of our life and relationships with others.

When our questions have unacceptable or poor answers, we are unlikely to learn well, to feel good, or be hopeful. We are unlikely to "behave" well as we are busy striving and defending to get fulfilling answers. When poorly answered, these become our "triggers" and "buttons." It is not as if our primal brain turns off. It is always working. When we have unacceptable or uncertain answers to these questions, we produce a fight-flight-freeze response. We might be sophisticated when we do, but we do. It is our human nature. We all know what it is like to try to do our job when we have strained relationships at home, are in unfortunate situations or are facing challenges with numerous uncertain outcomes. This taps into our Essential Questions. We will, with various levels of sophistication, strive and defend until good answers come. We need to persevere, yet some people give up—even three year olds or neglected newborns. Then again, you may be like Mrs. Lane-Rose who wears a T-shirt that says, "Too blessed to be stressed." Life is a positive journey of regenerating answers since the questions never go away and are always up for grabs. We are constantly looking for and assessing the Essential Questions. They are no less powerful or less intensely felt whether we are one or a hundred years old. Our brain and spirit are constantly on the alert for them.

To congruently answer these questions—implicitly and explicitly through the entire school climate and culture—builds emotional and physical safety, opens minds for learning, increases positive behavior and attitudes, sets the stage for perseverance and growth, and fills everyone with confident hope. Everyone will want to "attach." We have to be intentional and discern the primary questions to answer, but that is usually clear. Once you look and listen, they pop out. The Essential Questions came from listening to students, teachers, parents, people ready to die, sermons, the Bible, movies, news reports, therapy clients, nearly everyone I met, and myself. Listen—really listen—to the checkout clerk you meet or listen to a group of preschoolers chatting. Listen for the questions to unfold.

To answer the questions clearly and powerfully, you need the second main part of *The Essential Social Curriculum*: understanding social reinforcement and attachment. Being positive is not enough. These elements will determine a large part of your success at keeping your climate and culture going forward with utmost efficiency. Social reinforcement and attachment work almost at the edge of our awareness so my goal is to help you be fully conscious and skillful with them.

For a recent assessment on education, read *Forty Years Later – The Value of Praise, Ignoring, and Rules for Preschoolers at Risk for Behavior Disorders*, published in 2009. The authors state that praise, planned ignoring, and classroom rules have withstood the test of time in terms of empirical support. Indeed behavioral psychology has known how to have a powerful impact in classrooms with these strategies since the 1960's. The authors of *Forty Years Later* state these strategies can have positive effects, and "can form the basis of a safe, predictable learning community in which children of varying backgrounds, abilities, and needs can be successful learners." Indeed this is true because these strategies are a pivotal part of building a climate and culture of secure attachment. However, the authors continue:

"Notwithstanding the efficacy of praise, planned ignoring, and classroom rules when effectively implemented, a number of variables that require increased examination remain. For instance, researchers need to delineate and verify the precise attributes of these strategies that are the most essential in increasing and supporting positive teacher-child interactions. Child learning and behavior are embedded in the teacher-child interaction."

Note, the article is from 2009, and still calling for teachers to practice the basic behavior strategies that have been proven for decades to help children learn academically. The authors remind us that students' learning and behaviors are in the teacher-student interactions, not the lesson itself. This is because our personal example is interacting with the personal example of the student through the principles of social reinforcement in a dynamic, not didactic, evolving relationship. To get an idea how these behavioral strategies need to be implemented, consider Beaman and Wheldall (2000) who report that teachers use positive reinforcement strategies with students when addressing academics about eighty percent of their interactions. However, only about twenty percent of the messages teachers gave about behavior were positive. That leaves about eighty percent of interactions with students concerning social behavior as negative social reinforcements. Simply put, these articles are saying the teachers they studied are doing fine using positive social reinforcement with academic behavior, yet rarely use positive reinforcement with social behavior. Thus, teachers using negative social reinforcements increase problem behaviors.

This difference between being positive with the academic not the social, curriculum leads to a common teacher experience. They will say they already are being positive, and they are – with the academic curriculum. Yet they also have numerous classroom management issues due to almost equally high rates of reinforcement of social problems. They spend the day stating "good answer" to academics and "bad answer" to social behavior. This confuses teachers and students because the teachers are positive, yet negative things keep happening. When one understands social reinforcement, it all makes sense and the results are quite predictable.

The third component to *The Essential Social Curriculum* is creating a value-driven classroom. You may think you have a classroom with values because you have a reward program for respect or something else, but these programs usually inadvertently create followers. Follow expectations, follow rules, follow directions, and follow the example of so and so. If you do not follow, you cannot win. In my experience, such programs do not intentionally build up the values within students, and are often devaluing of students. In *The Essential Social Curriculum* a set of values is the center of every moment, the standard for all that happens, and is more valuable than any class rule. The rules are simply good ideas that point to/symbolize the values. In all aspects of classroom relationships and processes, values are driven through, connected to, and upheld. The goal is to create leaders of self, leaders in a community of conscious and conscientious citizens, and value-driven communities that lead themselves. I was in a first-grade class this morning where the teacher was asking the students, "How have you been being your best during independent reading time." In school about three weeks, the students gave solid answers as to how intentionally and eagerly they held themselves to being their best. The class culture centered on being one's best at all times. This component of driving values builds deep, rich internal guidance within students and creates citizens.

You can be praising behavior—what great focus; you sat down right away; thank you for being so quiet in the hallway. This still ties you to behavior and, importantly, just the moment of its occurrence. What I am proposing is that you run everything that is happening in your class and school through very high values over significant spans of time. This provides you with unlimited headroom to grow the values within your climate and culture, scaffold students from within, and invite them to BE someone of high values. This way you can arrive at December with a group of internally driven citizens who thoroughly understand the nuances and benefits of values like patience, kindness, trustworthiness, being a finisher, dedication to your best, and integrity. You can pick your own values. If you are only driving behavior—sit down; quiet in the hall; don't interrupt; get to work; remember the expectations—you will paint yourself in a corner of zero inspiration. Students either do or do not behave. If you attempt to run your classroom by having power over behavior you will probably fail because they—not you—are ultimately in charge of their behavior. Many will be glad to show you they are in charge of their behavior and, with certain Essential Questions, attempt to control yours. In April, you will still be trying to get students to behave. The class may be functional, but not growing in citizenship, emotional maturity, or internal intrinsic motivation. However, if you go for the spirit of the rules and not the behavioral rule itself, you can build and deepen values in the students and school from September to June. It makes a world of difference and hopefully a different world!

The fourth component to *The Essential Social Curriculum* restores students, along with the climate and culture, when there are violations, breaks, or drops in the values. When problems occur, there is action to repair, restore, and redeem the emotional well-being and dignity of everyone affected. The consequences require time and energy, but do not damage one's Essential Questions. In fact, the purpose is to add and strengthen answers to the Essential Questions of everyone involved. Traditional consequences in schools are usually what I refer to as "half strict." They nail students for problems, but rarely do they nail students as adamantly, as intentionally, and as often for all the students' best citizenship. Students experience us as seeing part of them, the part they struggle with at that. They also do not then have full integrity or full dignity as a whole person with us and often then treat us as a partial person too. Restoration helps them and us be seen and heal as whole people. How to effectively consequence and easily create consequences that restore the values in to action will be explained. In short, their consequence is to be a contribution to the values of the class/school culture.

When students and staff have their Essential Questions answered well, held to values and restored if they violate the values, the school climate and culture is stunning. In an alternative middle school where these messages are communicated deeply and richly daily, students gained three academic years as a class average within seven months. Attendance was ninety-four percent. Why? Because teachers provided abundant answers to their Essential Questions and filled their spirits. Teachers valued the students at a high level. Teachers had a strong vision for the students and grew that vision daily, creating a culture driven with values (not behavior). The students felt loved, and they were loved. Increasingly they disciplined themselves because they understood and experienced how they benefit from shared values.

However, all of the four components are practically useless if you are simply trying to produce a well-oiled machine of well-behaved minions who come in, do their jobs, and go home. You have to feed dignity as a human being. This is done through the capstone of creating value-driven classrooms and schools. When you drive the class culture with values, order evolves. If you drive the class with order, it becomes increasingly hard to experience the values. It will devolve into a battle over behavior, but the real battle is over worth and dignity. Again, if you only set out to teach a lesson and enforce behavior, you will fail because you cannot make anyone do anything. You can, however, be a captivating invitation.

If you go into schools to look and listen for the social curriculum, you quickly become aware of "the voice of the school." Just like visiting a doctor's office for the first time, you can immediately receive messages about your value, worth, and dignity as well as that of those around you. Consider school as a training ground for how you will fit in society; learning centers for what you can expect in the world; development centers for how students will see others and their own children someday. Through the personal examples of the staff, school teaches lessons on how to deal with social conflict, overcome failure, and emotionally cope. Most of the time, these major lessons are not the main activity or focus of the school. From what I have experienced, educators rarely discuss these issues or they see these issues as the parent's job. However, school cannot help but be teaching these lessons (as you cannot not have a social curriculum). Schools have to own this and be conscious and intentional about the messages exchanged every minute of every day. The gifted students I have seen over the years still need reassurance they are: seen, heard, good, belong, lovable and likeable, and can hope. From the beginning and in the end, it is the personal example, the Essential Questions, and the values that a person holds that helps determine joy and success in life.

Some teachers and administrators argue for a model where we need to prepare students for "real life." Does the law against speeding and speeding tickets keep you from speeding? If you got a ticket, have you never pushed over the speed limit again? Our values justify our speeding and, if caught, we might start playing Essential Question cards to escape hopefully with just a warning and not pay an actual price. Our students are not so different, yet we can get pretty demanding and threatening if students do not respect OUR authority and "pay the price" of their actions. If a police officer acted in a similar fashion, we would want their badge number and cry foul. We get a warning for speeding or get a lawyer to get us out of a ticket, then go teach the next day and ream students about how "real life" is going to smack them upside the head. Mostly I see that approach as one of appealing to some future authority (hard life) and hoping fear of that authority will help the students shape up today. The teacher has thrown his or her own authority out the window. The authority tossed out the window was the authority to fill the students with life that day, to instill hope (and not fear) in their future. Love does not appear to be part of these "real life" lessons and the personal "real life" example of the teacher is often not appealing. It is ironic that some people providing an academic education to open wide doors for students are the one's telling students it is too late for them and that real life is a done deal. Real life is not an actual thing. Real life is what you make daily through your actions, beliefs, values, and conclusions. Life is never completed. It only takes one person to totally change a life for the better and it can happen at any moment.

In order to obtain and fulfill the goal of producing educated students, many classrooms are driven by messages to behave. The teachers praise behavior and praise correctness, but nothing more.

"Nice quiet hands."

"Great answer."

"Good job."

"Thank you for sitting in your seat."

"I like how you remembered our expectations."

What are we teaching about them as a person? How do these teachers take a student forward as a learner? These boil down to a simple message: You are behaving well and I like it. How will this ever produce inspired, zealous learners or citizens? Such a focus in the classroom might translate into this imagined teacher evaluation:

Ms. Collins comes in on time and does her job all day. It is a good job too. She has a really quiet hand when she wants the class to pay attention, and has a correct answer ready at any moment. She is awesome and follows expectations all day. I like how she is so respectful. Her name is always on the chart for our special drawings. I am thankful for that. She should be proud of how she is a good example to others and follows expectations. She is always ready in line with a bubble in her mouth and voice off so students can model how to behave in the hallways.

Want that on a job search? No one would know about your personality, including: your values, your ethics, your social relationships among the school community, your maturity, how much you have done with what you have been given, your level of zest and joy, how you address your job requirements, your creativity, or if you were all that likeable or inspiring to be with. What do we expect students to glean from such a focus on behavior? We need to build students up with powerful internal guidance systems and dynamite resumes for the uncertain lives they face.

That internal guidance system would be our values. What do people really fight over, sometimes die for, lead businesses and churches with, stay married through thick and thin with, triumph, and persevere with? What keeps you going even when you feel like stopping? Values. I once met a teacher walking out the door the minute I was walking in her classroom! Fed up with her students and job, she had decided never to return to education. We talked about her dreams and values for school, and how to realize her dreams and values. She saw hope for her dreams and values, and kept on teaching. She became a force of joy for her students. She drove the class with high values and the class went higher and higher in manifesting them. Order grew. Peace happened, joy happened, love grew. She still teaches.

The last part of this book is "The Value-Driven Classroom." It is a top-down approach where you model and teach values in the class. It focuses on building a value-driven community throughout the school, in order for staff and students to weave the values in action. Who does not want lifelong learners or self-motivated learners? Who does not want students fully conscious of how they influence the social network, hold up their choices to high standards of moral and ethical citizenship, and recognize high values in others? As an example, Ms. Frazer was having trouble with her smart board and needed to reboot her computer. She asked her class, "What do I need from you right now?" A student said, "Patience!" Ms. Frazier celebrated and agreed. She then asks, "How will that help me?" The students answered, "Focus." Ms. Frazer agreed and got to work fixing the computer. After about three minutes the smart board is working. The students patiently and quietly sat. "See how your patience helped me," says Ms. Frazer.

This example is from a kindergarten class of about twenty-five students. These students need no reminders about behavior, talking rules, and blah, blah, blah. These students thoroughly understand the value of patience, hold patience as a value within them, and guide themselves with that value. Not told what to do, the students show up as people with values built up and reinforced, and celebrated as individuals in a community. "Show me your dedication to learning." "What will your caring look like during our assembly today?" They are already being great citizens and conceive the meaning of society in kindergarten. They can barely read and spell, but they excel at these values. They do not have to read and spell them, they learn by living them. This also does tremendous things for reading comprehension! Why? We fill them with the ability and awareness to comprehend the lives they are actually living all day long. They become leaders, not followers.

We all are motivated by, conduct ourselves by, and interact by our values. We will either strengthen or weaken our values when times are good, when times are bad, when the unexpected happens, or when temptation is at the door. Values are our guides and reference points for living. Many of the people I have met in prison or on parole did their crime because they thought they could get away with it and because the opportunity was there. They are floaters with no real internal guidance system. Values ground people.

Why are you teaching? Why are you an administrator, a school board member, or a school counselor? What values keep you going, keep you showing up? We will look closely at questions like these because I seek to create schools that build and instill amazingly good values in students so they show up with their best. Then they keep getting better and attaining deeper values to be the best possible learners and citizens. Like love. Like a lifelong learner, and beyond.

To get there we need to have great answers to our Essential Questions. They are the foundation of our attachments to our selves, others, and life. They are the questions and answers we will pass on 24/7 within the social curriculum. If we are having poor answers, we are likely to develop stunted values. If I have wonderful answers and abundant hope, I can really go places with my values. Poor answers lead to striving and defending which is sort of like treading water so you do not sink. Wonderful abundant answers lead to a network of caring, supportive, kind relationships with which we can then surf big waves, leap off the high dive, and jump out and try to do it even better.

The voice of the school then speaks through the Essential Questions and through the values being upheld (or not) within the social curriculum. It is our personal example and the congruency with which it speaks. It is hard to teach a value when you are not teaching it congruently, such as yelling at someone to tell him or her to speak respectfully. The social curriculum is always active, always teaching something about the Essential Questions and values by the personal examples of those citizens in the mini society of school as they interact. This book is about making the social curriculum as powerful as possible. The goal: citizens of high values who highly value others, pass on fulfilling answers to the Essential Questions of others, and love and live boldly.

This book is for you to be an inspiring leader of a classroom, a school, even a district. I am writing this book for you who have a passion to transform schools into great societies, who believe every minute in school counts, and that children come first and teachers second. It is for those who can draw a line on great teaching and inspire even greater teaching, who treat every student as gifted and talented, who believe schools are the best hope of our society, and who believe producing mature and informed citizens who have dignity is THE business of school.

I do not believe the primary answer to our educational problems lie in more technology, more curriculums, higher standards of achievement, or pedagogy that is more sophisticated. I firmly believe those may help, yet they are simply more of the same solutions already tried for decades. We need to be able to inspire learners who say, "Give me more!" and are ready with their best behavior, attitude, and values because **they want** to soak up more. The challenge is creating schools where students want to be, want to learn, and purposely contribute to the well-being of the climate and culture. I have no doubt that comes from the voice of the school inspiringly answering the Essential Questions we all have at our emotional and spiritual core. It also comes from being a leader that drives high values in ways others can congruently model and live by. Then you will have people who are giving their best, asking for more, and most importantly, wanting to be their best. In this way, we can produce informed and conscientious students/citizens hopeful and ready for an uncertain future of which they are unafraid. In simple terms, we as educators need to do what we want students to do. It is time to stand and thoroughly answer with the best possible answers in the social curriculum. This book articulates and operationalizes these answers so you can coherently send powerful, loving, and lasting messages that will literally change and guide the lives of everyone.

CHAPTER TWO
Dancing With The Essential Questions

When we were young and really did not have words to think with, we were learning a great deal in our bodies. We were forming patterns of actions/reactions, developing patterns to our emotions, setting stress levels, and wiring in chemical and electrical pathways, etc. They were being learned by our body, mind, and spirit. We are also born with built-in predispositions that we inherited. Several months of in utero experiences and our social living began to moderate or strengthen them. As examples, reading books aloud to unborn children improves their ability to learn to read. Just having books in the home, even if no one reads them, improves reading abilities over children not exposed to books! (This is why many libraries give books to new mothers.) We were also born with our primal defenses of fight-flight-freeze, which were reinforced or activated hundreds of times before we had any words to frame, contextualize, understand, and reflect on those experiences. We have hundreds of other experiences as well – which are hopefully predominantly loving, calming, joyous, and full of rich connection.

Even before we spoke as children, all these add up so that we had a sense of the degree we were loved, safe, protected, wanted, and could anticipate love and safety. This patterning of experiences, predispositions, and expectations over time became our attachment style. Attachment has been studied and researched for many decades. It has to do with dynamics of parent-child interaction. Specifically, how children separate from the parent, how the parent separates from the child, how the child interacts with the world around them once separated, and how parent and child reconnect upon reunion. We carry our attachment patterns with us as we grow and interact with the attachment patterns of others. There is no getting around this aspect of being human as we all have an attachment style/pattern. These neurological pathways wired in to our brains operate almost totally outside of our awareness. These patterns just seem to be "the way it is" as they operate without us really thinking about them. In this way, we are close to being like the fish in water. As we bump or sometimes crash into the attachment styles of others, we get some hints as to our style.

As language and awareness grow, we develop stories about self, others, life, and living. This is because our brains are made to think in stories (Siegel 1999). Eric Berne M.D. (1996) developed Transactional Analysis based in the premise that we all have a life story (our "life script") which we reinforce and sustain through social interaction. Since a great deal has already been wired in to us at a preverbal level, the early patterns we developed form a backdrop to the way we live out our life that is often cloudy to us but usually clear to others. With this backdrop, we try to make sense of our experiences and this leads to beliefs, opinions, expectations, reactions, and attempted solutions. These become the story of our life.

Here are the Essential Questions:

> Do I exist?
> Am I seen, heard?
> Am I safe—emotionally and physically?
> Do I make a difference—good or bad?
> Am I good?
> Am I enjoyable?
> Can I be me and reveal myself fully?
> Am I competent?
> Can I trust myself?
> Am I valued, worthy?
> Is there abundance?
> Do I belong?
> Am I able to love and be loved?
> Can I hope in me, in others, in life?

We live these beliefs, expectations, reactions, and solutions out in the ways we seek and sustain connections with others and ourselves. Others are doing the same with us. Our beliefs, experiences, and expectations collide with those of others in a sort of dance. Children bring what life has taught them about attachment to school and we bring ours to them. Sometimes we think the students should "know" how to behave, connect, react, and think when their life has clearly taught them an entirely different set of beliefs, expectations, reactions, and solutions than ours. We amaze them as much as they amaze us. Out of all the options possible, whatever they bring us is their best solution. Isn't that what we like to believe we are doing?

This dance is a major factor in the social curriculum. We begin to "teach" each other as a staff, as administrators, as students, and school boards what life has been like for us, what we expect it to be like, and we show each other how we seek and defend during our dance. We are all trying to balance our brains to reach some level of "sense," coherence, and an acceptable story. Most of the teaching of the social curriculum between people is implicit. Our tone, posture, rate of speech, inflections, eye dilation, muscle tone, physical proximity, eye contact, body position, movements of our body, pressure behind our speech, reactivity to what we see and hear, emotional level, breathing rate, depth of breathing, or head tilt say *way* more than the overt messages of our words.

What are we "teaching" through our implicit and overt messages? What are the concerns of the stories? What is our integrity and dignity built around? I put forth we are teaching answers to some specific questions we use to guide our lives, and teaching the probability of really good answers to those questions. This is why our personal example is so important. We are *always* sending answers and probabilities to ourselves and to others, just as others do the same. What do you begin thinking when you get a new job, are assigned a new grade level, a new administrator, new team members, new students? What do you imagine students begin thinking when they get a new teacher, a new parent, a new school, a new principal, and/or new classmates? I propose our style of attachment and our patterns of connection/interaction, are driven by Essential Questions we all seek to answer, by the answers we have found so far, and the likelihood of getting good/acceptable answers.

For now, consider that we are in a dance where we are seeking and sending answers from others, while others are seeking and sending answers from us. We send and seek answers at the same time others simultaneously send and seek answers. In systems theory, we are co-regulating each other. How I seek answers from you and whatever answers or challenges I send you regarding your questions influences what I receive back as answers to my questions. How you have sent answers to my questions and the ways you are seeking answers from me influences answers you get from me. For all practical purposes, simultaneously your attitude and words influence mine and mine influence yours. We are "seeking and sending" each other messages faster than we can consciously think as myriads of responses and cues fly back and forth between us. Then we walk away with a story about them and us that we built up from all the seeking and sending. This could be a story of defending and striving, or of getting fantastic answers.

All this dancing continues throughout life in various degrees and with varying levels of sophistication. We move forward through life with attempts to answer our Essential Questions while also being defensive for any further hurt/stress/let down. The important part is that we are all doing this so there is an interaction between **you**—seeking positive answers to your Essential Questions—and **me**—seeking to do the same. In addition, we are all defending against the possibility of a negative answer. We then engage in a dance of striving for positive answers while being on guard against negatives. Being pessimistic is one defense against negative answers. Another is to believe all things work toward the good and whatever happens is meant for my greater good. Put two people in a room that have these opposite beliefs and let the fun begin!

Usually, this dancing results in the fulfillment of our expectations. We could do the dance with someone with similar beliefs: the pessimist meets another pessimist, or the hopeful persevering person meets others as hopeful and persevering. Our being on guard, our defenses (our level of sophistication at fight-flight-freeze, our protective reactions, and protective expectations) can be too strong and put people off. They do so by triggering the defenses and Essential Questions others are bringing to the dance. It is often as though a person's defending and striving instills or provokes the same defenses and striving in others. They then wind up with similar questions and answers. A simple example is that irritable and fussy people often bring out the irritable, fussy part of others.

"No, I am not!"

"Oh, yes you are!"

"That's stupid!"

"That is *not* stupid—you are!"

A classic example is the common pattern of chase-avoid. Spouse A sees Spouse B as avoiding them. It does not matter who begins to create distance, just that the distance is too much to one spouse. So A begins to ask why, what is going on, what are you doing that for, why don't you spend time with me? Spouse B experiences this as aversive and becomes more distant. Spouse A is now sure something is wrong and chases, quizzes, and complains to Spouse B even more. B now sees A as intrusive, unpleasant, and complaining. B becomes increasingly angry, fearful, or passively avoidant with more and more lame excuses and vague explanations. This *really* gets Spouse A in an uproar as B now appears sneaky, evasive, snappy, distant, happier with others, and busier with others. At the same time, Spouse A's attempts also appear sneaky, evasive, snappy, and unpleasant. Now both see other people as far more appealing, increase time with others, and spend more time apart or locked in heated conflicts. Soon they are *both* feeling unwanted and questioning their commitment. They *both* feel validated that they *knew* something was going on and the other spouse didn't really care! Expectations fulfilled. Imagine the striving and defending in that relationship. If one of them had turned and answered the Essential Questions of the other, or asked and received a commitment to spend more time together, the escalating seesaw would likely not have happened.

Alternatively, it can be a student feeling stripped of dignity and that no one cares. This student presents a challenge to teachers because this student seems hard to engage. In fact, they bring a statement to the other: I do not and you do not have value. The teachers make some overtures to engage and receive a snippy, cold response. Now the teacher is being invited to also feel uncared-for and hopeless. If the teacher is secure with their self this challenge remains a student need. If the teacher does not feel secure and feels their respect and dignity is also in question, then there likely will be an interaction of more striving and defensiveness between student and teacher. The teacher may increase distance or try harder to push the student into caring via using enticements, bargaining, pleading, ordering, threatening, referring, and/or using organizational power to enforce punishments. Now the student is sure no one cares, acts worse, and invites the teachers to feel the same estranged, hopeless, and angry frustration. All involved can wind up feeling useless, "done," and that there is no value in the other person or the entire system of education. One or all may drop out of education.

What is the usual mood and topics in your teacher lounge? How is that mood and conversation both striving and defending? What Essential Questions are people really discussing?

Now for the full effect, let us reverse this scenario with teacher and student. The teacher could begin the year angry and distant. Students are treated from day one as problems or at least clearly as potential problems—the "don't smile until October" plan. The students then feel little respect or hope from the teacher, as the teacher did not give them a chance to be valuable, good, competent, and trustworthy. They are viewed with suspicion, as having poor motives, distrusted, and thus too controlled. They pay the teacher back in ways that reinforce the negative expectations on both sides. The teacher is convinced students are worse every year; the students are convinced the teacher does not like them or care about them. The teacher's attitude and expectations fall as "evidence" piles up each year. Other responses are always possible, but in this example, they did not occur.

In a fifth grade class, I watched the following dance build between a student and her student teacher. The student blurted out something about feeling all mixed up and then giggled to her tablemates. The student teacher tells her to keep working. The student soon said she just could not get it and giggled again. Her tablemates giggled and made faces, as if they were stupid too. The teacher tells the student to focus harder, and for the table to quiet down and get working. After a short time, the teacher wants the class to move to a new math problem and the girl blurts out, "I'm not done! I can't write that fast." The student has been sending messages she is not competent, and about five minutes into the new task, the teacher goes over to the girl to say, "Are you getting this written down?" The teacher is now reinforcing how the girl is not competent and expects the student will not be. The student soon blurts out how she is messing up the numbers. The teacher tells her to be quiet. Then a minute later, the student blames the teacher for confusing her. "You went too fast and mixed me up. Now I can't do this right." The student teacher accepts this and apologizes for not being clear. Now the issue of competency is on the student teacher. They both now share the same Essential Question and story as they have mutually reinforced the appearance of competency problems between them. The student teacher asks the girl if she is being clear.

Note that other stories and beliefs are certainly possible for both student and teacher. Yet without some intervention, these mutual questions of competency and the mutual reinforcements will grow and grow. In a system perspective, this is co-regulation. Students and teachers need to change the mutual asking and sending of messages about deficits of competency.

I urge everyone to understand one of the most common and repetitive cycles of human behavior. Daily, everyone goes through this cycle repeatedly. I watch students and teachers go through this cycle all the time. One problem is that teachers and parents usually only see part of the cycle and intervene in ways that then escalate it. Once you see it in action, you will see it everywhere. Some people cycle through all four steps in two minutes, some in hours or days. In our dance of trying to connect and get some answers, we go through a series of steps known as the **attachment cycle**.

1. We **try** something to get on the radar of another. If no success we then
2. **Try harder** (more intensely, louder, longer, more provocatively). If no success we
3. **Get disorganized.** This appears as random external behavior that has no apparent goal but is guaranteed to command attention (a discharge), or an internal response with random behavior (an attempt to self-distract). This is followed by
4. **Withdrawal** as we regroup to cycle back to trying again.

Regarding step 1, we can all think of ways we begin to seek connection. In classrooms it may be the raised hand, the pencil tap, putting their head down, getting out of the seat, dropping things, and many others. Motion almost always works. One of my favorites is when students get teachers to call on them and then say, "I forgot." In step 2 students wave that hand faster/ higher, shout out, throw something, slam a book, laugh way too loudly, pester peers, and other inventive ploys. Most efforts will be pulling on your emotional triggers. If that fails to get you connected, students likely become disorganized. The student may jump to withdrawal, but usually will go through a phase of seemingly random, mainly internal actions such as looking down, shivering, tearing up a piece of paper, scribbling, getting a blank look on their face, or dancing. Sometimes this disorganization is simply to take off running around the room. If that fails to get connection, there is a period of withdrawal. I watched a girl run through the first three steps, then hang her head for about a minute before trying to get the girl next to her engaged. Her neighbor smiled back and our girl joined in the class singing.

Teachers described one preschool girl as a terror who would get violent at a moment's notice. She would run around the classroom knocking all sorts of things down, and scream like a siren. As I watched the class in circle time, she would try to get on the teachers radar by wanting to answer questions. She would raise her hand many times and be ignored each time. Trying harder, she then began to bounce up and down on her chair or make noise while raising her hand. Those efforts did not work so she began to play with her hair, rock in the chair, talk to her neighbor, and look around the room. She began to shout out and interject things way off topic, clearly interrupting the class. Then she got in trouble and had to sit out. She withdrew in a little private world, eyes glazed and staring, and slightly rocking. After a while, she rejoined the class and, trying again, volunteered to help the teacher without any luck. She ran through the cycle—steps two through four—all over again.

I watched a second grader stand in the door of the class trying to get the teacher's attention by calling to her across the room. That did not work so he began yelling loudly and interrupting and jumping. He then ran right up to the teacher talking nonstop. That did not work so he began spinning around the room and knocked into numerous peers as he went. That got him on the radar. The teacher gave him a time-out and told him she would be glad to help him get started on the morning warm-up as soon as he showed his integrity. After a minute, he reconnected with the class for regaining his integrity. The teacher then began providing a lot of connection and pathways to keep this connection so he did not have to try on his own. He now had someone after him.

In a seventh grade class, there were three boys and one girl in a group. The teacher came by and praised the three boys, but not the girl. The girl quickly asked the teacher for help. The teacher helped and walked off. A little while later, this repeated. The boys received praise and the girl did not. The girl then began asking for more and more help and had the teacher on a short leash in no time. The girl was successful in getting "attached" to the teacher and kept reinforcing the teacher to keep helping. "Oh thank you, Ms. Cevartia." The downside is the girl made herself increasingly inept in appearance to keep it going. She actually was being highly successful in the social curriculum! Although she could have used numerous problem behaviors, she did not. The teacher could have cheered about this student's resourcefulness, independence, and determination, but she did not.

Note: As teachers, we are predisposed to help, so the girl's frequent pleas for help were OK with the teacher and not annoying. However, if the student had been yelling out goofy stuff, the teacher would have been annoyed — yet, more than likely, there every time to help the girl hush up. Either way, the social reinforcement continues the girl's behavior because it attaches her to the teacher. Either way, the student is striving. It is easy to observe this attachment-seeking pattern in every level of school, staff meetings, and in practically any group of people anywhere.

Often, we rarely see the" try". We often ignore the "trying harder", and just hope it will go away or socially reinforce it. The "disorganized" may get our attention and we misread the withdrawal as "problem over." It is just the end of the beginning all over again, unless we prepare to end the person's seeking and seek the person. Go after a peer or the students with answers to their Essential Questions, while reinforcing deep values and gifts they have as a person. Remember, if we are not conveying that they inspire us, what are they supposed to think? If we only stop for their problematic actions and attitudes, how should we expect them to seek connection and attach to us? The good news is they will most likely keep trying until we give them a better way. We often just get what we give. We also give expectations.

For decades, researchers have given teachers expectations about students and have documented the power of expectations or appearances. When teachers approach the students believing these expectations, they then appear to be true in the students. In one classic study, researchers told teachers that told blue-eyed students were smarter than brown-eyed students. They were! Researchers told other teachers the exact opposite, which became true too. Other researchers have done the same with learning disabled students and gifted students. Depending on the teacher's expectations, the learning disabled students became significant achievers and the gifted students actually dropped in achievement scores. There are many other beliefs and expectations in education.

The most powerful one I see year after year is the idea that students are "done" with school after state testing or coming upon the end of the school year. This is not true in many classrooms, yet some teachers throw their hands up and say, "Done." Is it a case of chicken or egg? It is usually a matter of co-regulation. Both can be true. The teacher could start fearing or acting as if the students are finished or a few students could begin to act "done." All it takes is for both sides to act a little more "done" and sure enough, it seems to come true. If one side does not act finished and somehow establishes that school is still full on, then chances are school will continue full on.

Think back to the girl at the table with three boys just a few paragraphs back. I hope you can see that both the student and the teacher quickly formed a set of appearances and beliefs that almost trap each of them in particular patterns. What do you think this teacher thought about the girl? If the girl becomes needy for more attachment with the teacher, what do you think will be her first choice of action? Many other possibilities could be equally "true." This is why it is vitally important for you to have your sights and intentions clearly aimed at the best and growing it nonstop. **The level**

of success you reinforce is the level of success you get. What is the best you could expect from the student without much confidence or ability? If you reinforce "trying" and "effort" the results are less than if you reinforce being "a finisher" or "persevering to the end." How high is your bar?

In medical experiments, people are given a placebo, told it is real medicine, and told they may experience specific side effects. From one-fourth to one-third will report those very side effects even though researchers gave them the sugar pill. A significant percentage of people report less depression even though they only took sugar pills when they expected real medication. Expectations influence us more easily than you think. What do you believe about your students, coworkers, or administration?

Years ago, I worked exclusively with military families in what was a grand experiment by the Department of Defense to provide service members and their family's state-of-the-art comprehensive mental health services. Often the children handled many transitions of towns, schools, social groups, caretakers, and parenting figures. The research and experience showed a clear difference between those that were able to socially transition well and connect positively with new people, and those children who had great difficulty with transitions and reestablishing social networks. In general, those expecting to be liked were liked, and those expecting rejection or marginalization were rejected and marginalized. Each group approached others and acted quite differently in their attempts to join in and connect/attach to others in new situations. They operated with different expectations and probabilities. The students who were generally rejected were striving and defending in ways that made them difficult to like or they didn't try and self-marginalized. The students who met new people and expected to be liked easily joined and successfully blended in to new groups. In systems theory, the same outcome occurs from a variety of sources so it is equally possible that a new student meets with great acceptance and richly connects before major striving and defending occurs. Henry Ford is credited with saying, "If you think it won't work or you think it will, you're right." How are your expectations keeping your beliefs about your students, coworkers, and administration alive?

Story Time: Never A Full Day

In a third grade class, a new student began in late September. Unbeknownst to the class, this new student had never been more than half a day in any school at any point during his education because of his severe behavior problems. We knew from advance information that he was way behind academically and hated school. His school file was over an inch thick with behavior problems. Because they expected violence, staff at the new school prepared a team of five who used walkie-talkies and coded messages. After about an hour into his first day, the student's new teacher stopped class and asked the class what they saw going well and right in the class so far. Then she asked the class what they could tell the new student about his being in class so far, "After all he has been with us a whole hour so we have probably seen many good things." (Notice how she defined the nature of her classroom social curriculum right then.) Several students volunteered speaking about his smile, how he was nice, and how they were glad he was there. This student finished the first hour and his first full day of school ever with friends, connection, belonging, value, and worthiness. This is what I referred to earlier as going after the student to answer their Essential Questions and eliminate as much striving and

> defending as possible. Imagine what would have happened with the girl and the three boys if the teacher had been after the girl and answering her Essential Questions.
>
> Two days later the new third-grade student missed his regular bus and took another bus he hoped would take him to school. In fact, he took two wrong busses trying to get to school that day. He eventually made it. He made it every day and all day the rest of the year. He exhibited no evidence of violence or acts of aggression or intimidation that had been expected. The walkie-talkies went unused. His mother cried to the principal how overjoyed she was that her son now loved school. The next year I knew that his fourth grade teacher had no idea about his history. At the end of third grade, they removed his special education label. After a few months, I asked her about this student. She said he is a little behind in his reading level but, "He never gives up and will find a way to succeed no matter what." How true! Or should I say, "How fulfilling of our expectations and intentions."

This is the power of the Essential Questions. His were powerfully answered the first hour of class, and his entire attachment to school changed. He no longer needed to strive and defend against poor, unacceptable answers. Relieved of that burden, his brain opened up to learning and he made great strides. The change can come from anywhere in the system. You can be that difference.

There are many other factors at play in research and social situations, but the big picture is we can often wind up reinforcing our expectations. The student above was certainly high risk of this. Reinforcing expectations occurs because we invite others to feel the same and think the same about their Essential Questions as we do. If this student had raised a wild disturbance, reinforcement would come from a thick file of expectations of his actions and hopelessness in him and others, his reputation and diagnoses reinforced, and his mom, the school staff, and his classmates all might have begun to hate school too. They may or may not. If the teacher handled the wild disturbance in a way that did not reinforce his negative answers and expectations, the possibility of a new story would remain open. **As soon as we are in a conclusion, we are finished writing a new story and left to retelling an old one.** So, if you arrive at or stay on a conclusion, make it as wonderful as possible. Right now, you could be thinking you/they will never change—or thinking change is always possible—or that true miracles are all over the place.

Several powerful skills help us not to accept the invitation to a conclusion and to provide great answers to our Essential Questions and those of others. They include understanding our "triggers"—Positive Behavior Facilitation (PBF) training is helpful at this. Using mindfulness skills to stay aware, understanding how we are the decisive factor (Ginott), and, in the words of Mahatma Gandhi, we can "Be the change you want to see in the world" We can train ourselves to stay in what is possible, "Be the Brain," and learn how to recognize and answer the Essential Questions. If we do one or some of these things, we can usually regulate the interaction. If not, we are likely to continue, and intensify, the defensiveness of our self and others. . This is likely to lead to inadequate answers rather than to satisfactory answering of Essential Questions. Both spouses above became more hardened to love and hope. Their striving and defending created a spiral, just like the negative expectations of the teachers and students.

If we are able to understand what Essential Questions a person needs answered, we can provide great answers and they can stop striving/defending so intensely. **We are often so intent on stopping the defensive and striving style of others, we miss their need, which goes unanswered and grows. As does ours.**

Our intentions mirror our expectations and communicate how we think/feel about others. If I expect my students are not to be trusted and will run me over if I smile before October, then my behavior and words will be guided by intentions to keep a tight rein on everything going on in the class and try to control it. As I go about controlling everything and not smiling, the message that they are not trusted, not good, and are not inspiring will come across loud and clear. Do not expect that to turn out well.

Story Time: The Bossy Devaluator

There was a girl in kindergarten who was one sneaky bossy bully. She repeatedly instigated conflict under the radar by inviting her peers to feel inadequate, less than her, or only good if they did this or that for her. Students would implode or explode. The student's actions drew the teacher toward trying to overhear, catch, prevent, be on top of, and know all so this girl wouldn't be able to pull her stuff. In other words, the student pulled the teacher into being a sneaky, micromanaging authoritarian too! If the teacher fully accepted that invitation, the teacher was destined never to be ahead of this girl, mostly a step behind.

The teacher recognized this pull but was not sure where to go. We began to assess this girl's Essential Questions. The invitation put forth by the student was built around never being good enough and never knowing where this message was coming from next – but it surely would. The teacher had direct experience of this with the mother of the student. The mother began a parent-teacher conference by announcing she did not want to hear about her daughter's behavior, she just wanted to know if her daughter was doing her work and making high grades. Period. The teacher felt devalued and simply there to fulfill the mother's need. The Essential Questions of being valued, good, and belonging were all active. The teacher felt the invitation to be devalued from the mother and the student, the student passed it among class members, and anger sprang up all over. Therefore, the answer we designed to come from the teacher was built around how the girl is inherently good just as she is, how she is enjoyable just as she is, and wanted just as she is. "I really like your choice of color. It makes me happy to look at it." "I just had to get closer to your smiling face." "When you're not here, it makes the class feel incomplete." When the teacher first delivered these messages, the girl looked in shock. After a couple of rounds, the girl came up to the teacher and asked for a note to her parent. "Could you write to my mom that I'm good?" Wow! When we answer an Essential Question, the response is clear and quick. Note that the girl was not directly told she was good, just treated as though she was. She downloaded the message all on her own from the attunement and intentions of the teacher.

How was the teacher an answer? She was accepting, kind, welcoming, validating, and upholding the worthiness of others. The teacher was now inviting, in clear and powerful ways, this student to change her attachment to the world. Before this, the teacher was on track to become more like the student, and if that happened, the entire class and the teacher would likely become like the girl in striving for any recognition. Now the student had a teacher to be like, a path to pursue, and a model from which to learn. The good news about secure, positive attachment is this: It is never too late for anyone to acquire or experience one! Hopefully that news just changed someone's story. Science has shown it is never too late.

Story Time: Always Out Of Control

A story I tell at most trainings I conduct is that of a fourth grader depicted as "always out of control, in the principal's office multiple times on a daily basis, needing to be medicated, and driving [the teacher] to the point of quitting." Once I began using the framework of the Essential Questions, this story took on clearer meaning and pointed to how a "lucky" response had a powerful impact.

The student had never been on green, PBIS interventions were not helping, and the student was basically being tossed from class to office to class to office. It was February when I visited the class. The class started to leave after forty-five minutes, and this student ran up to me and said, "Have you been writing about me? I'm bad." He wanted to know if he was making a difference and if he truly was bad. He was also asking for hope. He was striving (he pursued me in hope I have good answers) and defending (beating me to the same conclusion others had given him before). I told him I had not been writing about him, but I noticed three things. I told him I saw him pound his desk and yell out how he hated math, but then got right back to work and kept trying to learn. I told him I saw he was angry and complaining that he could not go to the special class (because he was not on green), but had been straightening all the chairs as the class was lining up. I told him I heard him be insulted by a girl in line and then loudly complain to the teacher - but he did not retaliate in any way toward the girl. He now knew he had made a difference and had done good things, but I had to go farther and provide the answer that **he** was good and could fully hope in himself. I asked him, "You know what that makes you?" His eyes and brain went wide open. "That makes you a man because a man does what is good and right even when he doesn't feel like it." He started jumping around the room smacking his rear shouting, "I'm a man! I'm a man!" He was restored as a person with value, goodness, dignity, hope. His spirit soared. Some of his questions were answered.

Two weeks later, I returned to the class and he zoomed up to me asking, "Am I still a man?" I asked him to tell me what he had done that a man does. He needed to be the one answering this question and, from his accounts, he had clearly done several things. "Those are you being a man." I said. He was only in the principal's office two more times that year and on the much sought after green level daily. Of course, the teacher's questions, defending, and striving changed too. So did the office personnel and the story of the school. Anyone can answer the questions for someone in the system and other parts of the system are likely to change for the better too. It's science.

Students will hand us their early learning, defenses, attachments, story, and provoke us to respond to their Essential Questions. We will also do the same thing. We will present to others our learning, defenses, attachments, and story. It happens implicitly and explicitly along a continuum of sophistication and power/entitlements. Life will go up and down and pull at our (and their) Essential Questions and defensiveness with varying intensity. At the same time I receive invitations, I send them to others. We all co-regulate each other in this regard, as we are all in it together as seekers of love, hope, competence, and safety.

I think this level of communication is why people have such variable respect for the roles/entitlements people have. The interaction is really around the Essential Questions and not the roles we have. If I am the teacher and believe students should just act right and follow directions because I am the teacher, then I hope my role has power. In my mind, my personal example will not matter as much as my role. If I have used my role as a defense against inner doubts and fears, regarding my Essential Questions, and appeal to the role—"I am the teacher. You need to listen!"—then students and other adults will easily know this and provoke me to experience my questions anew.

Story Time: Why Does It Always Have To Be Such A Big Deal?

As I walked past the high school classroom, a substitute flailed his arms and body as he shouted, "Why? Why does it always have to be a big deal with you, Romero? It is no big deal! Get over it and move on!" At this point, it evidently was a big deal for the sub, such that there was no significant difference between the student and the sub in behavior or attitudes. Big deal, meet big deal about your big deal. Student and substitute used the same tactics of striving and defending to make something happen for the good of self and others. This is not a good thing.

If our personal example conveys we have solid positive answers such that student concerns and styles remain a student issue, then we can be a provider of true answers to students who bring their poor answers to the dance. The substitute above might have been able to let Romero know he was making a difference and was safe in a way that helped him not to strive and defend so dramatically. We all need solid, affirming answers. When we do not, those also needing and seeking solid affirming answers will quickly engage us in a dance of seeking and defending. In the example above, the sub quickly engaged Romero in a dance of seeking and defending. Do you think Romero quieted down and said, "You're right, no big deal? Sorry."? Not even close. The substitute had not addressed what upset Romero. Only his style of striving and defending was. He received no new answer on how to be safe and make a positive difference. Romero got his style right back at him with an incongruent series of messages. The sub was saying it is no big deal at one level yet at another level unable to resist it as a big deal. To teach something new, we would have to show how to resist it being a big deal in us. That is the expectation put on Romero yet the sub was not living up to that expectation either. We are all seeking positive answers while striving and defending along the way. It is our shared humanity. I need what you need and most of what we do is imbroglio to get it.

Story Time: A Lack Of Commitment

Kris was all over the room and ended his roaming hidden behind a file cabinet. The teacher asked him to make a commitment to come to the carpet for the lesson. He agreed and sat right in front of her. As she ran the lesson, he did fine for about six minutes, but then began to crawl away from the group under some desks. The teacher looked frustrated so I spoke with her. I told her Kris had had made a commitment to be seen and heard for his best but she had not keep her commitment to see and hear him for that. She went over, apologized for not recognizing his commitment, and asked if he would try again so she could keep her commitment to him. He came right back, was a model student, and participated. The teacher was attuned and socially reinforcing his commitment.

The teacher was showing her commitment to his commitment and all was well. So many times we want students to be committed to high standards of excellence that are virtually ignored because we are not committed to their commitment. Would you expect someone to love you if you do not love him or her back? What Essential Questions would that bring out in you? Let us look closely at the Essential Questions.

CHAPTER THREE
The Essential Questions

The Essential Questions apply to anyone of any age at any level of ability at any stage of life. No one is exempt. They are questions of our spirit, our heart, and our mind deep within our fabric as human beings. More than knowledge, more than stuff, more than power, more than our own life in some instances, we need answers. In an ideal relationship, all these questions are richly and thoroughly answered. We can muster some great answers yet it is difficult to sustain them as permanent facts. The world gives us a generous helping of information to sift through about ourselves, and gives us challenging situations to overcome. We have daily opportunities to invite negative answers to our Essential Questions, and spew a few negative answers to the questions of others as well.

We need clarity in ourselves and the world in order to sift through all the information. Educators want students to know about science so that when they receive erroneous explanations of why the sky is blue or why the sun looks bigger on the horizon, the students can know exactly why, or at least have enough information to reason their way to the correct answer. In the same way, we need students to have lots of information about them as a person. However, even more than information about one's self, we need students who understand the social network they co-regulate within. We need conscious and conscientious citizens who desire to be their best and help others be their best too. We need scholars of learning and living.

Typically, students receive precious little information about themselves as a person. Recall the high school students who told me that they get grades on tests and marks on papers, but little information about *who* they are as a person or *how* they are doing in the big picture of life. Think for a moment about the praise and the comments you have given your students lately. What has it really told them about them? That they did a good job on something? That they know how to be quiet? That they are appreciated for following expectations? These tell them little of what they really need to know.

We also give students little about the social network within which they send and receive Essential Questions. My experience is that schools are so emphatic about following rules, that students rarely understand how those rules benefit themselves or others. I will get to that later in the book. For now, I will focus on the Essential Questions, and how students—and everyone else -- needs to know they exist, are seen and heard, are safe, making a positive difference, good, can be themselves, are competent at learning and living, can trust themselves, are valuable, have abundance, belong, are loved, and can hope. The foundation of being a scholar of learning and living occurs through answering the above Essential Questions with clarity, attunement, and intention.

Years ago, I was counseling a thirteen-year-old girl in foster care. Her mother presented a mixed picture of sweet words, missed visits, noncompliance with court requirements, and nothing substantial to get her daughter back. With this child's IQ below average, she looked at me one day and said, "My mom thinks I'm not smart enough to know she doesn't want me." She was a scholar of living. She could read life well. What does this child need to face the world? What do we need to go forward, not backward, when the world invites us or even tells us to? We need some clear answers.

SEEKING AND PROVOKING

Be aware that since these are questions, most often you will see students simultaneously seeking an answer while provoking the question further. We also do this but it is hard to witness it in ourselves. Here is an example: An angry kindergartner grabs her book bag and announces she is leaving the class to go home while she lingers in the door. Why linger at the door? Maybe others will stop her, but more than that, declare that they must have her with them. While taking herself out of existence from the class (provoking the question), she is seeking to exist by giving someone the opportunity to affirm her existence. Of all the luck in the world, a peer sweetly says, "Goodbye, Kemikah." This provokes that she does not exist, or at least is not needed, which is her deepest fear. She runs back into the class and runs crashing into her peers grouped on the carpet. She is popping them with a pointer stick. Peers yell out to make her stop. She literally is making the class feel her existence. However, it is overwhelming and rejection occurs. "Go away, stop, and leave me alone," rings out from the class as the teacher approaches. Thus, her existence is again threatened. She quickly hands the pointer to the teacher, hoping not to be rejected or removed. While the above events build evidence that existence is a question for her, even more evidence came.

The assistant principal walked by and noticed the disturbance. He took Kemikah to his office. With an elaborate field trip planned for the next day, there is no one to help manage this volatile student on a trip of this scope. Safety is a real concern. Since her parents have "placed" her with Grandpa, the assistant principal calls him. The AP asks the grandfather if he can come on the field trip tomorrow. The first response of the grandfather was, "I don't want her with me!" We found out later that the grandfather would send the student to her room for lengthy periods as punishment for misbehavior. As indicated by this student's experiences, questions often run completely through our social network. Where and with whom did this young girl exist? Who was communicating to her that she should exist? Who just couldn't resist her and wanted her to exist in full? We made a plan for just those questions and it worked. She no longer runs from class and loves being with her teacher and peers. She is dealing with other questions now.

This mix of provoking the question while striving to get it answered is common. Another student, written about toward the end of this book, had a history as a runner. He was not to leave the room, but would stand in the doorway and lean the top half of his body out the door. The top half is sending us a message and so is the lower half.

Consider another student who was spewing verbal insults while cleaning up the room he had just littered with blocks. Then there is always the students saying they want nothing to do with you, yet they refuse to leave you alone and follow you around. Half the picture provokes the question and half seeks an answer. However, the question remains unanswered because the method of seeking the answer often repels others and/or obscures the question itself. All we see is the striving and defending, which usually what we respond to and try to stop. This usually results in escalating the need for an answer.

Going back to the attachment cycle, each of the above students was still organized (not yet disorganized) and really trying to connect to a fulfilling answer. As soon as you deliver such an answer, students immediately recognize it and respond. Usually that response is to calm, become congruent in words and actions, and provide you more opportunity to answer even more Essential Questions.

However, some students receive a fulfilling answer from you — perhaps just the answer of their dreams — and they explode. It is as if their entire emotional and mental paradigm becomes overwhelmingly scrambled and they act out in dramatic, disorganized ways. Fear not. It is soon over and they are universally filled with guilt and regret over what they did. What, at first, may seem like the final straw or the worst ever, is actually the beginning of a new paradigm for a much better life. Wait and see if they do not express regret and a desire to make up for what they did. Often these students are immediately suspended, all the efforts staff made are considered failures, and hope is tossed out the window. That is very sad, as these students will be eager for a chance to overcome their shame, to do something to show you they are "good," and to love you for redeeming and believing in them. *Your belief in them — your devotion and caring — got them to reach a new and better paradigm in the first place. Do not remove it.*

CLEAR AS A BELL ANSWERS

It is important to answer the questions with sufficient intensity and clarity. If you are too vague or too general, the student may not hear the answer you deliver. This may lead to trying harder or to a disorganized response. For example, a teacher told me she was about to get a student from another classroom for thirty minutes of reading. She said the student throws himself on the floor as he comes through the door, and yells out, creating an on-going distraction for others. I presume this student is asking, "Am I seen and heard?" I ask the teacher to greet him at the door and tell him she wants him to read with her today. As the student enters she said, "I'd like you to read with me today, OK?" He walks to the far corner of the room. No hysterics or drama, but he certainly does not jump at the opportunity and seems to be provoking something else to happen. The teacher intensifies and clarifies by smiling and saying, "I want you to read with me now. Here is your chair right next to mine. Come on over so I can hear your voice reading." He came over, sat down, and was a perfect student the rest of class, even though the teacher had to leave him alone a few times.

A student in a self-contained class, known for being easily disappointed and going into fits of anger, wants help with math. But, his teacher is helping another student. He immediately becomes distressed and hollers that he wants help. The teacher tell him just a minute and the student tries harder by yelling, "No one is going to help me — you won't help me!" and begins kicking his desk. The teacher tells the student he needs to be quiet and sit still if he wants help. Notice that the student is not clearly hearing he will absolutely be helped. I prompt the teacher, who then says, "I have all the help you will ever need for math and I want to help you very much. Once you are quiet and sitting patiently all my help is all yours." The student immediately sits quietly and even raises his hand while waiting several minutes for the teacher. Sometimes you will need to deliver unequivocal answers that eliminate all uncertainty before the student hears it. After all, most people really striving and defending, like the above students, have been fed a steady diet of lies and half-truths, had the rug of hope pulled out from under them numerous times. They are desperate for a truth. Let us get to the Essential Questions.

DO I EXIST?

This is the most basic question. Some people feel invisible as if they do not exist. People may look at them and not respond, may look right through them, and may run right into them as if they were not there. They are like a ghost on someone else's radar. They may talk and no one responds or glances their way. They can be in a line and the clerk begins talking to the person behind them. Internally they feel a void, an empty longing, a nothingness that nothing fills, yet also feel a panic they may actually not be on any radar and truly null and void. You can think, but you are not sure "I am," so to speak. Some of these children have been given messages (overtly and nonverbally) they should not exist or it would have been better if they had never been born.

Outwardly, people living with this belief can be unresponsive or quite wild because of the panic, but, either way, they are socially disconnected. I watch young students get hurt, sit, and cry. They have no expectation of anyone responding. They do not know the names of peers or the teacher's name, even after months. They have periods where they run around with no focus at all. They run from this to that, with brief stops to soothe themselves in between, yet the soothing is still frantic motion with little purpose, like repeating the same motion twenty times fast. (Think disorganized. Think permanent step three because, in their mind, there is no one to try or try harder for. The panic usually prevents them from withdrawing in step four.)

Interaction only seems to happen if an adult is right in a student's face—and, I mean, eye to eye, a foot away. Rarely do these students chat or seek connection with the adults and, if they do, they use the adult as a tool or a means to an end. The student simply needs something only the adult can provide. As soon as the adult moves on, the child returns to own world, as if the adult moved a thousand miles away. These children are not autistic. Autistic youth have different histories and other characteristics than those not sure of their existence. The children I speak of here are, generally, in a sort of panic about their existence.

Sometimes the student exhibits this panic by running around in dangerous contacts with others, trying to run out of the room or school, or hiding in the school (but not too well). The kindergartner above was this type of questioner. Others may be saying outright that they wish they were dead, want to die, might be better off dead, and/or want to be anywhere but here.

As you might guess, having them in time-out, ignoring them, and harshly admonishing them only escalates the situation because they download these actions as messages that they do not, or should not, exist. To a certain extent, just talking to them, even with a comforting tone, has little effect. They need cellular proof they exist. Imagine young adults who need to know they exist. What extent do they go to get this cellular proof? By young adulthood they have severely withdrawn and/or are in to very intense cellular engagement. This may be cutting or some other means of body stimulation. It can be visible bashing into peers, injuries from recreational feats, getting beat up, or zooming all over while bumping in to walls, desks, or the floor.

With these children in classrooms, we provide a lot of physical contact by being close enough to gently bump them, give quick pats on the back, tie a shoe, give a high-five, count their fingers as we touch each one, hug them from the side, and mirror their movements and vocalizations. You can be creative, but not overwhelming, because you do not want them to recoil from overload. We just send a signal, "You are here, and I am too." Then all the comforting words and little conversations will have greater impact. These children are not sent to a time-out or to the principal's office for breaking rules until *much* later. Stop the students and direct them in kind, comforting tones. We want them to experience the benefits of existence with others and the joy of connection. The plan is to want them, enjoy them, and refer to them often. When the kindergartner above goes for the door, send a message that you see her by the door, you want her in class, and you have to have her sit beside you. At first, these children will have trouble modulating the excitement and joy of someone wanting them to exist, let alone to exist powerfully. Be patient as they work it through.

With little Kemikah, the teacher kept telling the student to sit next to her, to follow her around the class, and often patted her. In response, the girl crawled into the teacher's lap on occasions, hugged the teacher, and attached with more and more maturity. The student then discovered other people who wanted her, who were glad to see and be with her. She needed about three months of school to establish security, but that is a small price compared to the damage done if she had been rejected repeatedly for "bad" behavior. School would have taught her nothing new and worse, reinforced her question of existence.

With older students, you use proximity, make comments about events or objects external to them (so you are not prying information out of them), and frequently keep them connected to you. This connection can be comments like:

"I thought more about what you said yesterday about turbochargers and..."

"Oh good, you're here. I want you to help me get these papers out to everyone. Will you?"

"Nice shoes"

"I am glad you're here."

These let the student know they exist to you day after day, that they are present in your mind, even when not face-to-face, and their existence makes a difference to you. You can connect them to other people in the same way. "I think James would be lost if you weren't his lab partner."

What does it look like when someone knows for sure he or she exists? They know you exist too! They can take people into their experience, they can engage more fully in experiencing being felt in others, and reap the benefits of social interaction. As they learn the benefits of relationship with an adult, they can go to the next series of questions and grow as a person.

AM I SEEN AND HEARD?

Now that I exist, to what extent do I exist? Who and how many see me? Who and how many hear me? Perhaps the entire room will. A key aspect of attachment is feeling you are experienced within another person and understood within him or her. You know they know you, you know them, and they know it. With being seen and heard, students are not so much after the experience of being experienced, as much as they are after being seen and heard *more* than anyone else on your radar. This question gets people doing all sorts of things to provoke and sustain connections that convey being seen and heard. How many students do you know that do and say some outrageous things while scanning the room to see who responds to them? How many people do you know who are loud, brash, dramatic, and respond to about anything in the world no matter how insignificant? They listen in and jump in to hijack other's conversations, have poor boundaries with their movements and voice level, and want to be the center of the universe. Conversely, some students draw attention by visibly seeking invisibility and making a parade of withdrawing. For some, being seen or heard is too much, or even dangerous for them, and they clearly hide.

For some students, it is life itself to be seen and heard. It is not dangerous; it is the biggest thrill ever. Everyone wants to be seen and heard, so it is a matter of degree, moderation, and modulation.

"LOOK!"
"I see a bug!"
"I got the red marker first!"
"Hey everybody, watch this!"

These eventually lose their snap factor so adolescents gossip, get the latest gizmo, and disrupt classrooms through absurd attention-getting actions.

My favorite is the fifth grader getting nowhere trying to pull the class attention to her. After several failed attempts, she paused, thought a moment, and then exclaimed, "My left butt cheek feels way different than my right butt cheek!" I think mine does too, now that I think about it. However, no one gave her the slightest response. So, she then moved to the next steps of the attachment cycle. She looked perplexed, aimlessly shuffled papers around, sat motionless, and then joined the lesson and participated academically. Then the teacher and peers joined her, all tuned in and on task.

At the end of one class the teacher said, "Some of you have earned detentions." A chorus of students said, "Is it me? Is it me?" The teacher then said, "Some of you have earned positive notes home." The same students again chorused, "Is it me? Is it me?" They just want to be seen and heard, and it has to be direct connection. "Some of you" is too vague to matter. It has to be personal.

How often do you experience the following? While you are giving instructions, a few pay no attention and act up in minor ways that you periodically stop to redirect. As soon as you turn the work over to the class, these same students are the first ones to shoot their hands up and yell out for help. They try to be seen and heard for their behavior problems. If unsuccessful with that, they switch to academic problems.

A teacher switched the rules on such a group by finishing the lesson and announcing, "I saw several of you really thinking about the lesson and making the most of your education. If you need help, I will come to you first." Two, yes, two, of the students described above simultaneously stood up bellowing, "That's not fair!" I laughed aloud. They were instantly trying to capture the teacher's attention with an absurd argument. They instantly knew the rules of being seen and heard had changed and instantly wanted those rules operating as they had been. If, as the teacher, you give this argument an explanation, they have the rules of engagement back on their terms because you are now socially reinforcing their "problem," which is for you to be totally focused on them. The only difference is it is social, instead of academic. If you respond to their yelling out or disruptive behavior with calm, planned ignoring, or crisply deliver an actual consequence, you are excellent at keeping your mood and direction. This may sound confusing now, but will be fleshed out in later chapters. For now, just be aware some students are desperately striving to be seen and heard with social and academic strategies. When and how, and what we help is important!

Many students use tactics teachers love. However, it is all striving and excess as if there is not enough seeing and hearing to go around. In gifted classes, some students wildly wave their hands to answer. They raise their hands in the middle of the lesson to offer rich insights and intriguing facts, or blurt out fascinating tidbits of extra information. They cannot go five minutes without needing to be on their teachers' radar. They are desperate to be seen and heard, and use academics to make it happen. Everyone knows they have the academic answer, but they do not have the social answer—yet.

Students need a lot of assurance they are being seen and heard for whatever they are doing right and good, for positive values, and positive contributions to the class BEFORE they strive. This is what Dr. William Becker means by "catch them being good." We are to be after them like a hunter stalking the best catch ever! It is not a passive activity at all! We are not to be passively waiting and hoping they will do something "good". We are hunting them and stalking them for any "good" we can find. To create a value-driven classroom, we are after them for any manifestations of the values. We want to find them and reinforce them. We want to build up an ever greater, more enduring good. Becker knew social reinforcement was—and is—the most powerful reinforcement. He explained we are to be intentionally driven to "catch" whatever good we can find and reinforce it, build up the success, and build up positive qualities.

Students dramatically seeking to be seen and heard can be outgoing or withdrawn. I find two types of outgoing students. The first type of attention seekers are generally silly, funny, goofy, and break many rules in the process. Sometimes they are not funny, but fussy, complaining about everything and obnoxious in a cartoonish way.

"OMG, I hate grilled cheese!"

"I…can't…find…my…eraser!"

You might call them the class clown or the drama king/queen. What they have in common is that, as much as they push the limits, when they know you are really about to consequence them (NOTICE: This means they know you are going to stop fussing or ignoring them and actually do something.) they say something such as "OK, Mr. Thomas, I quit. You don't need to send me to the office, I won't do it anymore." They recognize your last second of tolerance and then shut it down—for a while anyway. Have they just talked you out of delivering that consequence? I hope not! We will get to that in later chapters.

The major plan with this first type of student is to see and hear their positive values before they begin to behave in ways that demand/ command you to see and hear them. At the same time, you actually want to deliver consequences for any infraction of the rules. Repeating a rule is *not* a consequence. A consequence is a time-out, a detention, a chore, or something that takes their time and energy to accomplish. We will get more in to what actual consequences are in later chapters. As Becker so clearly points out in Parents Are Teachers (1970), you do not want to be socially reinforcing more and more problems by fussing, reminding, or restating rules. This is especially true for students with this question burning in their heart and soul. When adults begin to see and hear these children and adolescents for even a small step in the right direction—and really pour on the praise establishing many moments they are reinforced or seen and heard as a good person, most students really bloom. Because they are being seen and heard, they no longer have to strive so hard and can relax. In the language of attachment, you are attuned and intentional with the best intentions. You are communicating you want to experience them within you in joy and peace. You are after them.

The second type of student with this burning question is not fun loving at all. They want *you* only, not the class. They go for fear and safety issues, provoking teachers and schools to be nearly obsessed about managing them. By putting the adults in the school in suspense, angst, and fear, these students command being seen and heard because they can be truly dangerous—physically or emotionally—and unpredictable. These students have your attention at home, at a party, sleeping, driving to school—everywhere. They make sure you *have* to respond to them or *really* bad things can happen. They can be three years old or seniors in high school. They do not know what to do with you when they have all of you; they just want to have all of you without sharing.

This student is not really about power, though they are often treated as such. Those after power have the Essential Question of "Do I make a difference?" These students simple want to have you seeing and hearing them and no one else.

Safety of others is always the number one concern with this second subset of seen and heard. Always ensure safety. That said, there is a difficult task ahead. The task is to boldly chase them down repeatedly with social reinforcement of when they are exhibiting positive qualities—not just positive behavior. This is important for three reasons. In the first place, these students are after total control of your direction so that you are intensely provoked to see and hear them. You must keep your mood and direction off fear and dread, relentlessly gluing your mood and direction to what you want to socially reinforce or build more of within the climate and culture of the class. The second reason is that, solely focusing on these students' behaviors will leave them in charge because only they can control their behavior. You cannot control anyone's behavior. You want to focus on the positive character qualities of these students so you drive the direction and have abundant freedom to find any number of positive character qualities. They cannot stop you from that. Thirdly, you actually want to show them they are likeable and good, in spite of themselves. This is important because they want *you* at a deeper level and if you focus on how they are behaving, they will feel you just want a well-oiled machine. It will not be personal and they want personal. If you just go for them behaving, they will escalate attempts to make it personal. They will take you down even farther on a path of fear and uncertainty.

With this second subset, because they will constantly break rules, you do not really want to be on them about the rules—except for safety—as they will take you down a path of constantly breaking rules. Again, this is so you will totally focus on them. Until the corner is turned where they relent and accept that it is better to be seen for good than bad, all but safety rules are on hold. You are purely laser-focused on their good qualities and, when necessary, going through the motions of securing safety for everyone. Someday they will act remorseful, be less intense, less frequently commanding, and give up sooner. Any of these is progress. If you see two at once, rejoice!

This second subset also will benefit from you letting them know you see and hear them when they act up in ways that do not trigger safety responses. While they pout and fume around the room, you periodically make nonjudgmental, nondirective comments such as:

"I see you by the mailboxes"

"I see you are angry"

"I hear you being upset."

This may sound like wacky advice but it helps these students calm down, and feel seen and heard so they do not have to escalate their actions into violating safety. It helps prevent them from dropping into panic that they do not exist to you anymore. That *really* escalates them.

Keep reading this book and you will learn a lot more about how to do this and what these terms mean. For now, these are general ideas. Wouldn't it be nice to understand everything at once? Just as "play nice" or "be a good friend" communicate a *huge* number of little acts and attitudes we expect children to get. We are dealing with social curriculum, character, values, and many smaller behaviors and attitudes in a vast culture and climate in the shifting sands of daily life. "If only I knew then what I know now, I would…." So, onward!

Some students act withdrawn to the point that you are provoked to crack them open a bit to become more outgoing. The temptation is to try to supply tons of outgoing cheerfulness that will make up or counterbalance how withdrawn the student is. Often though, when you ask questions, they give obscure, evasive, and vague answers. The chase is on. They keep moving the target you seek. They need basic, short messages that they are seen and heard, in a matter of fact way. "It seems hot in here. Are you hot?" They just need to see you as ready to move with them when they move, rather than push or cajole them. The task is to be the model of living that they need to adopt. Rather than trying to cheer up and crack open a student who seems withdrawn and sad, do be concerned, but primarily be a model of cheerful (not gleeful) and optimistic living.

AM I SAFE?

Being emotionally safe involves not being shamed, cast out, made to feel lesser than, or confused by others. It means your dignity as a created being is upheld. It means you can make mistakes, but no one says YOU are a mistake. It means the rules are clear and the information people give is easy to decode, someone has hope in you, and you get clear feedback that is coherent feedback. If you mess up, you may learn a lesson, yet can anticipate a reconnection to all of the factors above. You are able to reflect versus being pressed to act, and experience yourself accurately and fully in someone else.

This question also encompasses physical safety. How safe or dangerous is it to be seen and heard? I meet many children that recoil from eye contact because it has been dangerous to be on adult radar. Some literally jump when an adult raises their voice, even in happiness. The loudness sets them off. Other students constantly scan whatever is around, such as the door or everyone's proximity. Are students being bullied, insulted, hit verbally or physically? Are you a bully teacher? Does the administration bully you? Do you feel safe at school?

I visited an inner city school specifically designed for physical safety. There was the occasional shooting in the neighborhood and even on the sidewalk around the school. All the windows were frosted so no one could be targeted from the outside. There were no windows on the street level so you could not shoot straight in. Everyone parked in an enclosed parking garage that formed the first floor of the school. Guards monitored everything going in and out. The school enclosed three sides of a second-floor playground. The playground's open side faced single story buildings below. Inside the school, it was full of color, clean and cheerful. Everyone understood they were as safe as possible and students were glad to practice safety drills. They knew what the outside neighborhood was like because it was their neighborhood. Staff felt secure, so students felt emotionally safe.

All students in an alternative middle and high school I consult with are scanned to detect metal. Distrust, fear, and hassles initially marked this daily exercise. Now the staff have cheerful conversations during the process and thank students for helping the process go quickly, being responsible, helping them to be their best. Other benefits naturally occur. "You were a math-magician yesterday, Deon!" A new climate and culture evolved almost overnight, allowing everyone to send and receive different messages. This also happened at an outpatient psychiatric school. Staff could not believe how eager the students were when they returned the next day to continue positive conversations, and how smoothly the scanning went. Messages of comfort and safety replaced messages of danger and distrust.

Safety happens at many levels. One aspect is predictability. Can I be sure I know what is going to happen next? If something unpredictable happens, am I ready? Is anyone else ready? Is the hallway safe during passing periods? Is it safe when most everyone is in class? Are there toxic teachers and students that I cannot avoid?

Story Time: Drive By

Listening in the hall of the high school, I heard a student with a hall pass tell his teacher, who functioned as a hall monitor at the time, about the extra project work he had completed. Even though he was out of the previous day, he was proud he was ready for eighth hour. An administrator came up behind him, spun him around, and said, "You don't need to be out here. Stop your goofing around and get to class right now!" Off the student went. The administrator did not inquire into the merit of the conversation with the teacher, or even recognize the teacher. What could the teacher say then? She felt like she could not share her point of view or speak up for the student. What do you think would have happened if the student tried to speak for himself? What climate and culture was present for the administrator, the teacher, the student, and me as observer? We all individually walked away with the voice of the school speaking a message to us. What does that moment in that school speak to you?

When we are emotionally unsafe and/or physically unsafe, it is not so much that we are actually being hurt. It can be we are being stripped of our dignity. It can be we are learning helplessness, to be unseen or unheard, and not to exist. Perhaps it is not that we recoil and retreat, it is that we cannot really move forward to better things or better ways of being. Certainly, students come to us with chronic and acute traumas, neglect, and unstable lives. Yet students also come to school terrified they will not get into a prestigious college, will receive the grade of an A-, or are never good enough.

Story Time: Second Grade Portfolio

A second grade teacher told of how one set of parents came in to the first parent-teacher conference and wanted to know what the teacher was doing to build their child's portfolio because their child had to prepare to go to a big, prestigious college. Now the teacher is anxious, the parents are anxious, and the seven-year-old student is under pressure to fulfill the parental dream for, at least, the next ten years. How about living with the pressure to be perfect all the time? It is intolerable anything is imperfect because everything should be perfect. In a few schools where this "be perfect" standard reigns supreme, the tension is palpable in staff and students. It is the elephant, or gorilla, in the room. The barometric pressure drops when we discuss it openly. The staff feel unsafe because, at any moment, they might not be perfect and need to be perfect always and in all ways, which is impossible. Once in the open, there is big relief.

Many students I know live in poverty. That book bag is the only one for the year, as well as the pencil, binder, shoes, and coat. They may wear their coat all day. If they have to move away from their desk, they look to see who is looking at their stuff. They may yell across the room to make them stop looking. Looking is dangerous. "Don't touch it! Quit looking at my desk!" They have little security that their stuff is safe and cling to their belongings since it is all they will have for months. What does that do to learning when students are on alert for anyone even looking at their gloves, shoes, pencil, sharpener, binder, or eraser? What happens to learning when students realize the bus arrives in forty minutes and they have to deal with all sorts of hassles on the ride home, have to see if their little brother is safe, or if their dad has hurt their mom?

School is the most predictable, comforting, safe place for many. Schools have food, people you know, maybe medical care, space, kind, loving, and happy people. The furniture and toilets may be nicer and the lights and heat work—well, sometimes. A place someone actually listens, a place where adults or peers are not to hurt others, and a place where it is against the rules to be drunk, do sexual things, be drugged, violent, cuss, and threaten to harm. School is a place where someone agrees to help if any of those things happen and will try to stop them from happening. School is a place where weapons are not allowed. As a student, you may get to meet a nice police officer who cares about you and hopefully more than one adult who sees something special and hopeful in you.

Safety in schools has many dimensions that we do not often consider. Research on bullying shows there is more bullying when there is competition or conflict between teachers or between teachers and administrators. If people, or a class, compete against themselves, there is no problem. However, when it moves to a contest of which class is better or group is better, then more bullying occurs. Competition fuels the better than/less than idea, which spawns emotional and physical safety issues because it taps into our Essential Questions. This also is true if there is a lot of conflict between groups of staff. The more teacher-to-teacher conflict is present, the more bullying in schools. What do schools often do to decrease bullying problems? They have a competition. Sometimes it is lighthearted fun. It can also become emotionally or physically unsafe. Even adults riot after sports events, or they get angry when their daughter loses the beauty contest or someone gets the parking space before them. When competition fires my Essential Questions and negative answers ensue, I am in trouble. In addition, so are you, because it is personal now. What Essential Question am I grappling with when I have such high investment in my sports team winning, my daughter winning a beauty contest, or my side winning some artificially contrived game? I have a lot more to say in the consequences chapter about this topic.

Let us say I get personal and act the fool. Is there a way to restore my dignity and yours? Is forgiveness possible? If not, I am not safe, nor is anyone else in the system. I am damned, labeled, not forgiven, and unable to show I have learned, changed, and improved, and that you are valuable and important to me. Do you know that when students are suspended and expelled they experience shame? Do we really give them a way to alleviate their shame? On the contrary, we often shame and inflame. How safe can they be? How can they grow? What do we really expect them to do? Generally, we leave then in the position of "try again and don't mess up." What will they be most likely seen and heard for? That is not safety.

Let us go back to the students who take you down with anger and fear in their efforts to dominate what you see, hear, and feel. I recommended you let them fuss and pout as long as they do not violate safety standards or make teaching come to a halt. In terms of safety, not tossing these students out helps them learn they can control themselves, that you want them with you, you expect them to succeed, you believe they can overcome their approach to living, and you are there with clear boundaries or rules, and love and support, not fear and loathing. If you are overloaded with fear and loathing, they are unsafe with you because they are running the show. You are on your heels, not on your toes with a plan and mission to help them go forward with. It is important you regroup and find your level of safe so they can "catch" safety from you.

If you find you are fearful, loathing, shaming, blaming, and inflaming, find someone who can help you restore your ability to see the students as striving and defending, and help you be the experience they need.

We have to answer their burning question and the next higher question as well. In fact, you have to have hope throughout your climate and culture, or everyone will devolve into striving and defending over every little thing. To obtain hope requires character and values. Character and values come from perseverance. To obtain perseverance requires trials of one's beliefs and whatever one has faith in. We are on the road to hope!

DO I MAKE A DIFFERENCE GOOD OR BAD?

Yes, you do! Everyone makes a difference. You cannot *not* make a difference. This is a great deception in life—that we make no difference. It is impossible. You pull a small rock out of a mountain and it will make a difference. The quiet student who never talks to anyone makes a difference, the little fifty-cent item stolen from a store makes a difference, and the neighbor who never seems to come outside makes a difference. Those little pebbles and pennies may add up over time and really produce something new. Just like ignoring little problems with your health may eventually add up to make a significant difference.

This question is about something more immediate and interactive. This question asks if you have any power to influence anyone's mood or direction. In communications theory, this is known as being a difference that makes a difference. If you do something different and it makes no difference in the outcome, structure, or functioning of the system, then the difference is not "information" to the system. The difference had no power to influence the system's actions, qualities, direction, or outcome. In communications theory, it is then termed "noise." The question "Do I make a difference?" refers to how powerful someone is in making a difference that makes a fairly immediate difference in others and/or the culture. Some students are so legendary in making these changes that staff still speak about them for years.

This is important to understanding your personal power, and what I mean by authority. Your authority resides in your ability to control your mood and direction. If someone is able to alter the direction of your lesson, your class rules, and/or your mood, then they are making a difference that makes a difference. Otherwise, their efforts are noise without effect. We all have triggers that get us going. If it is not a trigger (makes no difference), then we just keep going with class. Just a little pencil tapping drives some teacher nuts. Other teachers don't even notice it. Students quickly figure out what difference makes a difference in their parents, their peers, and us. It is their job in life. In fact, when I am a grandparent, I will attempt to find the differences that make a difference in my grandchildren, and they in me.

Of course, students do this with academics as well. I was in graduate school and when a classmate mentioned the theory of Alfred Korzybski, one professor would change course and speak at length about Korzybski's work. He postponed test dates and cut short projects because, as a class, we were falling behind. All anyone had to do was say, "This sounds like something Korzybski might agree with," and the mood of the professor and the class direction changed.

Some students come to school hoping to make a difference—any difference at all, to anyone. They search for whomever stops to listen, who really thinks about what they say, or who changes their direction of motion or conversation or mood because of them. When we send students (or other adults) messages that they do not belong, we have no time for them, no help for them, or that they need to leave and be fixed, we communicate that they make no difference. Here is school, you do not fit, go away, or at least do not be seen or heard. You are a square peg in a round hole. We trigger them, often to the core of their existence, and they pay us back in unforgettable ways. They will make a difference you will never forget! Some just disappear or get hauled off in cuffs.

What are they really telling us? Please, please, please, treat me as if I make a difference to you. What if students hear something like, "I don't care if you graduate or not" or "I'm done with you. I don't care where you go, just leave my room." *Ouch*! At one level, as the student, I am not making much of a difference. I am not really wanted, I'm all alone, and I need to fit in the system or get out. Who *wants* me and says *yes,* you make a difference? At another level, I am making a difference. I am making a difference as a statistic, another student they will talk about at lunch, another dent in the shiny veneer of education. Yet, I will not really be a difference that makes a difference in my immediate life, and the system of school will continue as is without me.

Making a difference means what I say, do, think, and feel matters *and* influences the mood and direction of others and/or the system. My input is sought and counts for something that makes something different. It can be as simple as suggesting a game and people play it, or that someone walks briskly down the hall, but sees me and stops to say hello. It can be that someone is walking down the hall and avoids me like the plague. I can have a question and the teacher takes time for me, or the teacher notices that I do not feel so good today. Perhaps I am able to get the teacher off the lesson! What a huge difference! What if I can get the teacher so frustrated he or she starts yelling and arguing with me? Huge difference! What if I make them question their profession? What if I get them back on their heels so that they cannot stop looking to see what I am up to? I have remote control of their mind, emotions, and even their ability to propel a lesson.

The more you try to force these students to stop, the more they are running the show. As the teacher, you feel like you make no difference. Progressively you have surrendered your mood and direction and, therefore, your authority. You are in a contest over who will make the biggest difference and eventually appeal to greater authorities than yourself. As long as it is a contest, the student is winning, but both of you lose in the end. This question is about personal power, influence, and leadership. We want people to make wonderful differences and one of these is to be a leader in answering the Essential Questions of others in a proactive way. The main task with this question is to give power to the student so they can be a good and welcome difference. You want to give power away, not be in a power struggle.

What do you experience when you feel you make no difference at work, with a spouse, a son or daughter, your parents, the administration, or your team? What do you think students feel and experience in a school culture where they can create little real difference? Research tells us that the more students are involved in the government of the school and have a voice in the school, the less bullying and aggression there is. (Espelage and Swearer 2003)

You may know how it feels to be appreciated only for your grades, athletic ability, or the scores your students get on state tests. As long as you produce, you are gold. But, what happens if you can't or don't? This is no different than if students know that as long as they behave, they are gold. But, what if they don't behave? Do they have any dignity or respectability left as a person if they can't or don't? Sometimes we have to know and so we quit producing to see what happens. Are we a bad part of the machine that needs to be fixed or tossed, or do we really matter? Do we really make a difference as a person because we are a person?

I recently spoke with a seventh-grade student sitting in In School Suspension. He told me he had about given up on school because he cannot keep his mind focused. He said he takes medication, but it only helps some. "When I lose track, I ask for help but the teacher tells me I should have been paying attention and won't help me. So my grades aren't that good." He is learning not to ask for help in class. Guess what? He can get help in ISS. His hope is that teachers will help him in high school.

A number of students will not do any work until the teacher speaks to them. Then they get busy. When students come in, put their heads down, and are told, "Good morning! Glad you are here," their heads usually pop up. They are experiencing that they are making a difference—a positive difference—to the system. They are a desired component that influences the mood and direction of the teacher in positive ways. Remember the saying, "Whatever you give your time and energy to, you really love?" Who and what gets your time and energy? Who and what makes your head snap around? That is what makes a difference. This is what you reinforce socially. This is what is really inspiring to you. This is what you had better love, because you will get more of it.

When we start extracting differences out of others, trying to force it, we are in trouble. We need to be providing a difference that will invite others to respond with positive differences on their own. "Good morning. I'm glad you're here," is an example. Our tendency is to force the change. **The key to reinforcement is to follow success.** We will read more on that in the chapter on being the best coach possible. When you are forcing change, you are doomed from the beginning. You cannot make anyone do anything. Expect to fail.

As one develops, one may find that they indeed make a powerful difference, but in ways that drive people to meltdown frustration or to instant delight. I might be born with a natural charisma that draws people to me, or —born with an annoying voice, an irritable personality, or line of interests that repels most anyone. I will need to know if I really am a good person as well as find someone to fit with and share my life with. If I am a square peg in the school's round hole, not fitting in or falling right through, then I might be able to fit in with a gang that will make me feel I am making a difference, belong, and am enjoyable. Maybe students will tease me for my intelligence, but the science clubs and science fairs I enter celebrate me. Of course, there is also prejudice where the differences I make are imposed upon me simply by being seen or heard. What do I do with that power to influence people so strongly? What does that power mean about me? If that is how some or many others define me, who can I be seen and heard by so they see and hear *me*? Maybe they see my skin, handicap, clothing, accent, or whatever.

To help students experience making a difference in positive ways, let your head and voice snap for all the good you can find. Give the students jobs, have them take care of something valuable to you, ask their ideas, refer other students to them for help, stop class to praise them for evidencing a high value, tell them you feel better when you see them smile, and on and on. Tell them how they make you feel good, how they make others feel good, how the day would not be the same great day without them, and any other way you can communicate they make a positive difference in the world. Give them the power to make a difference with. This is an important part of consequencing. This is why "The consequence is to be a contribution." Bring a "good" difference back into the equation of the class climate and culture. There is an entire chapter on that.

I believe that a basic dilemma in human kind is a battle over how much of our true inner good we have to wager to fit in and be enjoyed. Another basic dilemma is how much of my heart can I wear on my sleeve and still protect it. How long can I wager my own dignity and integrity to belong and be enjoyed before I lose my sense of goodness or self? The reverse is true as well. Some students already have surrendered a lot of inner goodness or had it stripped away, and now fit in with a crowd of those enjoying each other and bonding as a group of "bad" people. It is a challenge for them to surrender this bond and sense of belonging that seems so secure, for something as already invalidated or surrendered as their innate goodness. They risk their group identity as well.

We want to make a difference and sometimes it is hard to be alone if we are lonely, waiting for that satisfying combination where we can be and feel we are good, belong, and enjoyed. I watched my daughter trying to fit into a new school many years ago. Little by little, she sacrificed who she was on the inside to be a part of what became a heinous clique of girls. She reached a point of too much inner sacrifice and got out. I hear some first-year teachers voice their dilemmas about the school culture. They directly speak about their values and hopes about coming to teaching and the incongruity of the culture they find themselves in. They fight internally about how much to let go of inside to gain something outside when there is disparity. If it all fits, great!

This need for congruity is important to our safety and learning. Later in the book, I address how your values will need to fit congruently with your attitudes and actions so they can truly be learned and experienced in others. If there is incongruity, there will be striving and defending. In order to help people make hard choices around fitting in and belonging, we begin with affirming they are "good."

AM I GOOD?

Even if I find I can only make "bad" differences—because no one has "good" differences on their radar—I still need to know I am good inside. I need to feel I am good even if my life circumstances teach me that to survive I need to be one mean dog. I might have a great mean dog skill set, but it does not have to be who I am. We may be so focused on the outward defending and striving that we can hardly see the question or the desire in the spirit. Perhaps we lose sight of this in ourselves, others, or both.

Especially in middle schools, I find students vary tremendously in their behavior and attitudes depending on the teacher they have for any given period. More than that, some students vary wildly in a driven, almost hysterical way. They fly back and forth between defiance and compliance. They intensely monitor peer connections. They appear in a crisis of questioning if they are good or bad and assessing what the social environment tells them. They do not really want to be "bad," but to feel they belong and are enjoyable, being "bad" may be their best option. Sometimes it is the reverse. They believe they are truly bad and are experimenting with good. Acknowledge you see and hear the "good", but do not shoot off fireworks and make a big deal over it.

Many students present us with a mixed picture. Like the student who had half his body following one rule and half his body breaking a rule, or the student who shouts out correct answers when you want to call on hands. We have to go for the good elements so we can grow them. I believe everyone has some gift. Some of us are humorous, magnetically friendly, powerfully observant, quite empathetic, or charismatic, and so on. Each gift has a set of pluses and a set of minuses. We have to master the gift wisely or it may take us down. We can be too humorous, too empathetic, too outgoing, too hung up on minutia, or too charismatic. We need to learn when, how, and to what degree to apply and use our gift. This is where we can help students see their gifts and then help them use them wisely. We are very likely to see the unwise use of the gift and possibly squish the gift in the process. Maybe a student is mean with their humor, or tells jokes at inappropriate occasions. We need to help them stop, but grow different elements of their gift with love and precision so they still feel innately good as a person.

Having a value-driven classroom, we can help students experience themselves as good people and find the class values manifesting in their actions and attitudes. We can just tell them, "You are so good!" We can ask the students questions such as, "What could a good-hearted person do in this situation?" You can ask the class, "How are we being helpful to each other today?" You can just write a note home that simply says, "Ms. Kirk, your daughter is a good person. We love having her in our class." You could just find students who are living out the values of the school pledge.

Avoid equating the goodness of a student with them following expectations or following rules. Avoid it like the plague. Do equate following rules and expectations with how that is helpful and giving, well intentioned and comforting to others. In other words, focus on the benefits and spirit of the law, rather than the law itself. For instance, let the students know that walking in their classroom helps everyone feel safe. Their being quiet helps everyone do their best. Do a clear download about the ways they help others feel good, worthy, and valuable. Just the fact that you focus on them to answer their Essential Questions, and deeply and lovingly help them use their gifts wisely, lets them know they are good. "Am I good?" closely ties to another question.

CAN I BE ME?

We are born with predisposed temperaments and reactivity to things in our environment, even our own emotions. Daily life then massages or hammers these into the background or foreground. The shy infant becomes an outgoing leader. The rambunctious toddler becomes a savvy diplomat. As we grow up, we may be able to define ourselves or others may define who we are. This goes on throughout life. However, some things are not so open for alteration. I may hate walking slowly, be overloaded by silence or too much noise, be incredibly attracted to color, thrive on new experiences or crave sameness, or run from or to physical closeness.

Students bring what life has taught them to be their best options so far. If we answer their Essential Questions well, they will be less defending and striving. They will feel safe to reveal more of who they are. We want this. We want them to show who they really are so they can learn how to fully be with other people and drop any deceptions or compromises. We want them to feel all the power they have over themselves. What are their real issues and hopes?

Here again is the dilemma of how much do I reveal about my true thoughts, true feelings, or real disposition to other people without putting my connection with others in jeopardy. How much can I just *be* me before we are no longer connected? Will anyone really "get" me? If they really get me, will it be OK and will they help me grow and find my life's real dreams? Children quickly learn what parents and teachers want. We almost constantly communicate what we like and want. When we meet new people in new situations, we instantly begin scoping out these likes and dislikes. We are all speed dating. I think it is a revelation to discover just how fast and fluid climate and culture operates. It is instantaneous, and you had better have both hands on the steering wheel driving climate and culture or it will immediately be driven by someone else.

Can I be me? Can I be the one standing at my desk while I do my work? Can my gift of humor be kept, just better used? Can I be hearing impaired and know that I am just like everyone else *except* for that? Can I be defended and striving, yet understood and helped? Can I enjoy what I enjoy? Can I be a six-year-old Black female who wants to be a farmer when I grow up, and find support and encouragement? (Emonie does!) Can I wear the clothing I like to wear? Can I love monster trucks, chemistry, and dance? Can I love what or whom I love? Can I be left-handed? Of course, these questions interact with laws, standards of kindness, religion, cultural norms, and fads. Can I like rap and country western? If I know I need space, is that OK for me to want, to need? Can I not want to go to college?

Interviewing high school students, I met an African-American student in her senior year already accepted at a well-regarded college. She spoke about how different that made her in various ways. She would see diversity in the hallways, but not in her classes. Where were her friends and all the other African-American students? She said she was only one of two black students in her math class. She would go out of her way to help and encourage other African-American students to work hard, to invest in learning, and to try for college, but they saw her as different from them. "You're smart and going to college." She connected to school through many extracurricular activities. Emotionally, she was strong and knew what she wanted to do. She sometimes had to work hard to get the guidance counselor to meet with her, to help make her dream come true. Her strength came from her family. What if her family had not been such a supportive and forward-looking family? Whom are you supporting in their dream? Whom are you writing off? How do you let students know they can tell you about who they really are?

AM I COMPETENT?

What am I good at? Academic success and social success are almost two different types of esteem. I might be a huge social success, yet have a mediocre report card. I might be a straight-A student, yet peers and teachers revile and rebuff me. On the other hand, I could be a big hit socially and academically. For students who have severely struggled with their Essential Questions finding academic success is important.

Story Time: Am I A Reader?

It was a fourth grade room in March and, as had occurred each day for months, Darion was at the kidney bean-shaped table with two or three other students doing some reading with the teacher.

He looked at the teacher and asked, "Can I read?"

"Of course you can," replied the teacher.

"No," he said. "Am I any good at reading? Am I a reader?"

The teacher told him he was, in fact, a good reader and gave him scores to show how much he had gained this year, how he was at grade level, had excellent word attack skills, and more. He was so proud. No one had told him how competent he was nor really anointed him as a "reader." Now he was, finally, in the fourth grade, two-thirds of the way through the year. What was his real "education" that day? No one had ever told Darion, a young minority student, that he was a reader, and a very competent one at that. Had he not asked, Darion never might have known and become one of the high school students mentioned previously, who told the college-bound girl they were different than her and weren't smart.

Students making huge shifts in their social behavior invariably report how they learned to read, write, do math, or draw, along with the changes they made in their behavior and attitudes. The key is to know how to do something and be competent in both the academic and social curriculums. Many students have told me the same clear process that changed the direction of their lives. First, the teachers believed in the students, and then the students believed in themselves. Once they believed in themselves, they turned on academically. They gained additional respect for themselves from their academic successes as well. When answering students' inner questions about their competencies, we can begin in preschools. A three-year-old student looks on the wall poster to find the letter "A" and tries to write it. The child is "resourceful," an "independent learner," and a "smart problem solver." If you want more lifelong learners, start early!

I consult in TMH classes where students learn to spell and read three-letter words, what one-half of something is, and add one-digit numbers. The teachers call them mathematicians, thespians, and writers. They are and they love it!

Sometimes students bring their hot potatoes to school. They have a problem for which they have no solution, and try to put it in our hands. I met one such child in a kindergarten class. As soon as anyone entered the room, this smiling cherub would begin all sorts of clever insults and provocations. He was being bullied by someone and he had no answer for it. (It turned out his teenage brother.) We could have consequenced him to death, but that would not help him respond to his brother. We needed to give him a response to bullying that he could use at home. Otherwise, he had no answer and would remain incompetent. Notice we are not telling him what to do. We are doing what he needs to do. We are the model of the solution. I decided the next time he tried me, I would respond with a bland, "I don't think that is much fun," and turn away to something else. The teacher and some classroom peers said similar things to him over the next few days. The problem disappeared in a week. Sometimes students bring us a problem where they need to be called a name or equipped with a solution so they can be who they are.

CAN I TRUST MYSELF?

A first grader, who had overcome great problems in kindergarten, was having some problems again in second grade. The teacher had sent him to the principal's office for acting out. He cried and told the principal, "I trust you and I trust my teacher, but I don't trust myself." We so underestimate the wisdom of little children! We need to help each child trust him or herself. We could spend hours trying to find the right punishment, the right incentive chart, the right person to relate to this child *or* anyone and everyone can be there to help him reinforce all sorts of moments so he is able to trust himself.

Such moments could be when he remembers something, when he stops doing something and then does something better, when he is showing self-control, and when he could be upset about something but does not act out. I especially like to validate the intuition children have. Our intuition is extremely valuable as a guide to us. Many things adults do really messes up the intuition children have. I like children to check out their hunches, feelings about situations, informed guesses, and inferences of what others are up to. Many people can be on the lookout for any moment like those. However, children could also be shown to trust themselves even when they are saying they cannot. They can trust themselves to know what their problems are and trust themselves to get help, rather than to act out. They can trust themselves to believe in other people even when it feels they cannot trust themselves. These are all valuable abilities in becoming a scholar of living.

Can you trust yourself? Do words and actions fly out of your body before you know it? When the moment comes to say what you have been planning to say, do you say it? Can you always say "no" to temptations? Are you keeping your word and completing your agreements? Can you trust yourself to remember things? Are you able to stand for what you believe in? We all have our moments where we falter, stumble, and drop like a rock. However, we have success too. As we build up students—with social reinforcement of those moments when they stand up, keep their word, resist temptations, keep agreements, and manage their words and actions well—we can build up trust in themselves. We especially want to build reflective, conscious minds. More on that later.

AM I VALUABLE OR WORTHY?

Do I deserve, as much as anyone, help, forgiveness, kindness, patience, dignity, a place in the social network, encouragement, recognition, utility, and the collective mind of the class and school? Do I receive enough necessities to feel like I have dignity? Maybe I am just part of a well-oiled machine and no one really says or acts as if I am needed. I just need to follow and fit in. Who will come after me so I feel wanted, worthy of the relationships and connections, and respect others seem to freely exchange?

Story Time: Joy

Because of a history of bad attitudes, poor achievement, and aggression, Joy was placed in the self-contained room at a middle school. The teacher in this room would give instructions and Joy would get all ticked off.

"I'm not stupid! Why do you talk to me as if I don't know what to do? I hate you. Don't talk to me. I don't want to hear what you say. Shut up and tell yourself what to do!" She would then toss her book on the floor, put her head down, and simmer in anger.

Now you might be thinking she is a terribly insolent and hopeless adolescent, but to me she was fighting for dignity and worthiness. We went with that hypothesis and when the staff gave her messages they recognized and respected her dignity, she actually became a joy! The staff began to ask her for ideas and say,

"Joy, you probably already know this but..."

"What do you think about this?"

"Joy, are you willing to help others on this?"

And, of all things, staff apologized when she voiced that she felt insulted. Wouldn't we normally do that to a friend or our own children? Often we can lose sight of that when we think our job is to fix people and stop them from striving and defending. We could look at her striving and defending and decide she is a lost cause, or we could answer her Essential Question and model the dignity she so craved. Within two months, Joy had become one of the most helpful, responsible, and fun students in the class. She smiles a lot!

Story Time: I Can Ride The Bus

Anton, classified behaviorally disturbed, usually sat in a special room for other BD students. He had a history of being aggressive and could really cuss! On this particular day, he had completed his task and earned some computer time, but as he headed to the computer, Bevan cut him off and got to it first. Anton looked disappointed and turned to cross the hall for another computer. The principal, who was substituting, praised Anton for making a good choice. After all, he didn't blow up. She focused on a problem averted. But, he did blow up. He went across the hall, started yelling, cussing, and threatening to tear up Bevan on the bus home. School was out in about fifteen minutes. The principal was trying to calm Anton, and find someone to take him home so he would not have access to Bevan. It was panic mode!

The Essential Social Curriculum constantly focuses on values. I spoke with the principal about how all the students in that program have social problems and, yes, a problem was apparently averted, but a standard of kindness was violated. It is easy to move from task to task and want smoothness without problems. However, when we overlook the values and standards of the climate and culture, we quickly head for striving, defending, and injustice. This spawns increases in bullying and anger. Bevan, who had no business being at the computer, had cut off Anton on purpose. The principal turned to Anton and said, "I am sorry, I made a mistake. I should have told Bevan to get up because he cut you off. The computer should have been yours to use." Anton stopped, looked down a moment, and looked up. "I am OK. I can ride the bus. I am OK now." The principal upheld a standard of kindness. She gave Anton dignity and justice, and valued him. She modeled kindness, dignity, and justice. When we nail the Essential Question and we are values in action, the results are immediate. It was not about the computer, it was about value and dignity. Anton really was OK and rode the bus without any incident.

I wondered, was Anton, and many others like him, labeled BD because he has a keen sense of when his dignity and justice are perverted? Perhaps he just can't stand when it happens because it happens repeatedly to him? Who can look beyond his striving and defending to see his question and build up his dignity and value? How much does he need? One thing for sure, he knows it when he experiences it. Note that when Anton received dignity, he showed us he could trust himself! "I'm OK, I can ride the bus." The school staff, his peers, and his parents could trust Anton more, yet none of this would have likely been possible had he not been dignified.

IS THERE ABUNDANCE?

Many children live have this question hanging over them. As do many adults. Is there enough love, stuff, time, help, recognition, food, enough…? Much of the time, the student issue in classrooms revolves around "Is there enough teacher connection?" At the teacher level, it is often a question of having enough time, permission from administration, and support to take the time. We want to teach abundance. Some teachers run ragged trying to put out one fire of need after another, or they pull way back because there is overwhelming need.

When faced with huge emotional needs from your students, begin going through the Essential Questions and you will probably find some grouping. Beyond the numerous needs for paper, pencils, food, sleep, clothing, transportation, medical care, and more, there will be the social-emotional needs. In spite of poverty, uncertain and frequent changes, toxic homes, homelessness, or other adversities, we can provide many daily teachings that students can take with them to nourish their life and spirit. Is there enough teaching of, enough abundance of daily affirmations and evidence for hope for them to go home with more than just the ability to survive?

Story Time: Could Have Stopped Here

I gave my coaching note to a third-grade teacher. In the notes were comments from her students about her. While I was in the class, three students had asked what I was doing. I told

> them I was writing about their teacher, and wondered what they would like to say about her. "She is an awesome teacher," said two. "She's a really good teacher," said another. I then asked them what made her so awesome and so good. They told me different ways she is fun, likes them, helps them, is patient, tells them they can understand something, and understands them. When I later returned to the teacher to discuss the class, she had read the note. She was happy about what the students had said since their comments clearly reflected the values she teaches from. I pointed to the first comments of "she's awesome" and "she's good" and said, "I could have stopped here." She immediately got how much she would have missed, how little she would have gotten, from just those generic compliments. Abundance breeds abundance.

Abundance answers many Essential Questions. When abundance is present, I can build hope, feel safer, learn resiliency, experience value, see my dignity, and learn greater and greater values. Being able to answer the Essential Questions for your students is part of that abundance. As you answer theirs, they answer those of the others around them. This starts a beautiful dance of answering back and forth. Remember, we are co-regulating a climate and culture constantly.

In an especially challenging first grade class there were six very high-need students, two who often became dangerous to others. We began by identifying the primary Essential Questions of each, and some practical ways to answer their questions. Two were the second type of people needing to be seen and heard. They wanted the total connection of the teacher through fear. Two were the first type of seen and heard, and did odd and dramatic things to be on anyone's radar. One was struggling with existence and often withdrawn and angry. The sixth student was autistic and little problems, such as not having an incredibly sharp pencil, easily derailed her. She needed abundance and hope. With this framework of knowing what questions to answer, the teacher felt less overwhelmed, had a plan, and was no longer on her heels with problems, but on her toes moving forward with provision. She could now literally see the student's questions in action and had answers. There were many complications to this class from outside and inside "help," yet the teacher made great headway. They all improved. The teacher ended the year confident with her Essential Questions answered in the affirmative.

I was able to follow three of these students into the next year and all three continued thriving socially and academically. The autistic girl was practically indistinguishable from her peers, easily moved through frustrations, and had friends. She rapidly learned how to socialize. The most unpredictably dangerous of the six is now a joyous second grader who angers, but reasonably so, and recovers quickly. He loves his teacher. He hugs her often. He learned there was more than enough and he could wait for it. He began to connect more with peers and grow emotionally. The third student I was able to follow is no longer striving to get whatever connection he can. He is focused, calm, successful, and staff and peers provided him with abundant, fulfilling connections. He is finding academic competency. Still a fun loving person, he is connecting more because he has win-win fun. Everyone wins as his winning social and emotional values manifest over time. **Before they manifest, we have to invest.**

We can spend many hours and many resources on stopping problems, when answering a few questions can change a life. When we answer the Essential Question well, the entire class and school benefits as a wonderful story is told which influences the climate and culture of the school. Parents will benefit too, and soon the community will have something wonderful to share. "That's a good school!" Or, even better, "Our community has good schools!"

Repeatedly, I watch this pattern occurring. I observe teachers going around the room helping students one-on-one, being pulled here and there by one academic dilemma after another. Then the teacher gets up, front and center, and begins to praise certain students and groups. In a flash, immediately a line of students forms in front of the teacher with students listing problems of all sorts. They strive to get the teacher off the positive connections with their peers. Not only that, but within their little crowd of needy peers they strive to get the teacher's help first. Many times are they are successful. The teacher abandons their connections to the most successful students and begins sorting through the ones lined up striving to get her. "You need to sit down if you want my attention!" or "Take you seats and I will come around to you." They fought and won, but what they won was not clear, positive connection. They won a frustrated teacher. There are ways for a teacher to provide abundance in a manageable way.

When students and staff act as though there is not enough, there will be many variations of striving and defending. Often people in schools act as if there is not enough because they have too many goals—all at number one—imposed by several other people at multiple levels. This is a real sinkhole for the human spirit to feel never good enough, hopeless, angry, and to become controlling to the point of bullying. You may ask, "How can there be enough when there is not enough?" or "How can I reach all these students when I do not have time?"

STRING THEORY

The key is to be living inside of the students, and for them to feel felt in you. This is the foundation of secure attachment and helps others stop zipping through their attachment cycle of striving and defending. To accomplish this, imagine a string between you and every student. If they pull and there is no tautness to the string, they yank the string to pull you in. If you can find ways to send messages down the string, especially many strings at once, and keep a flow going, you will be able to convey that there plenty of you to go around. As stated earlier, be aware that students yank with academic problems, not just social problems.

One way to provide is to state,

"You can all relax because there is enough of me to go around and I carry each one of you in my heart."

You might say, "Let me just stop and take you all in. I just love making mental video clips of you all to remember you by over and over." That is some love coming down the string!

"I know many of you have questions right now, but I want to pause a bit and just enjoy the sound of your collaborations and learning. Yes, that is the sound of great futures in the making."

Dr. Mueller, a masterful instructor, will sometimes stop conducting the high school orchestra, close his eyes, and just savor the music. "You sound so incredible, I want to fully experience you." Notice it is not the music, not the work itself, but the students. The orchestra always goes to an even more magnificent level! I get chills every time.

All too often, teachers get the right answer and move on. To send a message down as many strings as possible, you might ask,

"Who else had that thought?"

"How many other great minds were thinking alike on this?"

"Kiss your brain if you had that one!"

"Turn and talk to see if your neighbor agrees or has another thought."

I hope you can see how being focused on the answer and moving on has some serious drawbacks.

There is also scarcity in you being the only source of help, even though we often thrive on being a helper. It certainly adds to our positive answers around feeling valued, competent, and belonging, but it can drain us. However, if you can establish many sources of help—family, grandparents, library resources, posters all over the school, administrators, peers, Internet, other teachers, hall monitors, newspapers, and on and on—then you build abundance, hope, and competent, savvy problem solvers and part of what it takes to be a lifelong learner. You are teaching how to help, find help, use help, scan, prioritize, compare and contrast, differentiate, socialize, be creative, trust intuition, make educated guesses, and think abundantly, divergently, and boldly. Begin as soon as possible and fire yourself from directly answering and providing information.

Many teachers would love to have more homework turned in and finished. How abundantly is homework completion celebrated in your class? Often students just toss homework in a basket or hand it in. The creative Mr. Foli began saying, "Let's hear that homework!" and all the students with homework would shake their paper like crazy in the air. The noise was *loud*! Then they handed it to him as he roamed the room and he made comments to many of them. He had nearly a hundred percent of homework turned in. Students were alive in him and able to feel experienced through this little ritual. Think of every process in your day-to-day teaching, every transition, and each event. How can you send something down as many strings as possible at those moments?

Abundance also has to do with materials and peer connections. After nearly a century of institutionalized education and countless college courses, it amazes me that the issue of pencils and talking are still such consuming issues. In the first course any education major takes, the issues of pencils and the management of talking—when to raise hands or shout out, or how to train a class to manage their volume depending on the situation—should be taught thoroughly. That would save countless hours spent in educational settings, and who knows how many dollars of medicine. These two issues alone show the need for a viable social curriculum. Usually the problems stem from scarcity and not abundance. The more students talk, the more we want quiet. The more we prohibit them from talking (scarcity), the more they break the rules and talk, and the more they need to learn to be quiet. The more tightly we control, the more there are things that can and will go wrong, the more awful the students are, the more helpless you are and…then it starts all over again! When you look at these issues through abundance, things begin to look different.

Perhaps you could establish there is plenty of opportunity to talk, plenty of pencils, and then create or provide opportunity for them to students. What if you wanted them to have time to talk and made time for them to do so? Yes, there is work to be done. As students work, they may quickly turn and talk to a neighbor. When students work with stamina and diligence—even kindergarteners get these words—you might celebrate that by having talking time. "You worked so diligently, let's take time before the bell to talk!" You get time to talk to them, they to you, and they to each other. Powerful social reinforcement! How else might you provide abundantly?

As for pencils, some teachers have a huge basket of pencils willing students sharpen. To get one, you turn in your dull one. You can win pencils, buy pencils, or get one from the basket anytime. On the first day of class, everyone gets one free. Like the homework celebration earlier, on Monday morning, you hold your pencil high and the teacher or chosen helpers bring you a fresh one while celebrating students for being prepared, responsible, or whatever other values you attach to having a pencil. Abundantly and actively valuing having a pencil, they become a non-issue as far as striving and defending.

I moved to North Carolina many years ago and if even an inch of snow was forecast three days away, grocery stores immediately cleared of all bread, milk, peanut butter, eggs, and okra all over town. (Just kidding about the okra.) It was hoarding. Adults fight and shoot each other over the latest shoes or electronic gizmos if they think there is not enough—even though there will be more restocked in five days. Some freak out at the Cracker Barrel when they hear a waitress mention that the meatloaf is probably gone. There is a store in Champaign, Illinois, that hires people every year to carry signs on street corners announcing the store is going out of business. Big sale! Hurry! I have lived there twelve years and it is still going out of business in a newer, bigger store.

DO I BELONG?

Good in one culture can be different in another, and have a direct bearing on whether or not you belong with any particular group or subculture. This can be seen as students move from one class to another. In this class they belong and are enjoyed, in the next period they are reviled and unwanted. It may be within the same class as the teacher communicates that a student is wanted, but other students are not. The reverse could be true, or a mix where no one is getting a clear signal. The clearer we can send messages that others are enjoyable, missed, wanted, the more they feel they belong.

Story Time: Ugly Art- Beautiful Art

A third grade class was being delivered to art class and their primary teacher pops in to broadcast, "They are **really** a wreck today, beyond the usual. Good luck." I was aware there were chronic problems in the regular classroom so this was something special. Since the regular teacher had just given permission for her class to be a mess, they fully complied and were loud, defiant, obnoxious, and mean. The Art teacher tried the usual array of "If you hear my voice…," clapping, repeating rules, and other tactics intended to get students to behave. After about ten minutes, she came over and looked exasperated. "What now, Mr. Grove?" It occurred to me no one was really enjoying these students, really looking forward to them, not really wanting them. I asked the teacher to begin going around and simply find anything about each student or student's work that she enjoyed. So most everyone would be aware, she was asked to be fairly loud as she sent the messages out. She began to say things like, "Glad you're here Mark," "You chose a great blue for that," "I love the sound of your laughter Emily." The teacher gracefully roamed the class with messages of her delight in them. In three minutes, the class was timed in, timed on, and peaceful. She kept going all class. The class was directly experiencing they were enjoyable, that the teacher wanted to belong with them, and they were "good" people. At the end of class, she attempted to tell the regular teacher about how she had enjoyed the class, but the regular teacher drowned her out telling the class how they had better behave in the hallway. Back to striving and defending for them all.

Story Time: She Won't Let Us Fail.

I met a remarkable young man I'll call Val. He was acting up in high school most all the time and usually suspended or lodged at in school suspension. Yet, one class he begged to be in. Even if suspended from school, he wanted to attempt to attend! It was Ms. Sparkman's class.

I asked him why. He laid this sequence out which I am condensing here. First, "She believed in me. She said she saw something in me—something different but good. I would cut up and she would keep me in class! She would tell me to check myself and go on. She didn't hold a grudge like all the other teachers." Second, "If she could believe in me I could believe in me and I started doing my work. She wouldn't let us fail and gave us extra work to do so we could earn grades. I started respecting myself and even other teachers." Thirdly, "The other teachers started respecting me more."

First, we believe and see good in them. Second, they believe because we believe. Thirdly, we continually show them they are wanted, belong, and enjoyable. Then they pass it back into the school staff! How can we daily pass on—"You are good, enjoyable, and belong"—to each student?

When we convey to others that we would indeed miss them, we in essence tell them they belong. How often do you convey verbally or nonverbally that you would miss every student? After a school break, how clearly do you announce you are glad to be reunited with the students, that you belong together? For years I have observed that, after 3 day weekends or extended breaks, students give the teacher about 5 minutes to express how glad and wonderful it is to be reunited. If students do not hear that they have been missed as much as they missed you, they quickly enter the attachment cycle and get you highly involved with them by acting out. Answer as many Essential Questions as you can upon reuniting.

I have been a cog in a machine that was a real crazy machine. It was disorganized, confused, and on a couple of occasions I was ready to walk out, but I belonged. Truly, I could not enjoy Dilbert as it was too real, yet just like Dilbert, all the characters were deeply connected. The organization was a disaster but we were a close-knit emotional and mental team. I was so glad to leave that difficult organization, but sad to leave the people. Conversely, I have been in fantastic organizations that I did not belong in. My values and their values, my perspectives and theirs were irreconcilable at the social level even though the organization was fantastic. However, there is more to belonging.

Belonging is, in a large part feeling felt in others. Even if different values and perspectives are present, an individual's personal value and dignity are upheld. Bullying is all about degrading the personal value and dignity of others. I have met many students that act as if they want to destroy schools because school is destroying their value and dignity. School can make it hard for some to feel any belonging. School can be lonely. When students are suspended, they have the shame of not belonging. Can we really afford to have them turn that into a badge of honor? Or form a separate society of the non-belonging?

Story Time: Joe, Do You Smell Popcorn?

Joe was unknown to the middle school teachers he was supposed to have in the afternoon. He never made it. He was on the run, suspended, in the principal's office, or housed at in school suspension. He was legend though. He was the biggest class disrupter the school had known. Two staff would be on the front steps of the school every day waiting for Joe. Their job was to discern if he had taken his meds, and if not, to call mom and warn other teachers. Joe had a powerful and large adult companion with him who would always be about two feet away from him. He was there to help Joe behave. Lucky for Joe, he had Mr. Yacko first period. Mr. Yacko was determined to reach Joe and did. In fact, Joe had F's in all classes. However, once Mr. Yacko began with our plan, Joe was earning C's and turning in about sixty percent of his homework in six weeks! The plan was simple. Mr. Yacko would go after Joe with all sorts of causal questions, comments that were intended to help Joe feel valued and that he belonged. So, all of a sudden Mr. Yacko would say, "Joe, you ever heard anyone say mitosis?" Or many other questions like, "Hot enough in here for you today?" Comments such as, "I remember you said you like pizza. I could have pizza right now!" were common. Without *any* need to know *anything* academically, Joe's opinions, experiences, feelings, likes, and dislikes were sought, valued, remembered, and enjoyed. Joe belonged in class with everyone else and the teacher. He was getting many messages he was felt in Mr. Yacko, had dignity, and a valuable person to the class. Joe then acted as if he belonged and had value in better and bigger ways. This is the same sequence Val laid out.

The student Val recounted how Ms. Sparkman told him he was "different," but in a good way. "She saw something in me that I hadn't seen. That gave me confidence." That helped him feel he belonged in school. Ms. Sparkman had an earlier experience that helped her really see the need to belong and be wanted.

Story Time: (Snitch Sound) Only Twenty More Days With You, Ms. Sparkman!

Ms. Sparkman told me about a girl who had just graduated from high school and would come to class, zoom straight to her, and make a loud "snitch" sound. The girl would then look all put out and say, "I've only got twenty more days with YOU Ms. Sparkman." And so this continued to the last day of school. Ms. Sparkman asked me why the girl would do that every day like clockwork. They had not been on the best of terms and the girl was often antagonistic in class. I suggested the girl was telling her that she wanted something from her and was counting down the days hoping Ms. Sparkman would deliver before it was too late. Ms. Sparkman's eyes got big! To make the story short, Ms. Sparkman contacted the girl and they developed a mentoring group for other girls in foster care who had no real direction in life.

Who is telling you they need *you* to belong to them and want to belong to you? How many students are giving us a countdown before it is too late? This student was trying to belong, to be missed, and to connect with someone who she could trust with her dignity by the best options life had taught her. She was striving and defended, and, at first, her obnoxious methods were all that people saw. When you look beyond and see her as trying to become unforgettable, urgently announcing time is running out, and needing Ms. Sparkman in an intense way, then this foster child becomes an unforgettable keeper. Ms. Sparkman helped her get a job, open a bank account, and learn to shop and more. The girl had no help, no clues, and was so disconnected that she did not belong anywhere. She had many different foster home placements over the years. School had been the only place she could count on, but it was over. She counted down until it was done. Who really knew what those diminishing number of days meant to her? What obnoxious unforgettable student is seeking you because they need you?

AM I LOVABLE AND ABLE TO LOVE?

In our journey so far, we have gone from being seen and heard, to having emotional and physical safety, to making a difference that is valued, to really belonging in a world where there is enough. To have even greater intimacy and deeper affirmation of the Essential Questions, I arrive at love. There are several types of love in the literature. Ours will be on agape love. Can I love others for simply being on the planet, for having a spiritual presence because they are alive with questions like everyone else? Can I show others love simply for the sake of putting more love into the world to lessen striving and defending?

In the reverse, am I able to receive this love? Can I be someone that can be deeply cared for? Can I handle that someone wants me more than anyone else? Can I feel experienced in another and let them know I experience them in me? Is there anyone I will let know the truth about me and see if they still love me?

Far too many children seem to arrive at school with little love to start the day on. I have listened to parents screaming at their child as they exit the van for the beginning of elementary school. It is 7:45 in the morning, and their little life is full of anger and turmoil. In numerous kindergarten rooms, children repeatedly ask me to be their daddy. I compliment children and they often swarm to show me what they can do, to tell me anything good about themselves. Teachers often tell me they feel like the emotional needs of the children are almost overwhelming. They do not know how to fill the children up, and wonder if they ever can be filled. In 1969, William Glasser M.D. wrote about the overwhelming need for schools to teach how to love and be loved. It has not gotten any less.

So, straight to the point: Are you able to love your students and help them be lovable? Some students are traumatized, beaten down, hateful, revengeful, repulsive, and downright dangerous. As true with the general population, teachers are more eager and try longer to help anxious and/or sad students. We all have trouble with chronically angry and/or intensely depressed people. They tap in to questions about our competency and ability to sustain hope. They tap even deeper in to our view of humanity and value of humanity. I have heard people say things like, "I was nice to them for X weeks and they still treated me bad. I'm done with them." Does someone have you on a schedule of "X weeks and then done"? In TESC you are nice to be nice, not because it indebts people to be nice back, but to impart dignity, be a congruent model, and to socially reinforce more Essential Questions.

However, we all have our limits. These limits interact with the tools we have at our disposal to reach others. Our limits also interact with our beliefs and perspectives, our own Essential Questions. Can I be "done" in a loving way? Does my lack of success in helping them have to diminish their dignity or value as a person? No, it does not. If I lose hope and I feel I have hit my limit, does that mean the student should also lose hope? No, it does not if we lessen our involvement in a loving way, intentionally sustaining hope within them. We are at our best when we own our questions and our methods of seeking answers rather than blame, repress, devalue others. Others are doing the best they can too- just like you. We all fall short. How loving is it to know we are all after the same things with various levels of sophistication?

For many students we need to give them the experience of love because they have yet to know truly what it feels, sounds, and acts like. By answering the Essential Questions, we convey love, build love, and instill ways they can then love others. In the Value-driven Classroom, we are driving the value of love daily.

Some students are so wounded, they run from this. They have loved and hoped repeatedly, yet continually lost. To love means to attach, to hope, to trust. They fear attaching because they expect to be hurt eventually. So, they quickly flee. They provoke people to give up on them quickly too because the problem is replicated in reverse. You try to love them but they keep hurting you. Here is where you can overtly address several Essential Questions of the student. Can I be me? "Just because I really like you as a student does not mean you have to like me back." Sounds wacky, but this tells them they do not have to be close back. Their striving and defending is OK with you. In so many words we are saying go ahead and flee, I still value you and am not quitting just because you have issues valuing me. This helps them to belong, and to feel competent that they are doing something ok. It helps them feel understood, safe, even loved should they choose to flee. Love is about providing and we just keep providing care, compassion, and the best answers to their Essential Questions as possible.

However, this is done within limits and with limits so they can experience someone who knows how to give generously of their heart without letting anyone stomp on it and abuse it. This is an age-old problem. The way I manage this is not to be a moving target. Know what you are willing to do and to accept. Be clear what you will do and accept from them. Hold them to high values so you are not enabling them to continue destructive or unhealthy patterns. You follow their path, love them in failure, and set a limit—either on you, them, or both—until they succeed. You cannot make the horse drink the water but you can be kind to the horse as you make it thirsty, or make the water enticing.

Using The Essential Social Curriculum, I have teachers tell students, "I can't give my whole heart to you for that. Show me something I can give my whole heart to." If they do, you give your whole heart. If not, you wait them out or you give them a consequence. Another variation is, "That is hurtful and I expect kindness from you. Take a minute to think of how you can redo this with kindness and raise your hand when you have a way." For older students who are vile, I go with raw truth. "That makes me not want to give you the help you deserve. I want to help you with this because you need it to succeed. Can you stop this and be easy to help? I'm ready when you are." All of these make your intention clear, are done with kind tones, set clear limits, and create clear contracts. You do not chase them or cajole them because that makes you and your love a moving target. Hold the standard of being lovable for yourself and them in how you interact with them and what you want from them.

CAN I HOPE?

Hope can sustain us when all else is falling apart. People without hope can fall fast, give up and— literally—die. People with hope can live through impossible things, persevere, and even overcome. In general, pessimists who are physically injured take longer to heal, take more meds, and recover less completely than optimists. However, the main dimension I want to take here is that of time. Hope helps us see large swatches of time. I observe many people and it is usually immediately clear how big their swatch of time is. Some process in terms of short periods of time, others from hours to years to eternity. If something does not work in five minutes, some are done. No hope, no use. Others see months ahead, have an overarching vision, and do things daily to build their vision closer and closer to fruition. If you are going to answer questions of hope, you need a big swatch of time.

People with little hope often have little swatches of time with which they chunk life. I meet many frustrated teachers. Some will try an idea out for five minutes, five days and as soon as it does not work; there is no point in going further. Totally done. The baby, the bathwater, and the whole tub get tossed. They want immediate results and have usually run through many ideas already. Some teachers have the same experience of something not working, but hope to get better with the ideas and see what is possible. This is true with students as well. They may only operate in short chunks of time and if something has not happened in just a few seconds, they lose all hope and zoom into the attachment cycle. Most often, they become disorganized and act out.

Story Time: No Hope

You probably know someone like this kindergartner. If he got in trouble at 8:15 am, he was instantly defeated and angry the rest of the day. The teacher did not want to hold him to any limits, as the student would do no work if she did. She did a lot of management and fancy pleading to try to get him in a better mood and working. He was often destructive to boot! Being in trouble meant no hope to him. So, we taught him how to hope. The teacher would tell him she was having a problem of some sort and wonder aloud about how it would be solved. "I know it can be solved, I just wonder how. Can you help me with ideas?" The teacher pointed out to him how other students were having problems and solving them. With these and other interventions, we taught him problems can be solved, and, he was competent at solving them for others and eventually himself. Hope arose and meltdowns went away.

He could have gotten all sorts of anger management counseling, maybe medications, social skills classes, a chart to carry around, processed for an aid, evaluated for a special program, given incentives, and sent home. The value of the Essential Questions is that we all share them. When we struggle, we can help answer them rather than intervening to stop the striving and defending we exhibit when we do not have a good answer.

Blackwell, Trzesniewski, and Dweck, 2007 show that students who believe their intelligence is fixed run into difficulty and then believe they are unable to do better. They quit early on and avoid new tasks. Students who believe they can be smarter and grow their intelligence through effort will persevere, try new tasks, and have higher achievement. It is hope in what is possible. Tell every student they can forever get smarter and more intelligent as they learn more and more. The danger in thinking we are done, fully cooked, limited is too great. "See I knew I couldn't do it!" That student does not believe they can grow their brain. I know many teachers who routinely say, "Let's grow our brains. Who is ready to grow their brain with math?" Infuse hope. Make sure you clearly tell your students they can get smarter and more intelligent every hour of school. Why, in one week you can be thirty hours more intelligent! Kiss your brain!

How often do we intentionally model hope and teach students to hope? Here is one of the most fundamental factors to living well, being able to love, sustain friendships, and have patience. Without hope, we are immediately stuck in whatever we are stuck in. It can be the hope of forgiveness that overcomes my embarrassment, the hope of a recovery that spurs my immune system on, the hope of love repaired that keeps my heart from totally breaking, or the hope of succeeding that keeps me learning in school. We may say "good job" and "awesome" but those are about things in the past.

Story Time: Confidence

A fourth grader approached the teacher and expressed how she thought she could do more for the story she was writing by adding this and that. The teacher said, "Oh no honey! This is fine. This is really good." I asked why she said that to the student and she said the student suffered from a lack of confidence and she wanted to build the student's confidence. To me, this did not build confidence and was counter to building confidence. I would aim at the student's ideas as valuable, good, exciting, visionary, and celebrate how she understands writing and what makes it better. I want her to hope in herself and push the limits of what she can do, rather than hit the bar of good enough. I want her to reflect and feel the power of her decision making.

Story Time: Aw Gezt Ome Bahd—D-D—Dahr

I watched a little guy burst into tears over something a peer said to him. He was so upset he could not make words clear enough to be understood. The teacher softly said, "I know this really upset you and you cry all you need to. When you are done I want you to tell me about what happened, so I'll be watching for when you are done." The student cried another two minutes. When the teacher asked him if he wanted to talk about it, he said he did not. He had moved on. We could have added to his problems by telling him to calm down, been frustrated because he was blubbering, or fussed at the peer. The teacher simply extended answers to several Essential Questions. You are seen, heard, safe, valuable, good, making a difference, and loved. There is an abundance of time, and there is hope.

We need to give students every kind of hope we can. We know the world will try to take hope away, infect them and us with futility, try to convince us to give up, get us scraping to get through the day rather than to thrive vibrantly. We need all the hope we can get.

CHAPTER FOUR
Precision In The Social Curriculum

To teach a powerful social curriculum, the best learning will occur if you are precise in three main ways. You can be answering Essential Questions and driving values, be attuned and intentional, yet it can all go haywire if you are not clearly defining, reinforcing, and enforcing what you are after. In other words, you are defining and sustaining your direction. To do that, you need to (1) be congruent in what you socially teach, (2) be clear about what you socially reinforce, and (3) clearly stop – or minimally reinforce - what you do not want. In other words, what do you want to stop, keep, and grow in the climate and culture of your class or school? Usually teachers can immediately tell me what they do not want. Bam! When I ask what values they want their class or school to be known by, they invariably pause and ponder. You know exactly what you are after in the academic curriculum day by day. Do you know what you are after with the same precision in the social curriculum? Do you know it when you see it and know when it is not it there or even slightly off course?

We will first address congruency. If you are not congruent in the social curriculum, it will be hard to see the social lesson, hard to learn, and nearly always produce incongruent responses. After congruency, we will address how to stop, keep, and grow the values you want to build up in students and the school in general. Many schools have some program aimed at reducing behavior problems and incentivizing students to behave and follow expectations. The external programs that "manage" students might be good stepping-stones and have some beneficial aspects, but none I know of builds internally, value-driven citizens, who thoroughly understand and are personally invested in developing those same values with unlimited headroom. If you want students to be operating from a solid and rich internal code of high values, you have to build it and grow it and be it in action. Otherwise, it is just a good idea for those "other people" who just need to get on board with the program.

You are the program in The Essential Social Curriculum. You are already a program of something so it is just a matter of owning and aiming your program with awareness and precise direction. What does implementation mean? To most, it means you put a program in action. In The Essential Social Curriculum, it means you are the program in action. It is not external; it is you in action. Whether you answer the Essential Questions, drive values, or deliver consequences and restore others, you will need to be congruent in you messages, aware and clear about what you are reinforcing, and clear about enforcing your direction. From these the students can discern your intention to teach them how to love, and that they are lovable.

CONGRUENCY

While we are dancing, there are both implicit and explicit messages exchanged within the social curriculum. Implicit refers to how our actions and process/sequences talk louder than words. Explicit refers to the words, content, rules, and physical structures we try to make louder and more visible than our actions and processes. Implicit is mostly non-verbal and process based. Explicit is mostly written, verbal, and discreet events in time. Implicit and explicit communication is the difference between how we say something and what we say, how we are doing something and what we say we are doing, and how we are showing our feelings compared to how we say we feel. To avoid confusion or dilution, it is important to congruently answer the Essential Questions and build values at the implicit and explicit levels.

Sometimes our messages can add up and be clear. Someone may say, "I love you," and everything in their implicit messages—their voice, eyes, gestures, and body position—tells us they mean this explicit message with every fiber of their being. Someone else may say the same words and have a sarcastic twinge or a hesitation in their delivery that leaves us questioning. When the overt message (the content) and the implicit message (the process of delivering the content) do not line up, the message is hard to align and decode into one coherent message. A teacher, interrupted by a student, spent several minutes eyeball-to-eyeball telling him how his interruption broke a rule and, "If you want to get my attention you need to raise your hand." On the one hand, she was explicitly saying you will not get attention by interrupting, yet verbally giving him undivided and very emotional attention for several minutes. Therefore, the "lesson" (the social reinforcement) teaches that student, and every other student in range, to continue to interrupt to get undivided attention. In fact, because the teacher interrupted their entire classroom direction to address interrupting, no new learning about interrupting occurred. Even further, continuing to interrupt in the future was reinforced! Interrupting begets more interrupting and, therefore reinforced to occur even more via the process of social reinforcement. Or consider the teacher who yelled across the room at a student that they were too loud and should not be yelling across the room.

Another way incongruity occurs is when our overt message contains contradictions. One example occurred when a teacher announced, "Remember there are no more reminders today!" On the one hand he thought he was explicitly laying down the law, yet teaching there are indeed more reminders available. Therefore, it is not a rule. His comment was itself a reminder about no reminders.

Recently a teacher told a group," I can't talk to you until you're quiet." Well she actually was talking to them even though they were not quiet. While overtly saying she cannot talk to them she is actually talking to them. This is just the same as the substitute who made a big deal out of a student's big deal actually reinforced more big deals even though they are saying do not make a big deal out of it. When we mirror the problem—reminding about reminding, making big deals over big deals, interrupting to stop interrupting—we are actually reinforcing more of the same to occur.

Consider the incongruity present in wanting students learn to show self-control or to be kinder or more respectful while being shamed by an adult who is barely in control of their self, or being sliced and diced with skillful sarcasm, or being threatened with abject misery in the "real world". None of that is kind, or respectful, and so no new learning occurs. The student cannot experience the kindness or respect within and from the teacher that the teacher may be saying they, as the teacher, deserve.

Some may argue they do not need to be the congruent example or that the student needs to experience a tough message from someone who "means it." Perhaps you would like your evaluations delivered like this. Maybe students will learn more math or science if they are taught in these ways too. Maybe marriages would last if people said vows in such a fashion. Actually, most teachers would never think of doing anything remotely like that for academic problems, but I have seen some go there fast for social problems. We are too often desperate or placing a thin veneer over a need for great answers to questions about existence, value, competence, goodness, and hope. When we bust the veneer, it can be ugly. Teaching is one tough mission. It calls upon every bit of you as a human being.

If you accept that every school was built for the benefit of the children and young adults living in it—six to seven hours a day, five days a week, about forty weeks a year—then the goal of the social curriculum is to fully and deeply answer their, and our, Essential Questions in vibrant, loving, and hopeful ways. The more we act as if school is just there for the teachers and those interested in academics, the more the Essential Questions about our humanity and social future are shoved into the background. There is something fundamentally incongruent about that scenario, and when present, I see students paying those teachers back, seeking their answers from peers, dropping out, and looking elsewhere. A college bound high school student recently told me some students do not come to school with questions. Their questions remain unanswered or so poorly answered, they quit looking for school to answer them. They come to school to make statements. Wow! These students toss the incongruity back in our face by coming to school every day to show us they do not care about education or us. Do you think they will somehow come to their senses if they are repeatedly shunned, passed over, excluded, or punished? I think we should be listening closely to what they have to say to us and restore them. We cannot do to them what they are doing to us or there is no new learning.

William Becker, B.F. Skinner, and other behavior scientists clearly recognized the above dynamics of social reinforcement in the 60s and 70s. They were particularly concerned with ways to improve education by reducing incongruity in the reinforcement of student behaviors and attitudes.

Pioneers in communication and therapy like Gregory Bateson, Jay Haley, John Weakland, Paul Watzlawich, and Don Jackson from the 60s and 70s clearly recognized these levels of congruity in our messages as vital to healthy communication and good relationships. They even posited a theory of psychosis based on paradoxical messages. In paradoxical communication, such incongruity exists that no message can be downloaded which does not contradict itself.

"Do not read this."

"I'm not responding to what you just said."

Or the man from Crete saying, "All Cretans are liars."

"Breathe spontaneously."

All are such examples. By reading it, I disobey the command not to read it, but have to read it to learn the command. I say I am not responding but indeed I am. Is the man from Crete telling the truth or a lie when he says all Cretans are liars? If he is telling the truth he is lying, but if lying, he is telling the truth. How can one do anything spontaneously on command? Crazy-maker stuff unless you are able to meta-comment and make the incongruity overt.

If we send mixed up messages, we receive mixed-up responses, unless someone is good at decoding and stating the full truth of each level. If someone can do that, it makes the implicit overt and allows the possibility of clear coherent discussion. Or it could be all the people involved are good at decoding implicit messages and sending back equally implicit/implied messages that they understand. Think of Shakespeare whose writing is full of dual meaning, innuendo, and word play. Think of sarcasm, which makes it hard to decode the true from implied meaning. Sometimes we take things literally and miss the intended meaning. Grandpa asked his then three-year-old grandson to, "Come here and give me a hand." The grandson drew his hands back and said, "No, Grandpa!" Yet toddlers also can get idioms like

"Go figure."

"Driving me up a wall."

"That blows my mind."

I was in a third grade class as they discussed mercy and justice. Within this classroom, all the implicit and explicit communication and experiences over time informed them what these phrases and words meant. They could just as readily understand what it means to be compassionate, forgiving, efficient, dedicated, a good friend, kind, and so on. I know classrooms where three and four year olds grasp these values because they are provided such clear and prevalent moments to learn them.

The main point is that if we want students to value their education, to be outstanding citizens, to be kind and joyful, to be trying their best, and to feel deeply valued and connected to school, then we need a strong congruency in our overt and implicit messages. Truly, to be congruent and to expect students to be socially "intelligent," we have to be value-driven and committed to upholding great values in every class process and event. If we want committed students, we need to be committed to their commitment and honor it joyfully. If we want students to value and invest in their education with all they got, we need to value and invest in the student and show them all they have. If we want students to be reflective, aware, conscious people then we need to do all we can to be reflective, aware, and conscious with them.

I have been in classrooms and entire schools where students arrive in classrooms and receive gruff orders to sit, work, and not talk. "Be quiet in the hall. Stop talking, sit in your seat, and get to work. The assignment is on the board." It was 8:15 am, and that was the start of the day in numerous classrooms. These students, who given little to no positive comments for anything they do, are expected to sit and learn from uncaring, distant teachers who just wants to get through the lesson without behavior problems. Boring at best, harsh and punishing at worst, these classrooms and students have no positive messages about life or joy of learning. Driven by procedures like an assembly line, you are a bad, wrong, crazy person if you try to do anything other than sit, behave, work, shut-up. No wonder students tune out and act up. I have been in schools where students pledge every morning to be hard working, kind, considerate, respectful, and build peace, yet I have spent days never hearing any of these commitments celebrated, reinforced, acknowledged, or developed by many staff. Neither do I see many staff congruently manifesting the pledge. If the staff were not committed to the commitments of the students, what should they expect students to do? What do you think would happen if your spouse to be just finished committing to their vows of marriage and you said "Good. Now act like it. We shouldn't have to go over this again." Your commitment would be missing. Please post that on YouTube if you try it during your vows.

Story Time: Better Than No Love

A teacher I had worked with for a few months was wonderfully humorous, compelling in her personality, a strong teacher, and totally tuned in to her students. However, she was often sarcastic, often mad and frustrated with students who kept acting up. The students never did anything serious. She would fuss and complain, yet there was often humor tossed in too.

"What did *you* do now? Didn't I just tell you to be quiet? I'm going to have to just shout extra loud at the baseball game tonight to get my frustrations out about you. Now turn around and get busy before I have to shout out right here."

She was as frustrated as she was endearing. It was as if one part of her was telling students they drive her crazy and another part loved them mightily. They were getting many Essential Questions answered in confusing ways. The students responded in mixed ways to her so the dance continued. Gleeful teasing and pushing the limits of rules by students defined the class, yet they were sorry if they upset her. So, I asked her why she obviously loved her students, but was not clearly telling them. She said her first year of teaching she had totally put her love out there and the students ate her up. She vowed never to show her true full heart for students again. Yet, she loved them and could not contain it. It poured out in highly attentive, very connected, cannot wait to see what you pull tomorrow, thinking of you at the game tonight sarcasm. They could not *really* love her for that and she would not *clearly* love them back, but it was better than no love. The students went for all they could get by playing little cat and mouse games, feigning distress to seek closeness, and myriads of little teasers to frustrate her. She would tease them, feign distress (like above), and play cat and mouse games back. They were all so ready to love openly and yet clearly holding back because the messages were so mixed up. Everyone walked the edge, used the same methods, and set the same messages back and forth. I was overt, clear, and yet defined limits with her so she could have the experience of how she could do the same with students. It helped her be overt and clear. The Essential Questions she got answered in our conversation were that she could be emotionally safe and was truly lovable. How can you keep your heart safe if you wear it on your sleeve? Actually, it is the best place because you have maximum maneuverability. You can pull it in and protect it or hang it out there and find people who can take good care of it. Once she became congruent and able to safely love with her whole heart again, everything straightened out for the better.

Let's look at facts of the social curriculum in general. We know it occurs through verbal, overt messages and implicit, nonverbal messages, and problems often occur when there is incongruity between the overt and implicit messages. (Jokes often make use of this by building certain perceptions then suddenly switching context or meaning.) We know we send most of our communicated meaning nonverbally. We have begun to understand that if we apply a solution to a problem that mirrors the problem, we will reinforce more of that problem. However, a most basic fact is this.

It is impossible not to have a social curriculum. This is because it is impossible not to communicate. We are constantly sending messages by what we do and do not do, say and do not say, and the timing of what we say and do. Trying to "ignore" someone is usually futile as our "trying" often communicates we are irritated and whatever is going on is still getting to us. We are not able to focus our mind and emotions fully on something else as we "try." Our face, our gestures, our voice tone, and our words will all communicate we are still locked in, and not actually able to let it go or set it aside. It is hard to hide when we really like someone too. Our face and eyes will light up. We get perky. We stand and sit differently with people we like. Our gestures will likely mirror one another. Many other clues will pop out and show up as the messages begin to fly back and forth.

Just the fact that you do not show up at an invitational event sends a message. The person in an apartment you never see sends messages to all the other dwellers in the building. The student who is always in the back and never participates is telling us something. We will imagine something as we have to have a story.

Story Time: The Girl Who Stayed Outside

I was talking with a group of high school counselors and they told me about a girl (emancipated) that came every day to school but stayed outside in all weather. She would sometimes come for lunch, leave, and come in again after the last bell at the end of the day to get some books, her assignments, or speak to someone. One of the counselors said she had gone out to ask her if there was anything she needed, but no one really knew why the student did this day after day. Teachers and peers described the student as not saying much when people tried to engage her. There was a lot of speculation. There were many guesses yet little real facts. I asked what we could know about her just from what she was doing and not doing. Well, they decided she was dedicated to being at school every day. She was not disruptive to those arriving or departing. She did not mind bad weather. She was not out there playing digital games or calling people in the school with her phone. She did come in for books and some assignments, and if staff approached her, she would not zoom away. What was instructive from this is that nearly everyone had some story as to why the girl was staying outside but no one had really thought about what she was actually doing.

We know that this dance of mutual regulation and invitation, our sending and seeking as others send and seek answers, leads to another fundamental aspect of being human: **We will have a story.** As our primary attachment story interacts with the primary attachment story others bring, we bring about the same old story or perhaps something new. Who am I, who are you, what is the world like? Is there hope or not, do I belong, am I good, are just a few questions we answer in our dance with the questions and answers of others. Attachment Theory and Behavior Theory are really not theory as the principles, predictions, and reliability of the human qualities they describe are grounded in our bones, blood, and brains. To say they are theory is about like saying you have a theory there is a nose on your face. You may not always see it, but it is there in operation regardless. More than fifty years of research underscores this.

The cool part is that neurological science has evidence of how attachment qualities effect the development of young minds regarding learning, memory, empathy, resiliency, planning and organization, self-awareness, and other factors that are part of good and fulfilling lives. As stated earlier, secure attachment is wonderful for brains in every way. Our brains and therefore "we" in co-regulation do much better with secure attachment. This is true internally as well as externally in our social dance of mutual reinforcement and story making. Poor attachment—anxious, disorganized, detached—is neurologically connected to stressed brain function, less learning, and in extreme cases of chronic trauma, atrophy of the structures that create long-term memory (Siegel 1999). To have a mind and body ready and able to learn, secure attachment is the key. I say this. **The key to secure attachment is a life story that regenerates wonderful answers to the Essential Questions.** Amazingly, that story does not even have to be that accurate or totally true. It does have to be congruent and contain hope among other things. This is in part why some people go through hell and come out OK while others get a bad hair day and have a meltdown.

Attachment is an ongoing pattern and our life story flows from and mirrors this pattern. There is a variety of social terms and sayings connected this. Think of the unconscious, the "life script" from Transactional Analysis, how people seem rather blind to their own actions, the pot calling the kettle black, and the left hand not knowing what the right hand is doing. We are loaded with memories, emotions, and patterns that we are occasionally privy to. Our reactions and emotions seem to come out of us before we know what has happened. There are all the things we cannot consciously remember about infancy. To help us break into awareness we have sayings such as "Love your neighbor as yourself," and "Be the change you want to see in the world".

We can say that our brain and our thinking often fall in a rut. We keep firing the same old reactions, emotions, and thoughts, seeing things the same old way, and some things we do not see at all or dimly at best. The same story "seems" to be true all over again. We literally need to help our brain build new stories so that we can build and propel the best story possible. In this way, we can actually build new connections and circuits in our brain. Making new connections by having new ideas/experiences literally creates new circuitry in our brain. Most people have never heard of Neuro-linguistic Programming (NLP) or read much Milton Erickson, but building new circuits and patterns of circuits has decades of history and neuroscience to support it. Use that circuit often and it turns it into an expressway. It is hard to erase unwanted circuits and amazingly easy to build new ones. We will be far better off actually building new social actions, attitudes, and culture than trying to stop unwanted ones. "Fire it to wire it." Daniel Siegel writes. This is why precision is important. **You want be the experience you want to stick in their brain and then fire it over and over to groove it in. You need a precise social culture.** This is why you are the program. You are the experience, the change; you want to see in the world.

In simple terms, secure attachment comprises a common core that makes good marriages, great friends, incredible learners, and loving parents, helps children overcome trauma, and decreases bullying. Brains thrive on secure attachment. I conceptualize secure attachment as arising from having Essential Questions answered well such that we are validated as existing, accurately seen, valued, responded to, are able to learn, are helped and forgiven, belong to a community, and can trust we are emotionally safe with those in our community. All these factors take the stress and striving off the brain and let it learn, actually grow and integrate all the different areas that produce intellectual, emotional, and social efficacy. Your neurology literally is your sociology and, in reverse, your sociology is your neurology. It is co-regulation.

All the above makes for people who are happier, emotionally strong, able to resolve/cope with problems, and reach better outcomes with others. There is a strange "security" for people who experience chronic uncertainty, remain stuck with people who are unresponsive, punitive, abusive, invalidating, rejecting, exclusionary, and other harmful factors that degrade one's dignity, integrity, and connection with others. Think for a moment of youth in a violent gang. They pay a high price to obtain this connection but it is so essential to have some "security" that it literally can bypass anything rational or sensible. Soggy cornflakes trump no cornflakes. Some "gangs" we find positive. They benefit outsiders or we have no problem with their exclusivity. The desire to belong to one of these positive gangs can also override anything rational, and soon I am overspending to have the biggest yacht in the cove. In fact, that exclusivity just might make us want to belong even more.

What produces secure attachment and thriving neurological functioning fuels even better social functioning, and this builds continual opportunity to raise the bar mentally, emotionally and socially. Thus, a new escalating social dance is set in motion where our attachment to others, the world, life, the future, and ourselves all get better. A great story occurs. **To sustain the great story, we need congruent answers that are easy to decode and replicate.** When we are congruent, we are easy to decode, and likely are giving a model easy for others to replicate. From Jesus comes the second greatest commandment. Love your neighbor as you love yourself. Likewise, there is a tremendous truth in the words of Mahatma Gandhi, "Be the change you want to see in the world." Both of these call us to be congruent, and be the model for whatever you want back. You will be co-regulating those around you whether you want to or not, so put your best in the system.

CHAPTER FIVE
Precision With Reinforcement: Olympic Training

Now that we have looked at congruency, we will look at reinforcement, social reinforcement in particular, as elements of stopping, keeping, and growing your direction/ climate and culture. In his book *The Technology of Teaching*, the great psychologist B.F. Skinner explains how "behavior is built by reinforcing every response then every other response, then every fifth response and so on, waiting at each stage until the behavior is reasonably stable" (1968, 78). Then you add on another stage of progress and so on until the full set of behavior is there. The contemporary term educators often use is scaffolding. It is effective for academic and social curriculums. You frequently reinforce pieces, parts, moments of success and gradually do two things:

1. You lengthen the time between reinforcements for the well learned pieces, parts, and moments so they sustain the desired goal longer and longer.
2. Gradually add in new pieces, parts, and moments from the full set of behaviors until the full set is manifest.

This is done all the time in the academic curriculum, but rarely in the social curriculum. To have a great social curriculum, you need to understand effective reinforcement.

In general, the foundation of effective reinforcement is:

(A) Having a clear, *big* picture of what you are hoping to accomplish, and the many detailed steps and components that will need to be built and connected in order to produce that *big* picture,

(B) Being attuned and intentional in reinforcing,

(C) Scaffolding all the little details into the *big* picture, and

(D) Understanding social reinforcement – especially how it differs from material reinforcement.

Regarding your *big* picture (A), think of your ideal class or school climate and culture as a captivating movie. Watch it play out and make it as fantastic as possible. To create the final version of the movie, you need to start with many small snippets and hold your version of the final product firmly in mind as you watch the snippets of action. What are the actors doing that fits and does not fit in your final *big* movie? Which moments are exactly what you are looking for, which ones are close and need tweaking, which ones need cut? To create the *big* movie, you need to know all the pieces you are after and be alert to capturing them for posterity. With growing a value-driven classroom and school, you need to have a clear intention for all the details you want to reinforce and connect together to form the captivating *big* movie of diligence, integrity, kindness, trustworthiness, or any other values you are wanting to drive through the class. I have been in many classrooms and schools where there is no clear vision of an ideal climate and culture, nor a set of values that are intentionally grown and reinforced. Other than the edict not to be a behavior problem, do your work, and be good so you win a prize, there is no discernible purpose. In these school cultures, students are not intentionally developed and celebrated as conscious value-based citizens. They are celebrated for meeting expectations. Tell the one you love "Dear, I am so happy you are meeting expectations. Good job. Keep it up." Please also film that and put it on YouTube.

This points to another factor in having that *big* vision for your climate and culture. Usually the things that I hear commonly reinforced are really uninspiring and outright lame.

"Nice quiet hand."

"Very good."

"Good job."

"I see Tina knows how to follow expectations in line."

Many other praises like those above are not calling students to higher levels of social development. Such statements are not a high bar of morals or ethics. I think they are demoralizing as they have precious little to do with citizenship, community, or the future. What is the *big* picture for these cultures? It is not a *big* picture at all. It is focused on behave today and repeat tomorrow. Are students going to feel dignity from that? My experience is they do not. I do not think teachers do either.

Regarding (B), if you are not attuned and intentional, you are merely talking to the wind. Students will quickly pick up you are using a new program of saying many positive comments just to make them behave. Just being positive is not enough. To be attuned, you have to be tuned in, sincere, truthful, and communicating that the students are felt or experienced empathetically in you. To be intentional, you have to have that *big* picture and be communicating you have the best intentions for them. In short, you are communicating you see something unique and inspiring within them, and that you purposely have a vision for them. It is personal.

Regarding (C), scaffolding is important because many students do not come to school fully on board or equipped to help the school culture thrive and develop. They have gifts they do not know how to manage. They need assistance and we have to begin where they are. Two things are important to success with scaffolding. You have to be vigilant for any of the building blocks you want to develop in to the *big* picture, and you have to follow success. You cannot get ahead of the success or you are reinforcing failure. This brings us to the principles of social reinforcement.

Understanding social reinforcement (D) is vital to your success at growing a value-driven classroom full of conscientious and conscious students who are internally driven by high values. In Illinois at least, teacher evaluations will be based, in part, on the climate and culture of the classroom, and in particular, on how much the students are self-managing, propelling, and protecting a productive social culture. If you are precise and intentional with TESC, you will get such a classroom and probably get high marks on that part of the evaluation. Social reinforcement is something we are always doing but rarely conscious and precise with. It is why you are the most important and powerful reinforcement in the class. You are it because social reinforcement is always personal! **The truth is, since we are always communicating overt and implicit messages and "teaching" every second in the social curriculum, we already always reinforce something**. Rather than being haphazard or half aware of what we are and are not reinforcing in the social curriculum, we need to be clear, intentional, and aim carefully to build and sustain the best social curriculum possible for every student.

SOCIAL REINFORCEMENT

For five decades, behaviorists have known the exceptional power of social reinforcement. However, rarely is it used effectively and consciously. This is where the work of Dr. Wesley Becker in *Parents Are Teachers* helps readers grasp the nature of social reinforcement, the timing needed to actually be a powerful reinforcement, the specificity needed to accurately aim your reinforcement at what you want to actually reinforce, and how we can be the authors of our own stories (1971). Becker's phrase, "Catch them being good." is actually a rich, specific and intentional activity to build upon success after success to inspire thriving, industrious, kind, and hopeful people. His behavioral research forms the basis of countless other studies and programs to the present day.

It is nearly unanimous that behavioral principles work and are deeply a part of us. For ideas on just how deep, read Dan Ariely's *Predictably Irrational* for a lively group of studies that clearly show we are not as in command and independently minded as we like to believe. You might be shocked how powerful the implicit curriculum is on our decisions, spending, behavior, emotions, and health. You will never look at a commercial, mall, menu, purchase, or even what you read the same way again. This is just what I hope happens when you look at your school procedures, classrooms, and teaching styles.

SEDUCTION

Remember that with social reinforcement we are always reinforcing something. If we start going on about what is *not* there, what *should* be there, what *needs* to be, *ought* to be there, then we are reinforcing their continued *lack or absence*. In fact, we are growing *more* lack or absence of what we actually want. By focusing on what is there that needs to stop, we are reinforcing it to actually keep going! How is this possible? Think of it in terms of attunement, intentionality, and attachment. You would be communicating you are mostly/totally attuned and intentional about what is *not there* that should be or what is there that needs to stop. You are saying, "This is how to attach to me." Students will almost immediately seek to attach to you by doing what you are most attuned to and intentional about. This is why you want to follow their success so they will continue to be more successful. Then you want to be on the lookout for the next scaffolding step they take toward the *big* picture of success. Be much more inspired by what you are actually witnessing that you do want as opposed to what you do not want.

Becker explains this with research (1971). There is a seductive pattern to social reinforcement. You are often reinforced for complaining, fussing, admonishing, pleading because *short-term* you will likely see immediate improvement. I admonish a student to turn around, or a group to be quiet, and, by golly, they turn around or get quiet. The kicker is that *long-term* (sometimes immediately) I will have more and more turning around and louder more frequent talking. Soon there are more students turned around, more talkers, and so I do what worked before—I tell them to stop. (Uh-oh,

I just reinforced more unwanted behavior!) Short term they may relent, yet long term, I will likely get more problems. Thus starts a seesaw of fussing and problems that escalates into bigger and bigger swings back and forth. Why aren't these students behaving? I jerk out heavy-duty threats and punishments and (surprise!) out pop students daring me to heap on even more drastic actions.

"If this talking doesn't stop, there will be no…!"

"That's it. No recess!"

More than likely, they are already having recess at that moment, and you have become their game of choice. They may temporarily comply, but not for long.

Know that students want you to be the best teacher possible, and when you are not getting the social curriculum right, they let you know. If they had the best methods possible, they might politely offer you some ideas or engage in diplomatic discourse. However, they are most likely to simply throw our mistakes back in our face as a huge hint we are going down the wrong path.

Story Time: Getting What You're Giving

It had been a frustrating start to the day. Everyone seemed fussy and contentious when I entered the class. The teacher had brought the class quite far, but today seemed three steps back. Ms. Booth was rather confused about this state of affairs and was resorting to pleading, threatening, reminding students over and over how to behave and what the expectations were. Things just seemed to get worse. Ms. Booth wondered aloud why the class was like this. A girl approached her and politely said, "You're just getting what you're giving, Ms. Booth." This may have been a big moment of insolence to some, but Ms. Booth took it in and gave it value. She reflected on this idea and announced to the class, "You know, I have been very grouchy with you this morning and I apologize." She then returned to finding the best values in students, setting limits, and consequencing. The class climate became enjoyable again.

Know this too, that if you do have your social curriculum going really well, and have filled the climate and culture with forgiveness and restoration and love, when you do have that bad day where you are unwillingly strapped to a wild bronco of turmoil in your life, the students will still give you what you've been giving.

Students will extend you forgiveness, understanding, love, and keep being their best. You will have created a secure attachment with them, built up hope inside them, and been the model in action. They will not be so dependent on you, and will love you back with their best. This comes from following the success and scaffolding values to greater and greater heights. Just imagine what wonderful "lessons" Ms. Booth's students learned that day about her values, how much she really valued them. Accountability, dignity, and honesty prevailed! It could have been about power, yet Ms. Booth made it about truth, love, and the good of the community. She upholds compassion and dignity.

Story Time: Turn Around

I watched a class of twenty-six students doing excellent work, except one student who was turned around. The teacher walked over, softly told him to turn around, and he did. But three other students immediately quit working and turned around! Social reinforcement in action.

With social reinforcement, it is imperative to follow success. You want to reinforce what is actually there vs. what is not there. This is the importance of knowing the details of your big picture so you can reinforce and scaffold those into the story of the student, the class, and the school. Find the find the most zealous students in the room and reinforce them! Keep your direction and mood first and foremost attuned and intentional with them. You can always get to the problems later in ways that offset the reinforcement of doing so. **Remember this: Start with the best and then get to the rest.** However, if students are unsafe, get to them first. Never drop safety to second place, but where safety is not a concern, always go for the best you can find first. Let your mood and direction speak loudly and clearly through this choice. Keep the bar high on what gets you reinforcing or attached. With The Essential Social Curriculum, that bar is not on behavior; it is set on excellent values. I will not be after the quiet hand, I will be after the students being kind, helping others be and do their best, trustworthy, investing in their future, or any other values I choose to drive.

Note that being precise with social reinforcement means we need to be conscious of what we are doing, tracking the process of what we are reinforcing, and following success so we can grow more. Here are a couple of stories to illustrate how we need to be aware of what we are reinforcing through our process of teaching and reinforcing.

I watched a kindergarten teacher try to read a Clifford book to her class while periodically praising those students being patient and quiet at the drinking fountain in the room. Soon student after student was popping up to get a drink. She became frustrated and quit reading as there were more students in the drinking line than at their desks! She had steadily, yet outside of her awareness, reinforced the students at the fountain and so more and more went. She experienced a class problem. I experienced social reinforcement in action. Sometimes we may not have had a hand in something, but a good first thought is that somehow, as a teacher, I have reinforced this and I need to get my *big picture* back in focus.

Story Time: La La Land

A second grade teacher had a rockin' math lesson going. Energy and enthusiasm flowed wall-to-wall, except with James. He was in his own dream. The teacher called on him (a common management attempt) and he remained sort of in a daze. She casually remarked, "James must have gone to La La Land," a reference to a book she read to the class the previous day. The entire class went to La La Land. A girl said in a dreamy sing-song voice, "La La Land."

The class was gone! They all focused on La La Land and the energy on math was zero. The teacher looked at me and asked, "What happened?" I went up and told her she had accidently made their brains go to La La Land, and to be super energetic in voice and actions. She revved herself up and poured excitement into math. "Who has this one- is it you—is it you? Or *you*!" She got right in front of the boy who was in his own dream and he came alive—he had an answer! He came right out of his seat with his hand held high and others did too! In fact, he stayed so enthusiastic; the teacher had to ask him to sit down after he had stayed up for about five minutes all jazzed up on math. Whatever ideas and actions you put in the climate and culture becomes physically and emotionally present. Instantly. **This is because our brains *have* to make and actually think of these associations in order for us to process what is coming in to our senses and make meaning of our experience.** We cannot think of "La La Land" without all sorts of electro-chemical events occurring that summon up conscious and unconscious connections, emotions, and conjectures. Our brains are made to fill in missing pieces and hunt or search for conclusions. Even if you have never heard of La La Land, you will fill in the blanks and arrive at some conclusion or conjecture about it. If I add in a little girls voice softly slowly and sweetly saying, "La La Land," you have already filled in the blanks and imagined her voice, the cadence of her words, the articulation, the accent she speaks with, and the emotional experience of hearing her. You may have even filled in her appearance, facial expressions, age, or clothing. In fact, if you had not already done so, you probably did as I listed them. We really cannot help it. Whether communicated through your implicit or overt social curriculum, we are always making connections. Even when we do nothing, it sends a message, a connection will be made, and a response occurs.

Thus, we not only need to follow the success of the student to reinforce actual success, but we must be the success we want them to have! When we are the success we want them to have, they will process us and vastly increase their chances of being that success right then and there. Our brains are made to take it in and **experience** it. We are always co-regulating each other. This is why you are patient with impatient people, do not yell at people yelling, show kindness to meanness, and "Be the change you want to see in the world." You are inducing their brains to take it in and experience the solution firsthand. You could tell them to be patient a million times, but if you are screaming and hurrying them, they have less chance of actually experiencing it.

TUNING IN TO PROCESS

As you can see, being able to track your process is essential to keeping your mood, your direction, and clarity of reinforcement. This is another reason why being positive is not enough and your process might contain all sorts of inadvertent reinforcement of problems. As these will mostly be on the fringe of your awareness at first, you may need to develop that reflective monitoring and awareness. You can develop this on your own, but the fastest way is to have another set of eyes observing. I recommend you look and study with other people so you have a chance of getting an accurate analysis. Everyone is so sure of what they see and are aware of, yet there are huge variations in eyewitness accounts. For entertainment, read The Gorilla in the Room or watch the YouTube video of it. The basic experiment was to focus people in a room on some task and, while they were doing it, a man in a gorilla outfit came in and was active in the room. No one saw the gorilla. On the Discovery Channel, I watched a lost visitor (a researcher) asking for directions in a downtown area. Someone would begin avidly giving him directions and midway through there was a distraction. During the distraction a different man dressed about the same purposely replaced the researcher. No one noticed! The subjects of the experiment kept giving directions even though they have "looked" at and spoken with the lost person (researcher) several times. Even when the replacement was not dressed similarly, few noticed. I have been in the back of classrooms and watched students sneak into class, stand up and pop a peer, pass notes, text, steal, pee their pants, and more with the teacher totally unaware. I could easily see the situation where students were lining up at the water fountain and drifting off to La La Land. The teachers were focused on the content of the lesson and missing it. I ask teachers to consciously go back and forth between assessing "What am I doing?" and "How is it going?" as often as possible.

The bottom line though is that the process will usually determine the outcome. *How* you do something trumps *what* you do. How you say, "I love you." trumps that you said it. All the analog body language speaks volumes more that the words you say. How you raise a child matters more than the activities, school, toys, clothes. How you go on vacation matters more than where you go. How you cope with misfortune matters more than the misfortune. The patterns you set up in your daily teaching will determine more about the climate and culture than the subject matter or technology you use. Grow your awareness of process, as you need it to maintain your mood and direction.

I am not sure it is possible to be aware of everything in a classroom, so do not drive yourself crazy thinking you need omniscient awareness. I am sure when teachers try to act like they know everything going on and as if nothing gets past them, they are fighting a losing battle. Our humanity prevents it though we should certainly make conscious effort to be as aware as we can, and develop a clear and trusted intuition. Get a team together so you can observe each other.

Here is a bit of process. A teacher had about twenty-three students on the carpet and about every four minutes or so she was telling a particular student to sit down. After about fifteen minutes and several reminders, she told the student to take a time-out at his desk. He went to his desk but was up in just a minute or so. The teacher got up, put her arm around him, and said, "You were doing such a good job of being at your seat. Come on and show me another minute of how good you do a time-out." Almost every student immediately acted up. Why?

This has a logical answer once you understand social reinforcement. The teacher had not reinforced anything beyond "good answer" in about twenty minutes. *Every student knows you have to be married to the lesson, but what gets you married to them?* In the case above, the class discovered they could be the most married to the teacher while in time-out. The teacher socially reinforced the student in time-out with a hug and a sweet one-on-one moment. About fifteen other students wanted that too and went for **it the only way the teacher had established.** The "rule" she created was; if you want to be attached to me and get some Essential Questions answered, act up first. She got instant compliance. **You may not realize it now, but students are amazingly compliant with "social" rules that teachers unknowingly set up.** These students were just going for something they were born to seek deep in their brain: an attachment. They have to. It is perfectly natural and is at the root of social reinforcement.

What should the teacher have done? She should have been establishing a social rule in advance that focused on maintaining a set of excellent values and wrapping her arms, voice, and time around those. What can she do now that the class is near mutiny? Get busy and do what she needed to be doing. Find the best and then get to the rest. Immediately be reinforcing whatever you want more of so students seek you through that. Remember, by the rules of social reinforcement we are always reinforcing something. It might as well be the best diligence, compassion, power over temptation, kindness, integrity, you can find.

The kicker is this. If the teacher begins trying to suppress and squish problem behavior, the students would likely comply by going to their seats or doing some mass time-out. They then would be expecting what from the teacher? Sweet words and a hug. That probably would not happen on such a grand scale as 15 plus students. Chances are, the teacher will feel overwhelmed and escalate punishments when so many blow it. No recess, no this, no that. However, the students first need to make a good impression then blow it since that is the pattern she "taught" them. Some will behave, but for others the attachment cycle kicks in at steps three and four. Soon there is a mix of students in disorganization or withdrawal (submission). Some will go over the top and others will sit and behave. However, they will try again- they have to- and seek the door that opens to you. **This is why social reinforcement is seductive because they have to try again — usually by the same old rule- to obtain attachment.** If your rules and pathways about attaching to you are vague, confusing, and focused on problem behavior, you can expect a lot of confusion and problems back. "You're just getting what you're giving, Ms. Booth." This is so true because through your mood, intentions, and direction, you are constantly telling people/students how you want to attach to them. What have you been telling your students the social rules are for attaching to you? Just like the teacher in "Better than no love," they are showing you. There is the exception where students will bring an overwhelming experience from their life outside of school and show it to you to see if you have a solution.

One of the most common patterns I see many teachers oscillating in happens when they switch from teaching to the class as a whole to helping individuals. Once a teacher begins helping individuals, I usually see a huge increase in students needing individual help. Many a teacher gets bogged down with all the requests for help — unless the teacher is openly valuing *big picture* values, say independence and resourcefulness. When the teachers are really driving and reinforcing independence and resourcefulness, individual needs go way down and there are large increases in the number of students showing what they have accomplished.

How you "help" and what you are looking for will set up reinforcement patterns. A science teacher was going crazy running from one science station to another, helping students with their station projects. The rule was, if you needed help, you switched on a light at the top of the station. Students would turn on the light and wait for the teacher to get to them. Nearly all ten stations needed help all the time, accomplishing little. The rule itself had set up a social reinforcement pattern where students got rewarded with the teacher's attunement and intentionality to help. Flip a switch and get socially rewarded! People flip each other's switches all the time in real life and get socially rewarded. The frazzled teacher did not like what was happening but was unable to clearly name the process and see how she was rewarding a lack of achievement because she thought flipping on a light was following directions and she was supposed to be helping them after all. This is where another set of eyes can be helpful. To remedy this, we designed a plan to reinforce the values of resourcefulness, independent problem solving, making educated guesses, and showing initiative. The next class she began going around celebrating and cheering those students manifesting the values needed to be a scientist. Immediately there were fewer lights. If you did turn on your light, she would cheer on what you had done (followed success) and inquire how you could be more resourceful, or what educated guesses you might make. She held the students to the values she wanted them to show and modeled them during their interactions. If you were lazy and expected her to do it for you, she would tell you to come up with some ideas or thoughtful questions and that she would be back in five minutes to hear what you had to contribute. After everyone got the message, lights seldom went on, actual learning and productivity soared, and she was free to cheer on even greater levels of scientific attributes and social values. Have you been observed so you know who you help the most, the least, call on the most and least, smile at the most and least, "like" the most and least through the eyes of the class or another peer? Always be after the best values you can imagine with everyone you have. A great coach and trainer cannot neglect anyone on their team, nor lead with mediocre values.

To build your awareness of process,

1. Be observed by a colleague, friend, or film yourself.
2. Have a specific goal of what you are looking for. With whom do you talk to the most, help the most, ignore the most—or the least? What side of the room do you gravitate to, from, or are stuck in? What phrase do you repeat the most? How often do you praise social behavior compared to academic behavior? Who gets you the most involved? The least involved?
3. Map out to whom, when, and why you are smiling, and what message are you sending when you are not smiling.
4. If you have film, watch it with the sound off and talk aloud about what you doing as you watch. "I am writing on the board, talking to Selah, looking around…." Listen as you talk and see what patterns emerge.
5. Listen for how often you are answering any of the Essential Questions.
6. Some teachers pause in their teaching and have me provide short summaries of the last ten to fifteen minutes of class so they can learn to be reflective. Set your own clock and pause if you have no one to help you.
7. Ask a couple of students what they have noticed about the last ten to fifteen minutes of class.
8. Every five minutes write down how you are feeling and the class is feeling. What, over time, is the dominant feeling of the class climate?
9. Keep track of what you are saying. What happens next in the class climate and culture?
10. Develop a checklist so you can review the class if you do not have film. The class will generally love being filmed, if they know it is so you can be a better teacher. They want you to be.
11. Watch movies for process. Old classic dramas are best.

When you consider reinforcement as a process of installing exactly what you want students to experience, feel the difference between,

"I know it is a beautiful spring day out and you'd all like to be outside, but we have to finish these projects."

And

"It is so beautiful out today, but you are really focused and excelling on your exciting projects." Or,

"It is so beautiful out today and beautiful inside as well. You are so focused and excelling on your exciting projects."

Which associations would you prefer to be coursing through your brain and body? Which one is answering Essential Questions the most? I love how Trudy Walters would do the morning announcements. When it came time for the pledge she would say, "Let us stand and join our voices." So inviting and belonging. It powerfully reinforced belonging among the community of students through a huge network of social connections as everyone stood in unity to join together.

Here is a little guide to keeping your social reinforcement following success and building more. Let us suppose there is a student off track, not working, or perhaps not working up to the potential you think they have. Start with the best by praising the diligence and ambition of particular students.

1. Keep yourself first and foremost attached to the best values you can find in action.
2. Wait for some success to follow. When the student turns around, focus on that. "I also see your ambition going." Note you are reinforcing a class value.

3. Be the brain and tell the turned around student, "Focus your mind on achievement."
4. Do number one and then two.
5. Do number one and then three.
6. Use restoration by having the student name two things they will do in the next thirty minutes or next class to show diligence (or some other value). Then look for it and reinforce the student for showing that value.
7. Drive a value by asking the student turned around to show you his commitment to the value. "Dan, can you show me the diligence you had earlier during math now?"
8. Preface number seven with number one.

With any of the above, you are modeling the values you want the student to bring alive in their brain, moving you and them forward in a positive mood and direction, and providing great answers to their and your Essential Questions. You may have to reinforce every little step at first, but then you space the reinforcements out to build stable and long lasting effort. Sometimes we have built zealous learners from the mere fact that they came to school. I watched the incomparable Ms. Bonds scaffold a seventh grader with nothing on his desk. First came a pencil. Then he had 5 pencils out, then a sheet of paper, then his book, then an open book, then turned to the right page, then his name on the paper. She kept following every little step of his success, with answers to Essential Questions. It all began with "I'm glad you're here today." Just like with scaffolding academics, we begin where the student is actually successful and add. Look for the above steps in each Story Time.

Earlier in discussing The Dance of the Essential Questions, there was a story about a girl repeatedly acting incompetent and thus "inviting" the student teacher to believe it. The student teacher accepted that invitation and began to check on the girl to make sure she was getting the lesson. The more she checked the more incompetent the girl behaved! Eventually the girl invited the student teacher to believe she (the teacher) was less than competent too. You can apply any of the above eight ideas to that situation too. If you have a significant number of students who act as if being inept and incompetent are the coolest things ever, do one, then two, until the cows come home. The issue is not that the girl needs confidence, needs to do her work, is disrupting the class, or can do it if she tries. The issue is that you are guiding clearly the mood and direction of the class with congruent values, following the success actually there, answering Essential Questions, and building pathways of success that scaffold more success. You do not want to "manage" the student by telling her to get to work or stop disrupting, separating her from the group so she can focus, increasing help for her, or ignoring her. You want to drive every aspect of the mood and direction, the climate and culture, with great values.

REINFORCING WITH DETAIL

Too often, we assume students should know everything there is to know about being civil and social when they really have little experience or exposure to loving and fulfilling social process. I find that most students, even in high school, are extremely poor at understanding and articulating their understanding of social interactions and social process. They may say they were good at school today but unable to say what they did that was good beyond rudimentary behavior. "I didn't get in trouble." "I got a star." "I was good." How in the world are these students going to develop an internal set of values that consciously guide them in their life? How do you think they will perform on reading comprehension tests if they cannot even download the life they are living? I think students are handicapped by very poor reinforcement of their social best, and by very poor, uninspiring downloads of what that social network is. "Nice quiet hand." "I like that you're sitting." "Good job." "You've earned a reward card for standing according to expectations." If that is all the information I receive about how I am excelling socially, I am not learning a thing about me as a moral, ethical, self-guided person within a community of others. I am not learning a thing that will build a true value-based internal code to help navigate my life. I am not learning how my social actions influence and benefit others as a citizen of school. If we equip them so poorly to understand and conceptualize their daily life, will they be equipped to excel at reading comprehension? No. If you want to increase the scores or the school at reading comprehension, teach comprehension of the social curriculum in real time.

We need to be increasing their comprehension of the life they are living. My usual observation is that students are given a book to read or a lecture about love (or courage, compassion, kindness integrity), expected to cogently summarize what they read or heard, yet never "taught" **they** are loving, loved, or hear love cogently summarized in real time in terms of their relationships with others. Worse is when they read about love, integrity, kindness, but their teacher does not exhibit a congruent model to learn those values from. Sometimes the message is, "I'll make you miserable until you respect me and choose to act like a person should and not make people miserable." This is a totally incongruent message where students usually return the same message we send them: they act badly even though they know the rules and know how to be nice. In other words, they are fully compliant with the social rules.

To reinforce excellent values and help students to grasp social meaning, social process, and the social network, we have to give them clear details. We do this with truth in love, and with intentions to uphold their dignity. The most important lesson we can possibly teach them is how to recognize love, be lovable, and give love. Unable to draw a clear line on what love is and is not, leaves students open to many snares and traps. They need a clear line on love so they can raise great children who know love and can pass it on while protecting themselves. To accomplish this, to help them understand and comprehend the social world, they need detailed reinforcement.

There is research and opinion that generic praise (like good job, awesome, fantastic, and similar phrases) is actually debilitating (Kohn 2001). Such words and phrases lack any real specific detail and, as such, create uncertainty. What exactly am I doing that is so awesome? From an Olympic trainer perspective, I have told my athlete nothing about what to keep, stop, or grow. Sadly, some corporations have hired people to go around the workforce and be cheerleaders for the latest generation of workers. Instilled with vast amounts of generic praise, this generation has little internal evidence of their own competence. They have no internal reference systems to guide them, and are dependent on a stream of praise to sustain them. If they do not hear praise, they assume failure and become uncertain. Within a business, this equates with lowered productivity.

Being specific and providing ample positive reinforcement of success is even more valuable and needed in the social lessons being taught. The specifics do two things. The most important is that specificity communicates attunement. You are seeing, hearing, understanding. "When you got insulted, you didn't retaliate." "You told me the truth right away." "That came straight from your heart. I could see you giving your best effort." The second value of specifics is you are telling them exactly what to keep. Supplying ample positive social reinforcement for success also does two things. The first reason to be maintaining a high ratio of positive reinforcement to negative is that doing so defines your direction and thus reveals your intentions to build the best. This builds hope and happiness. The second reason is that we are always reinforcing something and thus you want to give minimal social reinforcement to what you want to stop. As problems are inevitable, you want to load the climate and culture with positive social reinforcement so that, in the balance, the reinforcement you give to classroom/ school problems seems minimal.

THE HIT LIST SO FAR

1. Know exactly what you want to instill in you and others. Know your *big picture* and the *specific* details of what to scaffold toward that goal. Intentionally build, build, build.
2. Build your awareness of process so you can track the mood and direction of the class and yourself. Look closely at the patterns of your daily teaching and schedule. These patterns are reinforcing and giving direction to a class culture. You want to be aware and precise.
3. Be the brain so you are being the goal with congruent words and demeanor/actions. You are the outcome you want them to arrive at. Be, be, be.
4. If things go a direction incongruent with your values or big picture, ask yourself how you may have unknowingly reinforced it. Then get back to your big picture and build it.
5. Be detailed and precise in explaining to students what you are reinforcing.

Aim as high as possible and link all you do to the values you want to define your class/school culture. Think anything is possible no matter what your situation. You can create a school full of citizens who are answering the Essential Questions of each other, are valuing everyone in the community of school, doing their best to be their best, and eager to learn more.

Here are some examples of detailed, attuned, intentional reinforcement of specific values upheld in a classroom:

"When you got insulted, you didn't retaliate. That was so kind because it gave them a chance to think a moment and apologize. That brought peace and hope to everyone."

"You told me the truth right away. You showed everyone they can trust you because you are holding to high principles."

"I could see you giving your best effort. Your dedication brought the entire class up."

"You are still cheerful and finished all your work despite numerous setbacks and obstacles. You are a finisher and that inspired many others to also persevere to the end!"

Notice they are hearing exactly what they need to keep or grow, and especially how they influence the values and people around them. This builds understanding of the social curriculum, how we affect each other, the value of values, and it answers numerous Essential Questions. From seventy-five to ninety people attended two recent trainings. All were educators and fewer than ten percent had ever heard anything specific from a teacher that positively affected their life. This astounds me. Many assumed a teacher was implying positive things, yet few had anything specific. How quick are you to articulate your favorite educational subject matter compared to your values? How quickly can you describe how the impact of these values and weave that through the social curriculum? Everyone is quick to tell me what he or she will not allow in his or her classroom or school. Few people can tell me, just as quickly, the values they uphold on a daily basis in their class or school. **If we cannot articulate our values clearly, are not attuned and intentional with our values, how can we hope students—or even our own children—will embody them and pass them on? Too often, we hope we are doing a good job when we can actually be a trainer of champions for the social Olympics of life.** We cannot haphazardly build common goals such as "lifelong learners" and "self-motivated learners" or students who say, "Give me more!" We need a *big* picture and *specific* details to scaffold toward to fill in that picture. Then we build it with attunement and intentionality, truth and love.

PUTTING IT IN ACTION

Before we leave this section, I want to take the major factors you have read about so far and wrap them together in an example. Using the girl who convinced her student teacher they were both inept, the first step would be to figure out what her EQ may be. She could be acting inept and quiet about it. Instead, she makes a production out of it. She is attempting to get some peers in her club of the inept and trying to get the teacher in the club, too. If I take her tactic out a little farther, she would eventually work her way to be the leader of the club. Therefore, I surmise her desire is not only to be seen and heard, she wants to make a difference and run the club of the inept. It is more about power. She wants to be the difference that makes all the difference.

Now that I have an idea of her question, I can define some classroom values or even individual values I want to build up in her. In general, with her question, I need to find moments of success where she makes a positive difference so I can find ways to highly value her. I want to make her methodology of acting inept unnecessary by replacing it with something better. I want to build up other tools and pathways for her to use that truly make wonderful differences to everyone in the class. Notice, I am accomplishing this by literally installing new and more rewarding pathways in her brain. I want her to feel valued and to be a leader. I could spend a lot of time and effort trying to get her to stop interrupting, work harder, pay attention, and wondering if she needs special help. Suppose she stops. What then? What has she learned, how has she grown, and what path is she going to go down now? If I have a *big picture* for her and know the details and scaffolds to reinforce, I can take aim and actually teach, grow, and build a champion of wise power, leadership, and value.

What might I specifically look for to show her she is making a positive difference of leadership, wisdom, and value? I might look for instances where she says something helpful, pauses to consider something, empathizes with someone, asks a productive question, takes some initiative, volunteers, goes first, encourages, acts efficiently, joins in a game, uses a strategy, is needed by a peer, thoroughly completes a task, or makes good use of advice. Further ways she might show leadership can be contributing to the peace of the class, extending grace or forgiveness to another, bringing good-humored laughter to the room, doing something without being told or asked. She could be caught remaining focused while someone else is distracting, playing a game at recess, writing something moving and inspiring, or walking in the class allowing others to keep focused. Once I know what I am looking for, I am sure to find it. I can reinforce a multitude of moments to connect her to the BIG picture that she is making a great difference, is wise, leads in valuable ways, and is an important contributor to the school/class culture.

She will then hear messages such as,

"The way you organized that game with your friends showed your leadership."

"You really saw to the essence of that. You have wisdom."

"You know how to help us all have a good laugh."

"There you go again showing your willingness to lead and take the initiative."

"You were so wise to just ponder that remark James made."

"You are helping everyone around you do their best simply by you quietly doing your best. What a help to our class."

She will know she is being seen, heard, experienced, and valued by someone attuned and intentional with the best of intentions for her. I will show her she has power in many ways, and does not need to seek power by appearing inept. My power is to give her power, to guide and to grow it within her. There is no end to how she might attempt to stay inept and I will surely become more inept at trying to stop her from that.

I am *not* going to talk about how she is behaving well, following expectations, remembering to be quiet, how I knew she could all along, or how I like how she is doing anything. Those do not take her further along her path of building wisdom, leadership, and value to others. Likewise, just showering her with a bunch of positive compliments will not provide the precision attunement, intention, or direction needed to build specific pathways aimed at her being a leader, wise with power, and valuable. The above will also not clearly answer her Essential Questions. They lack rich attunement, and lack forward moving intentionality. I need to be the values I want her to catch and internalize. I will show her by my personal example of precise social reinforcement how to be a wise leader who imparts value to others.

GROWING WITH COMMITMENT TO VALUES

Using the value of commitment has been sensationally powerful in helping students turn themselves around; go for new heights academically and socially, and greatly reduced the need to use consequences. We are asking students to be more attuned and intentional with themselves by asking for their commitment. It is silly simple. You find the student or class doing something or manifesting some honorable value, you tell them what it is, and ask if they can/will commit to continuing it, or even take it to a higher level, for some defined time limit. "You have been so patient waiting for our guest. Raise your hand if you can commit to being this patient five more minutes." Suppose the class is not being so patient and starting to unravel. Rather than speak to that, ask them for commitment. "Our guest is not here and I am wondering who can commit to being patient for five more minutes?" Imagine a student is up wandering around. Ask them if they will stop and commit to five minutes of being their best at math (or whatever the task is at the time) If they say "no," ask for three minutes. Scaffolding in action! This lets students "show up" and not just do as told. It sets us up to be following success. To succeed at their commitment, they will be building more and more attunement and intentionality within themselves! This is how you build self-motivated, lifelong learners and reflective, mindful citizens. Often I advise teachers initially to not ask for more time or more effort. At first just ask for a repeat. "You have all been amazingly focused on your reading for the past five minutes. Do you think you can commit to doing five more with this same focus?" Hear the attunement and following of success in that? If you are telling them to keep it up, (especially saying "Keep it up I know you will")you are not letting them "show up" Most likely someone will hear you as having more investment in the task than the integrity and effort they are bringing to the task (and having some special power that knows they will). They will quickly let you know that you have erred and show you that they have the power—all the time—in an attuned and intentional way that unzips your composure in a second. Do not take it personally. They are trying in a backwards way to help you be the best teacher possible. Ask them for a commitment, and the issues of who has the power and integrity are restored quickly.

Suppose I do not get commitment and need to send stop messages for behavior or attitudes violating the values of the classroom and school? What consequences can I put in place to keep the students and myself as their teacher on the path of making a positive difference? While I definitely need to tell students what to keep and grow, sometimes I need ways to send "stop" messages and get the students back on the path of growing values within them. Let's go to stopping.

CHAPTER SIX
Prelude To Management And Consequencing

Delivering effective messages to stop or change unwanted behaviors and attitudes has confounded educators and parents since the first school and the first child. It is not easy, and there is no perfect way. We do our best. During trainings someone will ask, "What do I do when a student is (fill in problem of choice)". I think a primary reason obtaining impressive social and emotional citizenship has been so hard is that people wind up shooting themself in the foot with most methods. Not only neglecting to reinforce the positive actions, attitudes, and values that grow better climate and culture, there are usually problems with the way limits and consequences are delivered, the consequence itself, the focus of the consequence, and what we do after the student has been consequenced. With so many ways to go wrong, it is challenging to produce a right.

There has to be precision in consequencing, like in reinforcing, because when you consequence you are actually reinforcing either the unwanted or the wanted. This is the concept of social reinforcement, that you are always reinforcing something all the time. If I am going to consequence unwanted social behavior, I had better be aware and precise with my social reinforcement. Typical disciplinary processes rarely reinforce the wanted outcome. Why do you keep seeing the same students in the office? Why do the same problems occur repeatedly in class? Behavior science says it is mostly because typical methods of management and discipline reinforce more problems. The only reason a student is difficult is we have not found a solution they can use. Their behavior and attitudes are a solution to something, and we need to offer a better solution than theirs to that something. We will not have much success punishing them for the best solution they have found so far and trying to get them to stop it. They need a better solution, and so do we.

In the next two sections, I will speak to the perils of "management" and then the elements of precision consequencing. Specifically, we will cover how to address problems and set limits in ways to keep the mood and direction of the room moving forward. I will look at the foundation to consequencing, a framework to measure progress, and ways to restore the values of your classroom if someone misses or violates the high standard set by the values. You will learn what it means and what to do so that "their consequence is to be a contribution." This prelude to the next two sections focuses on the fundamental factors common to each. The first is this.

Keep in mind that you are consequencing that the values are not upheld—not the behavior. If I have a classroom value of "caring" or "kind," then I am consequencing anything less than caring and kind words and actions. I am after the spirit of the law, not the rule itself. Consequencing in this model is designed to:

1. Manifest the value through your actions during the consequencing process.
2. Establish the value back in action as soon as possible through the student(s).
3. Restore the value within the entire classroom and school.

Remember that with social reinforcement, you are always reinforcing something by your presence, along with the degree of and length of attention you give to anything. With this in mind, I want you to think of yourself as having a door to you that swings open or shut. If you open the door for students manifesting the highest standards of the values defining your class, they will stream through that door. If you open the door for violations, for missing the mark, then students will begin to stream through that door too. Either way you are reinforcing more of whatever door is open. Your objective then is to have your door open for missing the mark as little as, short as, possible. You want your door for students upholding high values wide open as long as possible. By doing one above, you can have your door open for missing the mark and still be upholding the values (reinforcing the values) by your personal example (your mood and direction). You will still be giving affirming answers to their Essential Questions. You will still be teaching love and a model for them to use as a solution.

I am not saying totally ignore problems. I am saying keep that door open as little as possible for problems. Most of the time, you will be holding the values of the class culture high and consequencing anything less. If you eliminate the "management" of problems that you already are doing, you will initially be quite busy consequencing problems, yet actually reducing them over time. Ignoring and even the concept of "planned ignoring" are terribly misunderstood and rarely used effectively with precision. You will read about that in the coming pages.

Across the board, the face of public education is changing in nearly every classroom. Thus the administration of and preparation or teachers for school is in need of change too. Out of about a thousand educators I have asked, fewer than ten told me they had any sort of behavior management class in college. Even then, they only read a book or listened to a few lectures. A recent report from the National Council on Teacher Quality (www.nctq.org/dmsStage/Teacher_Prep_Review_2013_Report) looked at 1130 teacher programs and made the stunning statement that overall, these programs are "an industry of mediocrity." Of course, there is some pushback to the conclusions, but the overall message is that teachers are not being prepared to master their soon to launch career. What I find most of the time is that teachers were given advice such as "Your discipline plan is your lesson plan." Most teachers are woefully unprepared for the classroom management challenges they will face. It is like going through graduate school in psychology and never learning to do actually therapy only treatment planning. Then there is the ground level advice like

"Don't smile till Christmas."

"Show them who's the boss the first month then be nice."

If you are frustrated with classroom management, no wonder! Maybe you were lucky and got a fantastic teacher for your student teaching. I hope so. At the same time, more and more veteran teachers tell me they are struggling with the evolving sociological climate and culture of education. President Obama's head of education, Arne Duncan, has called for a complete overhaul of the educational system. While we wait, here is the second major factor to effective consequencing.

While you are driving values, you need to be fully strict. Fully strict means you are nailing students for all the wonderful values they manifest, all the wonderful scaffolding steps they give you to build more sustained and rich values from, just as intentionally and attuned as you are nailing them for problems. In brain terms, you grooving your circuits on the best you can find, just as intently, if not more so, than you are stopping problems from being grooved in to the student's brains. Our brains actually store and recall unpleasantness, problems, and danger faster that the good stuff. *Literally, you are the external brain of students and waging a mission to fill their brains with abundant good and help with recall of the good.* It is imperative to be intentional, attuned, and precise in this mission.

You want to have your door swinging open for excellent learning and citizenship, not just open for problems. If you are only inspired (opening your door, nailing, naming, attuned, and intentional) by problems, —you are only half-strict. To be fully strict, be inspired by the whole student, or you are only having a relationship with a part of him or her. This is experienced by the student as not being seen and heard as a whole person of dignity and integrity. Would you—do you—feel whole if someone zeros in on only part of you and that single part is a problem? You have to, not just should but have to, be after students for those moments you can celebrate, cheer on, and reinforce for all the elements of your BIG picture of value-driven citizens. You do so with the same precise exactness you find them falling short. If not, it will be hard, by the principle of social reinforcement, for you to grow a dynamic culture because you will be actually growing more problems.

Being fully strict also gives congruency to the academic and social curriculums. When students have academic problems we meet them where they are and encourage, help, cheer, reinforce, support, scaffold, so they can understand and attain more competency and success. When students have social problems we are likely to fuss, chide, complain, punish, and/ or embarrass. One teacher refers to this as "the shame, blame, and inflame" process. The research shows that teachers are positive in their responses about eighty percent of the time when addressing academics but only twenty percent of their responses to social behavior are positive. Thus, with academics we are usually using positive social reinforcement, and with social issues primarily using negative social reinforcement. By being fully strict, you align your academic and social curriculum around positive social reinforcement. This gives the academic and social curriculum congruency, which vastly increases learning in both. Achievement scores go up as students are more "timed in" with you and "timed on" learning.

To be fully strict you will need to stop managing problems. I have devoted the next section to the perils and pitfalls of managing problems. This is a plague in the classroom and school in general. Teachers often feel so much pressure to produce scores and get through lessons that they can begin to tolerate, overlook, and just end problems while actually solving nothing. The same problems resurface and every day becomes an exercise in getting from one moment to the next as the academic lesson is shoved along. Administrators sometimes approach teachers as if there should never be problems in school and so teachers will try to eliminate problems as quickly as possible. You may feel there is no approval or tolerance for actually resolving problems over time. Some people want instantaneous fixes for lifelong problems. School is education, not fixation. It is about growing not stowing. In the next sections, I will give you a framework for assessing progress so you can see the direction you take bearing fruit and keep hope alive. Now we arrive at the last and most important piece to effective consequencing.

You're it! For decades, maybe a century, it has been clear that the primary reason for success in education resides in the teacher-student relationship. But what does this mean? What factors comprise this relationship? We wonder why students could care less about incentives and chasing the thrill of earning points. They want you**.** They are after a personal relationship with you because biologically we are made to attach. Even that group of eighth graders who act as if they don't care work very hard at showing you they don't care. Why work at it if you truly do not care? **Points and incentives cannot love them back, validate them as someone lovable, spend time with them, speak unforgettable words, fill their heart, forgive them, understand them, or clearly answer their Essential Questions.** My points and I do not have a future together that is building into something more rich and deep every day. **Only you can provide that.** Even if you think the children love the points, it is only because you do. If you love the points, then it is how the children will seek significance with you. It is the main doorway you have open for them to connect to you. In the absence of other doorways, many go for what they can get. However, some will care less about the points and still go after you in whatever form they can get. Make showing excellent values the main doorway and they will go for that even more so. What is your door open for? **To be effective at consequencing, you need to understand there is no external consequence that will be more effective and meaningful than your loving mood, direction, and intentions in your relationship with the student.**

If you do not care about the student, do not really want them in class, and do not have any desire to make their life a joy, you have already dealt them a huge consequence for existing. Adding on trips to the office, detentions, and in-school suspensions are nothing in comparison. In fact, they become the primary settings for the student to strive for existence. If you are not teaching love, even in your consequencing, you are teaching something else. Success resides in the teacher-student relationship because it is personal and we cannot avoid it being personal. No matter how impersonal you may try to make it, it is always personal. We should really be listening to those students who still show up to make "statements" as they truly need something personal and meaningful with us. Remember, first she respected me, then I learned to respect myself, then I began to apply myself, and then I respected others. Are you as done learning and developing as you think some students are?

CHAPTER SEVEN
Managing Problems Versus Driving Values

Much of the time, I see teachers struggling to manage problems of attitude and behaviors. By manage I refer to attempts to finesse, expediently end, or deflect problems. Two students may be arguing and then seated apart. A student may insult another and they are told, "Say you're sorry." As soon as they say they are sorry, the teacher tells them to get busy doing what they should have been doing. "Now get to work on your math." Two students are arguing and told to stop. A student throwing a tantrum is cajoled and finessed into a better mood. We tell the running student to walk. As long as the problem or disturbance ends, that is the end.

Recently I have seen an explosion of low level but incessant bickering, instigation, picking, and harassment among students in the early elementary grades. Often the teacher is striving as they try to plow through, over, and around this undercurrent of distress. They may try to find the magic lesson that hooks the class, but usually that is short-lived, even if they do. The teacher may try to make whatever he or she is saying *super important* to hook the class:

"I have something **really important** to tell you, you need to hear this or you won't know what it is!"

"Oh, *look,* everyone! Look at *this.* Isn't this *cool*?"

"I have something *really neat* to show you but you need to be quiet and sit down first."

What new rabbit will the teacher pull out of the hat next? These attempts to be seen and heard eventually lose any power they might have had, even if you have a hundred rabbits. Sometimes teachers become defended and rationalize it as "just kids." The result is a slowly festering climate of anger, fear, excitement seeking, and retaliation. Then seemingly, out of nowhere, major conflicts and extreme behaviors burst forth.

The drawbacks of trying to finesse, expediently end, or deflect such problems are more than the eventual explosion. The main drawbacks are that no one, including you, can develop a climate and culture of growth and peace, nor develop much academic learning. No one can move forward because the next act of danger, instigation, and harassment is just around the corner. Everyone, including the teacher, begins to stay on alert for the next thing coming his or her way. They are either moving to withdrawal or attack mode. The class, including the teacher, becomes consumed in watching for the next attack, stopping, or blocking it somehow. Those in distress are not soothed, little brainpower or emotional connection remains for academics. This includes the teacher. The class is like treading water in a shark tank. The whole school may become that way depending on the administration and how they respond or react to these issues. An even greater drawback is that all the students know the teacher is striving and defending **with** them, the **same as** them. The teacher and students are all in the same boat. The teacher is teaching nothing new to the students as they are all doing the same thing in the social curriculum.

A student tosses a coat around and hits another student in the face with it. The student who was hit cries and the student with the coat is told to either put it on or put it in their book bag. The hurt student may hear a quick "I'm sorry," but nothing soothing or restoring happens. A student has a minor meltdown because they did not get the book they wanted. The teacher tells the student it is no big deal and to pick another. Two students are bickering over a marker or a spot to sit on the carpet and told to stop. "You sit here and you sit here." A student walks by the desk of another and grabs something away from the student at the desk. The teacher tells the grabbing student to give it back and not to do it again. A student, sent to the office for picking on another student, eventually walks back in the class with the message not to do it again. There are no commitments or clear intentions by the student to make the class a safe place to be. It is just "try again."

I can confidently say these management methods only dig a deeper and deeper hole for teachers and students even if the teacher is being otherwise uplifting, positive, and encouraging. Even if the teacher is giving students time-outs there will be little progress. The time-out is usually spent festering rather than truly moving beyond the problem such that it stays lodged in the emotions and minds of the students. Nothing has happened to resolve the emotions (mood), and create a clear pathway (direction) for good feelings and experiences to occur or to be expected. No valuable values are upheld in the process and Essential Questions remain in jeopardy.

Actions that actually resolve the problems are needed that move the student to a new conceptual class/group of behaviors and attitudes. Systems theory or cybernetics calls this the difference between Type One and Type Two change. Type One is usually referred to as "more of the same" because Type One solutions usually replicate the problem, thus keeping it going. The interrupting student is often dealt with by the teacher interrupting whatever they are engaged in to deal with interrupting students and telling them to stop interrupting. Type Two responses do not involve replication of the problem because they shift to an entirely new conceptual level of thinking. The teacher would finish their task and then get to the interrupting student when convenient. In this way, the problem behavior does not replicate at the teacher level.

Type One change would be for pioneers to want faster horses. Type Two would be cars and trains: an entirely new paradigm. Type One change is for an alcoholic to not drink. Type Two change is for that person to develop new character qualities and thinking patterns unlike an alcoholic. Type One was Newtonian physics, Type Two is quantum physics. Type One parent interventions would be to take the child's TV away, allow no phone, give lectures, warn, yell, forbid friends over, take away privileges, send to their room, and restrict the child to only thirty minutes of computer time. While the parent may say they have tried everything, all are only one class action: punishment via deprivation and threats of more to come. Type Two parent interventions would be new classes of actions such as use of natural consequences, earning privileges, doing restitution, community service, using praise and encouragement, or being truthful in loving ways. Type One is yelling at the yelling student how it is *not a big deal*! Type Two smiles calmly at the students and validates their concerns, then asks them to change their method of expression. Type One is finding many ways to avoid the obnoxious spouse or coworker who keeps chasing you. Type Two is to turn and talk to them and make clear agreements and understandings to end the chase and avoid pattern.

The most common example of "management" is in dealing with contentious, picky, argumentative, instigating, drama seeking students. This has become alarmingly prevalent in my experiences from pre-kindergarten through third grade and beyond. The teacher may try point charts, incentives, taking all sorts of fun time away, calling parents, detentions, sending students out, ignoring, and losing their cool by yelling and bullying the students to be good and nice. While the teacher may feel they have tried many things, they have from a system perspective only tried one class of action, **which is exactly the same class of action in which the contentious students are engaged**. The students are, and the teacher is, trying to get mean fussy people to quit being mean and fussy while being rather unlikeable, mean, and fussy themselves. Everyone becomes mean and fussy too, or beat down and semi-helpless. Are the teachers *really* mean, fussy people? Are the students *really* terrible little people? From a system perspective, mostly the answer is "no." It only appears that way because they are in a system feeding upon itself with no new "information" or "differences that make a difference." When truly new information, a new class of action is taken, and differences that make a difference are put in the system, everything changes. That would be Type Two change. For a deeper understanding of change, read the book *Change* by Watzlawick, Weakland, Fisch, and Erickson, 2011.

There was a worm that was always afraid of birds. The worm found a magician and asked to be turned into a squirrel. While as a squirrel, he was again afraid of hawks and larger animals. So, he asked to be turned into fox. Yet, he was then afraid of wolves and asked to be turned into a bear. In short measure, he was afraid again and asked to be turned into whatever creature never had to fear. The magician said "For that you need a change of heart and that I cannot do." In essence, only one solution was ever used and a complete change of concept and class of solution was needed to solve the actual problem.

For rooms loaded with mean, contentious, picking, excitement seekers, the Type Two interventions are usually built around the teachers being a model of kind, joyful, calming, uplifting fun with the students, in combination with real truths that reflect a *big picture* to the students of who they are being or could be in that moment. The exact content is not important. What is important is not to replicate unpredictable, fussy, mean, pointless, transient, narrowly focused unfulfilling social interactions. **In short, you are the solution you want the students to experience and adopt**.

An elementary school was totally stumped by a first grader. They had tried many interventions of praise, point systems, check and connect, consequences…you name it. What emerged was that, as a kindergartner, he had moved through five schools in one year. This year, due to stress on his primary teacher, the school put this student in five different small group settings each day. This is Type One where more of the same keeps happening. To not move the student, to provide permanence, and build in support for the classroom teacher in class would be a Type Two change. Sometimes the "more of the same" is in the patterns of our life. Next time you find yourself stuck in a problem, list your attempted solutions and see what commonality they have. How are they replicating the problem? What would be 180 degrees different? What would be totally different?

There was a second grader very much into power and pushing limits. He wanted to be the difference that made all the difference. Typical Type One responses would be to "get tough" and "show him who is boss." This would become a power contest. Rather than getting in to who was more powerful, the teacher focused on reflecting who the student was being (not what he was doing) in those moments and providing alternative choices of who the student might be. "You are powerful at making people upset. Can you use your power to make friends because you deserve good friends?" All of the student's power was kept in the student, all of the teacher's power was kept in the teacher, and the teacher just followed the student's choice. The student wanted power and he got it. It was his power, and he became a much more conscientious user of his power. We just had to make him fully conscious of it and let him feel it. The teacher was also a model of using personal power. If we had tried to make the student powerless, he would likely have escalated his displays of power, learned more techniques from the teacher on how to make people powerless, and never learn to appreciate, feel, and use his own power. If you go after behavior, you are digging a deeper hole for yourself, the student, and the class in general.

Another aspect of managing is that it, perhaps exclusively, is overly focused on behavior. Consider just how many times a day you tell students exactly what to do. They are given one task after another. Line up with your voices off and hands to your side. Walk to your seats and get your math book out. No running. When we are in the hall, voices are off and stay in a line. Stop at the door. Raise your hand if you want to talk. On and on students are given one task, one goal, one set of behaviors to do. When they do not, the typical response is to intensify the focus on their behavior. They may lose recess, lose points, get calls home, and soon become even more prevalent behavior problems. Typical Type One outcomes.

Rarely do teachers actually speak to the process, the way they want tasks approached and completed. To build aware, conscious students, we need to speak to process. By defining the values the teacher wants to see in action as tasks are completed would be a shift to Type Two. For example, the teacher may say, "We are about to line up. I will be looking for safe and considerate students as we line up." "While we are in the hall, who can commit to being kind and supportive of the others learning in the rooms we will pass?" Or upon re-entering the classroom, "Today I am looking for students who are efficient and ready to be their best once back at their desk." "On this project, I am looking for the level of teamwork that would make me gladly recommend you to any employer." Isn't this what you really want more of anyway? Aren't these the abilities and values they need for life? It is a common complaint that "By this time they should know what to do!" I agree, and believe they do know what to do because that is all they ever have heard. Do, do, do. They are missing how to be. They have not been seen, heard, valued, or reinforced for having a personal code of inner guidance. We want self-guiding citizens, but we get stuck too often in treating them like robots behaving or not. We become robotic. Speak to values. Name them, download them, celebrate them, model them, and make them clear in the classroom process.

Another handicapping aspect of management is that we wind up stuck in a small moment of time, and thus become unable to given the student a *big picture* in a loving, hopeful, truthful way. This is closely connected to being overly focused on behavior. We wind up giving little pictures (you are losing recess, no TV tonight) or overly dramatic unloving gigantic pictures (you will go to prison and be in Bubba's harem). You want to be able to tell the truth in love and give the student a realistic, true picture of what is occurring in the social curriculum at the level of values. *Really* spell out the social truth.

"You could keep refusing to do your work or you could really invest in bettering your future and help me feel great about my investment in helping you achieve a great future."

"If you keep calling others names, they will probably not be able to like you with their whole heart. You are a good friend when you take turns as you did with Timone today. I want people to like you with their whole heart. I hope you do too."

"I really want to trust you. When you do that, I cannot. And if I cannot trust you, it is hard to be fully happy and relaxed around you/recommend you to the AVID program/have you on a field trip. All of those are things I would like to be able to do. I want to be able to say you are trustworthy and have integrity. What do you want me to be able to say?"

Notice how all the above call upon the listener to consider a large span of time, a big picture. Notice too that all the above are closely patterned after the assertiveness framework you will soon read about. They have no blaming or shaming in them, are personally true, lovingly, respectfully, and hopefully said, and do not end in a demand or threat or promise of punishment. If the problem persists, just deliver a consequence as a matter-of-fact. We will get to what the consequence could be in the next chapter. WAY too many classrooms are built around short term, narrow, tiny pictures and leave the BIG picture totally out or vastly distorted; most all unlikely to occur and easily discounted by students.

The object is to give the student a model of conscientious thinking, to experience a decision process, to feel their power directly over self and others, and to put fate in their hands with informed love. This is a significant factor in students who should know what to do but do not know how to be. We rarely share our being and they miss a valuable education in the social curriculum. When we share our being in a safe, kind, informed way, this immediately creates attunement, intentionality, and answers nearly every Essential Question. I am not saying to share your deep secrets, cross boundaries, or be their friend. They already have friends. They need an adult they can model, grow into, and become.

Using the Type One and Type Two distinction, the response to a contentious classroom would begin with the teacher finding every reason to like the students and enjoying the daylights out of them. The teacher must avoid replicating the student behaviors of disliking others, being on others about every little thing, and especially being defensive and trying to make others stop with threats or retaliation. The teacher then upholds the values of kindness, helpfulness, and being a good friend and drives these values through everything that happens in the class. The students are seen, heard, valued, and enjoyed for their kindness, helpfulness and acts of friendship at every turn. Joy and good feelings are infused in the fabric of the room from every angle.

Rather than attempt to stop the conflicts, conflicts are resolved. Personal slights, insults, rudeness, and disrespect are all consequenced by restoration and contracts where the student actively contributes the values back in to the class. So, if you put hurt feelings or unsafe feelings in the class, you are asked to do something to show kindness and show you can be trusted again. When the above actions are taken, classrooms change immediately. Deep in their heart and mind they will sense you are building secure attachment, and will really show up with their best when you do.

It is quite common for there to be misunderstandings between students that end with, "See, they didn't say that about you. You misunderstood." Typically, the upset student is expected to accept this head knowledge and calm down. It was cleared up, let's move on. Typical management. However, I think more is needed. Some Essential Questions can be answered to restore the class/students and move on in much better ways. A restore would validate the offended student or put some good feelings in the relationship. Maybe things like, "I wouldn't say that because I wouldn't want to hurt your feelings." "Don't be upset because I never talk bad about you." "I'm sorry. I actually think you're pretty cool." Now the upset student can focus on how they have a positive relationship, or at least a neutral one, and feel valued as a person. This is why I advocate you have a clear intention to uphold certain values in your classroom and focus on the Essential Questions. The head knowledge that there was a misunderstanding may suffice as a solution to a problem, but it does not help model kindness, positive coping, respect of dignity, nor propel good feelings forward.

Change the dynamics and the system/classroom becomes different. If you find yourself barking and fussing at all the fussy students, expect more of the same. If you become the experience you want them to be: kind, patient, joyful, truthful in love, and contributing to a positive mood and direction for the class, then you will get more of that. You will have jumped into a new class of actions and attitudes which will be a difference that makes a difference, and thus change the system dynamics. In system theory, more of the same (Type One) does not make a difference to the system and is termed as "noise." If the system does change, it is because some difference made a difference (as Type Two change is a change of class). This is called "information" to the system. If you re-read many of the stories in this book, you will be able to see how the student was presented with a new class of information or responses and then changed.

Very often in trainings, there is concern voiced about the negative colleagues people work with. These negative and sometimes toxic colleagues yell at students, are sarcastic, thwart change, and create a lot of division among staff. Unless they are stirring a boiling pot of negative attitudes, they are not happy. What happens when you attempt to finesse, deflect, and avoid these people? They fester and degrade the climate and culture of the school. I know many teachers who avoid the staff lounge because the conversations are so negative and depressing to hear. Like many students, I know of teachers who have been written up numerous times yet continue to disturb, disrupt, and degrade those around them. Nothing "new" occurs and the "noise" continues.

As with your classroom climate and culture, these negative and ultimately destructive social interactions need addressed. The longer they continue, the worse they become and the more they are grooved into the system's mind and emotions. Just as you would do with your classroom, you begin by finding every reason to like these colleagues. You do not finesse, manage away, or expediently ignore the distress they create; you openly address it. If not, it becomes a giant elephant in the room that people deny experiencing, or they suffer under its load. Just as with students, you move to resolution, contracts, and pathways to build love and strength in them.

One simple, but useful way of speaking the truth in love and working within a contract is the classic model of assertiveness. You can set personal boundaries with it, stick up for yourself with it, diplomatically work out agreements and plans with others, resolve conflicts with spouses, children, friends, business people, you name it! Here are the four basic components.

1. You factually report what you see/hear the other person doing. You have no attitude or judgment about it. You do not say what you think they mean by their actions or words - just the facts.
2. You report how you feel and/or what you think about the above.
3. You offer what you would like to have happen or how you would like things to turn out.
4. You ask if they are willing to pursue that outcome, do what you would like them to do, or not. If not, go back to step one to address that.

Here is a sample. "When I hear you raising your voice at the class, I feel you might be frustrated. I would like to work with you to offer some ideas that might help. Are you willing to meet with me?" Notice they are not being accused of anything, demanded to do anything, blamed, left alone, or simply told to stop. They are seen/heard, valuable to me, and offered a path to something better. If they say "no," then I start over toward a new agreement or set a limit. Supposed they say, "No, I'll run the room the way I see fit. These kids need yelled at or they don't respect you." I might use a shortened version then. "I think respect is important too. I am much happier since I found some other ways to get their respect. If you are interested talking about those in the future, just let me know." The point is NOT that they have to agree with you or do what you hope they will do. The point is you have modeled the respect you hope they will opt for. You have given them the EXPERIENCE of respect and a path forward they may take someday. This comes from you being congruent with the values you profess.

Suppose you are really brave and totally had it with their yelling at students. Your response to them may be like this. "I hear you saying that yelling seems to be the only way. I find it hard to teach and my students find it hard to learn when we hear it in my classroom. I would like you to think of what might help reduce the impact on my room. Will you talk with me more about it tomorrow?" Notice I am not going for a solution then and there because right now they see no other way. I want to stay in what is possible, and it is possible they will talk more about it with me. It is possible they may come over to watch how I am getting it done so I might invite them over. It is possible they cuss me out and tell me to mind my own business. At that point I would ask them, "Is this really how you want it to be between us and for you at school?" I just keep going for the possibility yet I am also asking them to make a clear yes or no. They might tell me to go away or walk off. They may not want to change one thing ever. However, I have helped my colleague who yells experience the process they can use with students to convey and grow respect, and to set limits. Now let's go further with driving values in the classroom. By driving values, I am going to be primarily in Type Two levels of change and keeping a *big* picture going on my climate and culture.

CHAPTER EIGHT
Value-Driven Consequencing

On the ground level, the requests for help in the classroom are not for assistance with one or two challenging children, but four, six, eight or more challenging children per class. I am not going to give you some fancy point system you can use on your smart board. Point systems are sometimes effective at jump starting a class toward better social and academic behavior, yet if you do not quickly move to build up internal guidance systems based in values, you will hit October striving. You have to build a community of students internally driven by great values that guide them at ever-increasing levels. I am not going to give you more ideas to make students miserable or ashamed or excluded from education. Too many already come to school that way, and there is no support for such tactics being beneficial. You can buy a ton of books and spend huge dollars on programs with tactics and gimmicks aimed at enticing students to behave and follow expectations. I want you to have more than that. I want you to have a room full of conscientious, conscious, value-driven citizens who know how to love and be loved, and are zealous learners. In the words of a fourth grader, "My teacher taught me to do my best even when I don't know what to do." I love that!

What I will give you are ways to guide and consequence students with love, hope, and dignity so they can actually learn something about those values from you and the school culture, internalize them, and most importantly, grow those values in the entire school culture. Then students will give you back their best. If you use a Response to Intervention (RTI) model, and in the process of using interventions do not convey love, hope, and dignity, you will not get far. Similarly, if all I have is the later, I may not have clear pathways to success or a direction. Just as with an Olympic trainer, I must have a plan (with direction and limits/guidelines), and be a superb advocate too. Either alone will not help create champions. I know students will help you be the best teacher possible, when they know you are after their dignity and clearly have your mood and direction set to uphold yours and theirs.

STORY TIME: DRIVE HER CRAZY

In one fifth-grade class, there were about fifteen students who were openly rude, loud, disruptive, insulting, and doing their best to make the teacher feel totally worthless. In fact, that group had already blown a veteran teacher out of the classroom in less than two months. Now they were plotting to do the same with the replacement- of course a first year teacher! How did we know they were plotting? They told a male mentor who was also part of the district administration. They told him they had numerous teachers each year and none of the teachers liked them. This was true. So they set out paying the system back for failing to value and like them. They actually planned their strategies before school. In self-fulfilling manner in the dance of the Essential Questions, they were unlikeable! The replacement teacher was yelling and threatening the class all day, and so appeared to dislike the class immensely. The students knew they existed and were compelling others to see and hear them in unlikeable ways. They definitely made a difference but in escalating lose- lose games. Although marginally competent in academic skills, the bottom line for the class and teacher were the questions of being valued, wanted, and loved.

This class did not need to hear one more word about rules, how to behave, expectations, and punishments. They did not need one more chart, point system, or incentive program. They did not even need to hear they were behaving, or how the teacher was pleased and liked their behavior. They had chewed up all those things and spit them back at the school/teacher. They needed something real from the gut and heart and spirit of the teacher. It was personal. It always is!

THE FOUNDATION TO CONSEQUENCING

It is always personal and any attempts you make at consequencing students need to be completely prefaced by a multitude of positive, affirming, sincere answers to their Essential Questions. Otherwise you are employing another gimmick, an external tool, a depersonalizing ploy to wield power over behavior. You are devalued in the process and so are the values we need to be building up in students. Once you begin employing tools to externally enforce behavior, you have taken the power out of the student too. They need to experience their power and ability to self-direct so they can experience their dignity and worth as a person.

Once you move from a relationship based community to a financially (points, prizes) based community, you have begun a bartering system and your hopes will not be fully realized. It will be about the prize or the cost-benefit ratio for acting up rather than developing values and internal guidance based on those values. It will be up and down, up and down, and work against you getting the relationships you need to have in a real community/class/school. It will be chasing rabbits. From the book *Predictably Irrational*, comes a story where a school was having problems with students brought late. Many letters, phone calls, and curbside conversations occurred with parents to reduce the problem. After little success, the school decided to charge a fee for late comers. Lateness increased as did the number of late students. The school had made it "worth it" to be late. When they took the fee away and tried to go back, there was no improvement. The relationship basis had been broken.

When teachers and schools start taking away, depriving, and making it all about points, they are setting up a cost-benefit economy where it may be worth it to break rules and act terrible. How much can you really take away, how severe can you get, how much freedom to act the fool can you really take away? The value of people and the building of a community are lost in the process. The danger of an allowance for chores is someday your child will say, "If you want me to keep doing this, you need to pay me more." Notice how little love and value would have to be present for that to occur. If all you have is a business model, expect the business. Keep it personal.

I see most incentive programs as business models and causing more problems than success. As soon as incentive programs are announced, some students immediately act out and blow their chances. Others act out along the way but then begin shaping up to undo referrals and eventually go. Teachers may begin to use the incentive as another power tool to threaten students. "Stop that right now or you will not be going to the incentive." The main issue is that incentive programs are not really reward programs. A true reward program would follow success such that on an unknown day, students who had already been showing a certain level of excellence would have the reward dropped in their lap. "Congratulations! You have been an outstanding student and we thank you with this pass to our dance this Friday." Boom! Reward! Who knows when the next reward will occur? Maybe it will be a choice of rewards! True rewards are extremely powerful. Incentives create bargaining and rabbit chasers.

This is similar to incentive chart systems. Following expectations gets your name on the chart, but that is not enough. You do not "win" unless you are lucky. What lesson in life is that? Is that how we will possibly get into Heaven someday? "Welcome to the eternal afterlife. You were exceptionally good, but not so lucky. Sorry." I do not want students working hard to follow expectations but overshadowed by some need to be lucky. With people and attachment, I am blessed every day all day, not just on Friday afternoon by some incentive. The cost-benefit of the respect chart is fine for those students who are already hopeful, patient, and having some higher level Essential Questions answered. It is a game on the sidelines of their already fulfilling attachments with others. However, incentives, points, being on green, and pieces of paper will never really answer any Essential Questions, replace your value in doing so, or replace your valuing and love for a student. These are your powerful gifts to their spirit and dignity. They are worthy of being experienced, known, loved, and forgiven. You are so worthy that students will immediately respond back to you with the same. **They want you to be the best person possible.** More and more students are desperate for you to be. If you are your best for them, they are going to feel deeply valued and secure.

Many schools pass out slips of paper or points to students for following expectations. Again, I see these usually becoming a business/ bartering system where the paper slips and points become the reward in itself, or a new threat to hang over students. My experience is teachers use them primarily to manage their most difficult students and the truly best students get very few if any. I will never forget the day I was in a classroom and a bunch of college athletes showed up to reward the problem "high flyer" students who had made enough points on their charts. All the most difficult students in the school left with the athletes to play games on the playground. The students who were actually the best citizens ran to the window to watch all the known problem students having a blast. How would you explain that to your best citizens? My view is these pieces of paper and points are best used as markers, mementos, tags, that the student was bringing one of the community values to life. "You were really upholding Dan's dignity. Would you like this (paper) to remember this by?"

To me, if I make the movie, party, whatever more important than the values driving the community, I have devalued the values and made them secondary. I have also taught short-term thinking and stunted student's vision for long-term achievements. If the only goal is meeting expectations, and everyone in the school meets those expectations, there can be many parties and rewards week after week, but what will actually be growing in the climate and culture? What is there to actually instill, develop, and deepen the values within students so they are leaders, not just followers?

With all the above in mind, do not begin consequencing students for misbehavior, rule breaking, or other problems (unless they are really unsafe) until you have really been socially reinforcing the best qualities and values of students, and have clearly established a direction to keep doing so no matter what! If they can get you to revert or sink to nothing more than someone trying to get them to behave, they will feel they have lost their dignity with you, their value as people to you, and will seek revenge on you. In other words, if the above happens, you are no longer a source of positive answers to their Essential Questions and they retaliate by going after yours. They will show you that you have no real control over what they do try as you might. Soon everyone is in a battle over who will do what when, where, and how. Values and a path forward will be MIA. You fall into a trap of acting as if students will not be "good" to you until they behave. You will be acting in ways that will not invite them to be "good," and since they always have the last card to play on their behavior, will pay you back for treating them like bad machines that just need to function correctly. They will be "good" for a while then pull the rug out from under you. They will show you they are holding the last card in a game of lose-lose, unless you begin and continue to value and enjoy them. Then you will always have the last card.

Back to our story of Drive Her Crazy. With the class plotting to drive their latest teacher out of the room, we began with the step of simply finding everything possible to like and enjoy about the students. They could not like her, but she could like and enjoy them no matter what. She began to delight in their smiles, the colors they wore, their drawings, their questions, that they were creative, moments they shared with peers, any helpfulness, any effort to work, that they had friends and were being a friend, and much more. SLOWLY the class began to treat the teacher as if she mattered, had worth, had valuable opinions, and was likable. Within two weeks, the disruptions were far less frequent, intense, and/or long in duration. Within a month, most all were listening when she spoke, would ask her opinion, wanted her help, volunteered personal information, and invested in learning more. It all began with the teacher sending unmistakably clear messages she liked and enjoyed them. She held on to her worth, then they were worthy, then she was to them, and then education was too. **This pattern is one I have seen over and over in so many settings, and heard come from so many students that I consider it the foundation of any success you will have, and totally a prerequisite before any consequencing of problems. First, consequence/ reinforce how worthy and valuable and likeable they are.**

PROGRESS

Just as in academics, we have to scaffold progress in eliminating undesirable behavior and attitudes. Too often as people and parents and teachers, we want a magic bullet or pill that wipes the problem away instantly. Progress can occur like that, but mostly it is a process. I use four signs of progress. Any one of the four is progress.

1. It is occurring less often.
2. When it happens, it is less intense.
3. When it happens, it is of less duration.

4. The problem becomes more intense but the student is obviously running out of ideas and begins using desperate if not absurd measures to pull your mood and direction back to confirming their worst answer to their most intense question.

Bill comes in the class while the teacher is teaching and does not sit down. He approaches the teacher and interrupts her. He is ignored and, still standing next to her, raises his hand. He is given no response so he wanders over to an empty desk, puts a knee in the seat, raises his hand, and is ignored. The teacher is just calmly continuing to teach. He then goes over to his desk, sits, raises his hand, and is soon acknowledged by the teacher. "Bill thank you for so considerately raising your hand. What do you need?" Every step of the way Bill was making progress as he progressively gave up his intensity and moved closer and closer to his proper seat.

A first grader had been used to driving the mood and direction of the teacher for weeks but lately had been unable to use the keys to the teacher's emotional car he thought he owned. He intensified by becoming louder and more disruptive in class which had been landing him quickly in time-outs in the assistant principal's office. After a few days of clear limits, he was sitting in the office arguing that, "I am being kept from my education and you are not letting me learn!" This first grader was making progress as he made more desperate and outlandish arguments to have his way. He had not acted like a serious learner at all in the past few days. **This student, like every one of us, has a certain "Fix it" level that we must reach before we actually do something about a problem.** Often we fight and fight until we are out of options and surrender to change. It can be fixing the car, the faucet, the health issue, the marriage, the annoying task at work, whatever. Until we fix it, we are managing. How far do you have to go until you fix the whatever?

Sometimes the escalation is not more sophisticated verbiage but plainly regressed actions where they act and sound years younger than usual. A seventh grader was running into strict limits with his language arts teacher over his loud and impulsive talking. One day after receiving a consequence, he squeaked out in the smallest child-like voice, "But… I just want to talk." This was progress and a turning point. NOTE: If the student regresses and becomes truly wordless and helplessly distressed like an infant, it is not progress. It is time to soothe and comfort, and call the social worker.

Sometimes progress is a mixed picture. A student with a mean and repulsive vocabulary had thrown little plastic blocks all over the room and scared a few students verbally. He had been disruptive to the teaching process and had just returned after a short break to regroup himself with an aid. Back in the room, his words continued to spew venom, yet he was picking up all the little blocks. The aid told the student he was being helpful and kind by picking up the blocks. The student then offered to help a peer with the math lesson, did for a moment, picked up more blocks and sat down. The verbal venom and disruption ended, his mess cleaned up. **Since we are often living in an Essential Question, we are often simultaneously trying to answer it while also provoking it.** Such is this student who was being "good" and "bad" at the same time. Here is another example where the picture is mixed and the teacher has to decide which aspect of the total picture to reinforce.

A first grader, repeating first grade, famous for violence, disruption, and running out of the room, had his toes on the tile seam in the doorway to the class. He knew if his toes crossed the line, he was going to get a consequence. The rest of his body was leaning out of the doorway in to the hall. Technically, he was "in" the room and abiding by the rule not to run. Half his body was still out of the room. Which would you pick to address? The teacher said, "I am so glad you are following the rule and staying in the room because I really want you here with me." The student went ballistic and trashed some of the room. After he calmed down, he was genuinely apologetic, ashamed, and set out to repair the room. This was a huge turning point for the better.

`Many extremely challenging children change for the better with that pattern. It is as if their brain explodes in a massive rewire of old patterns, habits, emotions, and beliefs. In fact, I encourage you to see the student being half in and half out, half cooperating and half defying, quite literally as his brain in conflict. It also puts your brain in conflict just figuring out which aspect of his behavior to respond to. How many times have you seen an angry student half-smiling? How many times have you wanted to say yes or no when many other parts of you want to say the exact opposite? These explosions usually come after weeks of progress when staff began thinking the "really bad" problems are behind them or at least a truce is maintained. When the explosion comes, many people are discouraged and see failure. It is actually the beginning of the best ever. **It is attachment in action.** It is common in many settings. You may have been or witnessed a child rejecting the new step parent over and over, then after a period of what seems to be calm truce, an unforeseen blowout occurs followed by reconciliation and growth in the relationship. Do not lose hope. See if they have not resolved their internal conflict before you do anything rash. I know a first grader who has a depressed mom, two older brothers in their late teens who have alternative education histories with serious criminal records, and a dad who emotionally abandoned him about 8 months ago. He idolizes his older brothers. School wants him to be, and do, many things vastly different from his brothers. He is certainly in conflict. He can be wonderful and then horrible in class. He has had to learn to not care, but he does and will risk it. If the teacher is in conflict over caring about the student, nothing new can happen but more and more swings between caring and not caring. Someone has to care, to be the lesson he can use to solve his conflict. We also give him all the power and the information to choose who he wants to be. "Elijah, you could stay mad like this or you could make things better by helping Brian read. I hope you use your power to help others." The teacher is not invested in Elijah picking one or the other. The investment is in helping Elijah choose and feel he has all the power to direct his life. When it will happen, I do not know. I only know what will happen if the school models him, verses be the model he needs. Progress will be one or two of the four signs above followed by an extended period of success, followed by an explosion.

BUILDING ON THE FOUNDATION

Now we can look at ways to send some stop and start messages, how to set limits, and design consequences to help students be their best ever. All that follows has to be built upon the foundation above.

IGNORING

You do not have to "ignore" behavior though many teachers feel they must. Ignoring is one way of sending a "stop" message. You can choose to not socially reinforce behavior so it will eventually be extinguished, which is commonly known as "actively ignoring". Active ignoring can be powerful, but there are a few "ifs" with this consequence. **If** they do not have Essential Questions that will be escalated by being ignored, **and if** you can truly not be triggered internally and externally, **and if** you can keep it up for weeks, **then** go ahead and use active ignoring. **And if** the attitude/behavior is progressively reducing over time in any one or more of four ways (less intense, less frequent, less lengthy in duration once it starts, more desperate justification), then keep going with it. Note this would not work with the girl promoting herself as queen of the inept learner club. She had the power question of wanting to make a difference if not to be the total guiding difference in the room. **Never ignore students with existence questions or wanting to be the total difference.**

Other versions of being ignored include being moved, given a time-out, sent to a time-out spot, having to put your head down, and put in the hall. Such messages as these are messages that you will be ignored for a little while and the above criteria apply. These may work but if you cannot meet the criteria above you will wind up reinforcing more of the behavior you want to stop. This can occur by losing your mood and direction toward the best values possible. Their mood and direction will then prevail. It can occur by the child escalating into unsafe behavior you have to respond to. It can occur by you giving up too soon when you are getting one or more of the four signs of progress.

In the beginning, never use any versions of ignoring without also communicating a clear pathway that the child can take to restore. Do not leave them guessing when, how, if, you will attach to them again, nor leave any guessing open about your direction with them. What the heck does this mean you ask? It means you say things like:

"Take a moment and think of a way you can show me your trustworthiness."

"While you are refocusing, I want you to find the patience you had this morning during math."

"I'd like you to think of two things to do before lunch to show your integrity. Do not tell me; let me see if I can tell what they are. Will you do that?"

"Can you commit to being diligent and build stamina at reading for the next five minutes?"

"Are you being the best you can be right now?"

NOTICE: I am being the brain, going for a better future, giving a clear path to it, and going for values- not behavior. As a student, I know exactly that you want me to be a better person, view me as a better person, and how I can best attach with you. Once you have clearly sent these messages for a long enough time that everyone in the class knows you want them back with you, and are after their best, you can begin to use some version of ignoring without these messages. Even when everyone knows, I still recommend speaking to the pathway back. That way there is no question they are significant and belong. If you use ignoring with even the slightest hint the student is not significant, nor wanted to belong, expect these feelings and messages served back to you on a sizzling platter.

LIMITS

Notice that several of the examples above contain some definite end point – before lunch, five minutes from now. These are limits and very effective. The student and you know something is expected to happen or to change at a specific point in time. A middle school teacher had told three eighth graders to sit down three times. She looked at me with a questioning face and I told her to tell them, "You need to be in your seats in three – one." They literally ran to their desks and we struggled to hide our laughing. I have a saying. **When you do not know what to do, set a limit.** This helps you avoid the quicksand of management, adds structure, and lets students know a consequence is about to occur. Limits are also at work when we tell others they can do X or Y. By doing that, there is a limit on their choices. Limits can be set on the order things will occur in; such as when a child is told to first eat their supper and then they can have dessert. Of course, they can take all the time in the world, they can invent their own limits, but usually people of all ages stay in the limits. I again refer you to the book "Predictably Irrational" for more examples and discussion. You can have students put limits on themselves by asking them for commitments. "Will you commit to three more minutes of quiet on the carpet?" One very powerful and respectful way of setting limits is to use to most powerful forces on earth: truth and love.

TRUTH IN LOVE

Sometimes it is much clearer, easier and faster to tell the student to stop something. Again, do not give a "stop" without a "go." Toxic students or co-workers often do not download ignoring as a "stop" and may consider it permission to continue. They need a clear message. The best way to do this is to use the assertiveness skills from page 85. You will be consequencing difficulties between you and others with straight-up truth, honesty, ownership, kindness, dignity, and moving the relationship forward to something better, rather than striving and defending toward a stop. The other person or persons will hear how they are in a dance with you, learn about social connections, and be an equal partner in making the future clearer and more agreeable: even if that future is to end the relationship.

With this framework, you can tell students they are doing something they need to amend, revise, undo, stop, and reconsider without blaming, nagging, shaming, or any other pothole in the road to understanding and agreement. Many marriages have been saved, and a great deal of diplomacy has occurred by the four simple steps of assertiveness.

It can be difficult, but avoid judgments and conclusions. Just stick to the basic actions seen and heard. You do *not* load it with conclusions or judgments such as, "When you act like a rude infant I just want to scream. Act as if you have some brains. Will you stop acting so stupid and grow up!" That follows the framework but violates the intention to speak the truth in love. Here are some examples where the intention is fulfilled.

"Devarion, when you call Josie a name like that, it is not kind. I would like you to say or do something kind for her in the next five minutes so she feels better and we have a happier classroom. Will you do that?"

"Fredrick, this is the third time you have been out of your seat. I am distracted by that. Will you use your diligence to stay seated until the end of math? That will be really kind and help me be a better teacher."

"If you choose to do that I will have to give you a discipline referral. I would rather have you succeeding in class. Will you avoid that temptation and do something I can honor about you now?"

Keep it personal as long as possible. You might end with a limit rather than a request. You may reach a point where you have to follow the discipline code, but even then you can use the framework.

"Devarion, when you call Josie a name like that, it is not kind. I would like you to say or do something kind for her in the next five minutes so she feels better and we have more kindness in our classroom. Sit here and raise your hand when you have an idea of what you will do."

"Marleena, you have hit another student and that means I have to call your parent and write a discipline report. Before I call your parent, I would like you to show me you are committed to making our school a safe place to be. Will you show some kindness and use your self-control in the next period so I can tell your parent how you brought safety back to our class?"

Sometimes, abbreviate it. "That is not going to help people trust you or make you easy to like. Can you turn that off and do something easy to enjoy?" The girl wanting to be queen of the inept needed to hear these messages. The class seeking to drive the teacher out did. Everyone does.

ANSWERING ESSENTIAL QUESTIONS WHILE SETTING A LIMIT

We do not always need to jump to a consequence. Sometimes we can answer an Essential Question and add a limit to restore a positive mood and direction. Limits simply define a specific time period, number, or choice such that there is a clear yes or no response by the student. "You need to show dedication to growing your brain in five seconds." "You need to have that written by 1 pm." "You can stand here or there as we wait." Limits set a deadline after which something will happen. Just telling a student to sit is not a limit. It is something they can agree with. "Yeah, I should. You're right." "Sit in five" is a directive with an implied "or". Earlier I wrote about a student in a self-contained classroom who we knew needed the ability to hope. He was yelling at the teacher because she was helping another student. "You'll never help me!" She was giving him a common limit. "Sit quietly and I'll help you." He kept wailing, "You won't help me!" and started kicking the desk. She then turned and told him she wanted to help him, had more help than he could ever need, and would definitely help him as soon as he sat calm and quiet. He instantly did. She first had to answer his questions of abundance and being valued. He had to hear she *wanted* to help, *had plenty* of help, and he was in control of making help happen. Bam! He sat down and was quiet. He even raised his hand. Just the limit did not answer his question.

There are many students in your school right now living with so many mixed messages about their Essential Questions that they are completely bamboozled. They come to school and drive us nuts. They are doing what we all do. They pass on their striving and defending hoping for better answers. They have parents who don't show for visits, parents who lie every day and promise the world every other day, parents who love/hate them, parents choosing drugs over them and food, and parents who feed enough lame excuses to fill the oceans. I know a kindergartener who is proud as can be of his mom and grandmother because they are so good at stealing from stores. He steals from the school and peers several times a week. We need to be clear, easily understood people for these children. We need to be answering their Essential Questions in clear powerful ways before we go setting limits on them. Just the limit devalues them and provokes their questions deeper. It is not that we are in a battle only about stealing; it is a battle about love, pride, belonging in relationships. We first have to supply a relationship of love and pride to attach to this young child. Many a marital argument would be over sooner if the first words out of someone's mouth answered the Essential Questions of the marriage relationship. "I want you to be with me and for this to work out so we are happier and more in love. I don't know how we'll do it but I want it to work out like that." Settle the goal, then work on a method or set a limit. Lid up or lid down?

Be clear what the limit/expectation is. I have watched many a teacher telling various students to take a time-out in some fashion(Reset Bill; Take a chill Franklin; Take a moment Vanessa; That's a minute Halenna), and the class gets worse because no one knows what they are being timed out for. One way of being clear is using contracts and commitments while keeping everything focused on the values of the class or school. Now we will look at driving the values though consequencing.

THEIR CONSEQUENCE IS TO BE A CONTRIBUTION

Notice how in every case I am asking for a return to upholding values of the climate and culture of the class, not just for them to behave, follow a rule, meet behavioral expectations, or stop acting out. I am not promising a reward or incentive. I am asking them to make a positive contribution to the mood and direction of the class climate and culture. I am putting it all in their hands because that is where it is anyway. I cannot make them do anything and I can only be the best invitation and congruent example I can be. The rest is up to them. This message is powerful because many people have already tried to "control" them. With this intervention, I am making the reward and incentive their own power and ability to answer some of their own Essential Questions.

By having their consequence be a contribution, you can end the considerable effort often put into thinking of some punishment. You can drive the climate and culture of the class/school forward while clearly providing fulfilling answers to Essential Questions. Just by using this idea, the student will "hear" you communicating "You can trust yourself, you make a difference that makes a difference, you are wanted or belong, and you are fully competent". Even preschoolers will hear these messages and respond with their best. You get to maintain your mood and direction as well. Whatever the student does gets measured against the values. The students may want to play a game of lose-lose with you, but your response is to uphold the standard of the values. "I understand you are upset. However, when you…, it is not kind, helpful, or contributing to value of others. Take a few minutes to think how you can bring kindness, helpfulness, to (peers) and our school." Notice how this follows the assertiveness steps with a limit. If they do not, if they refuse, go to a consequence. "Since you are not willing to bring kindness back to our class after having time to consider how, you are getting a referral." Note: not will get, not going to get, but are getting. It is a done deal. If they immediately shape up, too late.

Even preschoolers can think of something that restores the values of the class or school. They will come up with some way of being kind (or whatever values you have for the class) almost always. However, some truly do not know what to do to help other people. Even middle school students can draw a blank- but you turn this into a little project for them. Who would know? Whom can they talk to? What book have they read that might help them, or movie? Who at home might be of help. Anyone but you can be a resource. You are the guide for their learning.

It might go like this:

"James. That is not showing integrity. Sit here until you have two ways to show you are trustworthy this afternoon. Raise your hand when you have two ways."

After James identifies two ways he will be seen as trustworthy, you ask him to commit to doing them.

"Those are great ideas James. Will you do them in the next hour?" If he agrees, you be on the lookout for them. If the student dawdles and takes too long to think of a plan, you can always go with limits:

1. You pick a way and ask the student to commit to it.
2. It becomes homework.
3. You have a well-known rule that if the student does not think of a way in a reasonable time, they have to spend some recess time thinking. "Once you have shown the class you are committed to being kind I can let you play with them."

The main components are that (step one) they are contributing the value back into the class culture, (step two) you and they have a clear idea what it will look and sound like, and (step three) there is a clear and spoken commitment from the student. The most important component is that the teacher will be committed to reinforcing the student's commitment.

Here are some simple ideas to help your design your own consequences that are contributions. You imagine what needed to happen or should have happened that would let you honor them for outstanding manifestations of the class or school values. A common consequence for running in the hall is to go all the way back and walk. You may actually get better results by having the student stand there and count to twenty-five or think of three nice things about their teacher to show they are patient and thoughtful. They could also be your line leaders that then help their peers walk to show they are contributing safety and kindness. They can be hall observers that cheer and praise other students who are walking. Running in the hall is just one of many examples where students have trouble controlling their impulses and cave in to temptation. One student, who was supposed to be on his way to class, zoomed in the gym, took a couple of shots at the basket, and then chased out by an adult. That is not strictness. That is managing. To have him do a consequence, you might have him stand at the door to the gym and resist the temptation to shoot baskets. You might have him walk by the gym a few times while peers try to tempt him to come in for a quick shot. He could become a hall monitor who thanks peers for walking straight to class. The aim is to strengthen the internal values, the internal guidance system of the student.

Unkind students are required to put kindness back in. Students who act up in another teacher's classroom are required to demonstrate the citizenship and productivity they should have had for whatever time they were not at their best in the other teacher's classroom. If I often blurt out goofball stuff and disrupt the class, I will need to prepare questions and facts that will contribute to the lesson tomorrow, plus apologize to the class for taking away their time from learning and for not being kind. If I am creating conflicts between others, I need to come up with ways to be a good friend to others. Of course, all these ideas are done with love, meant to restore the student to the best they can be, and make the culture of the school the best it can be.

Two middle school girls had a big confrontation and the next day are sitting with the principal to discuss how they will get along in school. The principal was doing most of the thinking and the girls were agreeing with his ideas. However, when I asked the girls to tell me exactly what they would do when peers began to egg them on, when they heard a rumor, they did not know. We discussed what they would specifically do, and, rather than commit to the principal, I asked them to commit to each other. This opened the door to their past friendship and that began to restore. They left as friends again with commitments and specific actions to sustain that friendship. Despite clear instigation from some drama-seeking peers, they have remained friends.

I have met so many students that have been so thoroughly "behaviorized" that they think it is perfectly fine to run up, say excuse me, and keep right on talking. They are indignant and surprised when they told to take a minute/take a time-out because they think they have said magic words. "Why are you giving me a time-out! I said excuse me!" They have no understanding of the actual social network or spirit of the rules. In general, school does not teach them about values and the social network. They are mainly taught to behave, to follow rules, to meet expectations. They say, "I'm sorry" with no real connection or attunement because they have been managed to no end. They hurt someone and all they hear is, "Tell them you're sorry." They do and it is back to driving the academics. We go through the motions and think the problem is over. Maybe so, but a bigger problem is left growing: students who have little attunement, little understanding of their true impact on others, and the idea that the lesson is more important than the moral, ethical, social issues in the climate and culture of the class or school. This is why I am not in favor of students being sent to In School Suspension and given academic work without first addressing and repairing the violation of values that landed them in ISS.

Think of yourself as a famous movie director. You would never tell the actors, "Now act right and go do a good job." You want to prepare and direct the action every step of the way. You want a clear vision of who, what, when, where, and how it will all happen. You want it to be the best possible scene ever. All the while, you also have a vision of the finished film of which this scene is a part. You want to regulate the voice, the climate, the messages sent through actions of the movie. The next section helps this process happen.

CONTRACTS AND COMMITMENTS

In using the assertiveness model, you may have gleaned that you make a contract and ask for a commitment to fulfill it. You can use these frameworks to get huge developments in the social and academic curriculum. Rather than telling students to stop, threatening them, or dropping a punishment on them, try making a contract and getting a commitment. We want to focus their brain exactly what we want more and more of so the mood and direction of the class culture can build. For this process, scaffold and get commitments.

Especially in early grades, I have watched students run around and tease, insult, and harass each other. When timed out, some of these students will say they do not know what to do when they are to think of ways they will bring kindness back to the class. All they know is retaliation and defense. We then scaffold as described above. Who do they think does know, who might have ideas, what books or stories have they heard, who can they see being kind right now, what can their imagination think of? They cannot use you other than to imagine what you might say. You are their coach and the model as they learn how to be resourceful and informed about kindness.

They do not need the answer from you; they need to learn the process from you. "Since you don't have an idea yet, think of two people you know who are kind and might have some ideas. Raise your hand when you have two people picked." Then you go back to the class, as it is the class who are being their best. That is who you want to give the most social reinforcement to. Go for the best then get to the rest. Not every problem needs solved right away, and you do not want to just "manage" problems. You do not even want just "resolution". You want to build a culture of active, intentional contributing. Simple commitments are effective ways to send a "stop" and get a "go," a contribution.

Sometimes I do not need a "stop." I just need to set up the next section of time or activity. James may be doing nothing wrong, in fact, he might be bringing his best, but I want to build his stamina. Or the phone may ring, I need to answer it, and I need quiet. To those ends, I might say:

"James, will you commit to working independently for the next five minutes so others can see what dedication is all about?"

"While I talk on the phone to the office, who thinks they can be totally committed to quietly and patiently wait for me to finish?"

I might prepare the scene for being in the hallway with the following:

"We are about to walk in the hall while other classes are still working. Who trusts themselves so much they know they can help the other classes do their best by being quiet while we walk?"

Other situations may call for questions such as these:

"We are too loud. I need you to commit to a level one voice. Who is willing to commit to level one for the remainder of our science period?"

"I need to think about that. Can you help me by letting me think about it for a while?"

"Who trusts themselves to be so respectful that they really don't need a (whatever) to remind them?"

Any time you use management tools—like students holding a bubble of air in their mouth to promote quiet walking on one side of the hall, assigned seats in lunch, or hands raised to be called on—you want to move beyond them as quickly as possible. You want to build up value-driven students who are orderly, thoughtful, kind, self-managing, and trustworthy all on their own as quickly as possible. Short-term contracts and agreements can get the class there in a hurry. **We leave the training wheels on *way* too long and pay the consequences. It is all about the scaffolding and having the most fantastic *big* picture possible. It is hard to grow a mind while trying to get the spirit to behave like a machine, or degrading it. Grow both mind and spirit.**

CREATING LEADERS NOT FOLLOWERS

In typical school discipline, it is common to have students do a time-out when they are being a problem. For example, two students horse around, so the teacher has them sit on the carpet until they can be still. After a couple of minutes the teacher says, "Thank you for sitting still. You can go to your seats and start working on your project." While this may be considered a time-out, it does not really require much brainpower, reflection, awareness, or forethought on the part of the student. It is efficient, but if I am a student who is not adding up my experiences, then I am merely sitting until the adult says I can get up and move on. I have not really learned much that will make the future better.

To build a leader of self, we need to impact the student's awareness, ability to reflect, and increase forethought. To build a leader of self, we also need to drive values. It is not going to accomplish much to ask if they know what they did was wrong, or even to ask them "What did you do that was wrong?" They probably know, but not always. For example, I have met many students who think that if they return what they just stole, they are not stealing because they gave it back. Sometimes students really do not know. To build a conscious and conscientious student, have them do some thinking in that time out.

"Dale, are you being principled (or helpful or safe or…) right now?"

"How?"

Or, you might say, "Dale, I am looking for your integrity right now. How can you show your integrity now?"

Perhaps you say, "Landon, what can you do to show your self-control while you are in time-out?"

Then go even further. You want to have them to hear your intentionality and have them plan so you have something to look forward to and enjoy about them. "Landon, what self-control will I be able to see once you are back at your desk?" If they cannot tell you, then you have just learned returning them to their desk is pretty much a crapshoot. They have no clear trajectory where you may have assumed they were adding up experiences, learning from their mistakes, and should know what to do. Far from it.

Test for understanding. Do not think serving time is of much help unless you are quite sure students are actually adding experiences up and building an internal guidance system. The process above equips them to be a leader of self and thus a better citizen. Of course, this process is done calmly and kindly according to the foundational conditions of consequencing given earlier in this chapter. You may be thinking elementary students are too young to do this, or that you do not have time. Would you keep teaching math to a student and not be checking for understanding? No. Same with the social curriculum. However, this understanding has to do with awareness, thinking ahead, and upholding a value.

There are many preschool and kindergarten classes where the students understand, discuss, and intentionally demonstrate integrity, efficiency, kindness, diligence, dedication, and trustworthiness. These values are taught from day one as all activities and processes of the day are rotated, revolved, and refocused on those values. Imagine what happened to their verbal comprehension scores compared to classrooms solely focused on rules, points, and earning things. Imagine how resilient these students are when bullied, or faced with change, or disappointed. Some of these students are quite economically poor, in need of early intervention, have difficult homes, and IEP's. In spite of all those challenges, they have dignity, integrity, value, and belong in a community where they are wanted and loved, filled up with hope, and understand the value of the values that they are increasingly manifesting.

"Take a moment and consider how you can do that with even more efficiency. Is there a way?"

"Greg is so proud of his math. How can we show Greg we are proud of his dedication to math?"

"Sasha has been diligent by practicing her fluency at home. Who can take a minute to give Sasha their full attention while she reads to us?"

Kindergartners can figure this out if you let them. "Let's see if we can figure out ways to take turns talking without raising hands and without interrupting each other. Who is willing to try that?" This way you create a bunch of scientists who can experiment, evaluate, and eventually self-monitor as a class. You have also just built a pathway to success and can follow the success as you head for the interstate and then the Autobahn. Scaffold the management tool out and scaffold value-driven self-guidance in.

I know many classrooms where the students have discussed and selected the values they want their class to have. They are committed to the values and have discussions such as, "What are some kind ways we can help each other get back on track? If you see someone doing something that is not respectful of others, how can you respectfully tell them to be respectful?" The teacher helps them become a reflective, self-governing body of value-driven citizens. It is *awesome* to hear the ingenuity and compassion and truth spilling out of students when we let them show up!

STRICTNESS AND CONSISTENCY

This is a confusing subject as parents and teachers are often told to be strict or consistent with rules above all. It is highly desirable. We cannot learn a sport, new culture, card game, or how to behave—*without* rules to guide us. Our brains demand rules so it can regulate itself. In the absence of rules, our brain will invent them—even if they are crazy rules. However, the mantra to be consistent can lead adults to feel like prisoners to the rules and as if they are violating their own sense of values. In the same way you do not want to make your climate and culture just about points and prizes, you do not want to make it all about adherence to the rules. Instead, make it about the spirit of the rules and how the rules benefit the community. **You cannot always strictly enforce the rules, but you can be strict and consistent with the spirit of the rules, or in other words, the values you uphold in the classroom and school.**

This conflict between consistency and the spirit of the rule happens on a small scale every day when students, who are supposed to be raising their hand, holler out the correct answer. Under the rules, it is the right answer in the wrong way. Some teachers go with the answer, and some ignore the answer and say, "Next time, raise your hand." Some think it is a great to have competition where students are trying to answer the fastest so they encourage it until it gets out of hand. Another common occurrence is a teacher has just told the class they have to be quiet in line before they can go to the assembly or field trip, and a few students refuse to be quiet. If you're late to the assembly, the whole class disturbs it, or the other classes have to wait for yours to board the bus and other teachers are ticked off because now everyone is late—and trapped on the bus with a bunch of wild things! Do you go for consistency, go anyway, call for help to keep a few back while the class goes on? How many times have you said, "I'm waiting for quiet," and a few chatter away as you wait? Here are a few things to keep in mind as we go forward.

Stating the rule is not a consequence. To be stating the rule over and over is social reinforcement to keep breaking the rule. Use all or a combination of reinforcement, limits, or consequences.

The longer a problem continues, the deeper it is weaving in to your culture. This is why you want to be very careful with ignoring. Use ignoring to extinguish problems only if you are getting some of the signs of progress given earlier. Do not announce you are waiting for success/ quiet, find some and go for it! With the talkers in line, go for the best and get to the rest. Celebrate those showing integrity and helpfulness to others by helping the class get to the field trip as soon as possible. Then ask the talkers to commit to quiet or tell them there will be a consequence later. Then go. You could also reinforce the best then just go, only later you give the consequence. Remember, not every problem needs solved right away.

Everything against the law, in general, is against the law because it diminishes the human spirit and creates social unrest by messing with our Essential Questions. (Jim Crow laws are a completely different story where the law itself messes with Essential Questions.) You can have the talkers restore the class values later.

This swinging back and forth between consistent rule enforcement and practical matters occurs at the program level too. What I see in several self-contained and alternative school programs is a general confusion among staff as to the rules and how tightly to hold students to rules. In general, the students are in danger of dropping out, most have terrible social environments outside of school, they have a lot of potential, and staff sincerely want to help the students succeed. The program cannot operate with the same standards and rules of regular school, the student already failed at those—often because of many factors. Some accommodations must be made, yet there must be rules too. The accommodations begin, the student pushes the limits, some staff call for tighter rules, and the student begins to be less successful or blows the rules big time. To help the student stay in school, there is then a swing back to accommodations. After several cycles of unsuccessful accommodations, some staff will advocate going back to tighter rules or declare the student beyond the program. This leads to splits between staff who are "uncaring hard liners" and those who are "enabling pushovers." Too soft, too hard and we have a dance between them. Just as parents do, when one is too hard and the other too soft, each side gets more extreme until they are each far from any middle ground and consequently a huge field to play in is created for the student. However, both sides are usually after the same set of values from the student. Most often, both want academic growth, signs of accountability, responsibility, self-control, problem solving, and hope. When there is staff division, the student is divided.

The focus needs to be on what the student is doing with **their** contracts and commitments. What are **they** saying they will do, do they do it, and, if not, what will they commit to then? We scaffold and cheer whenever possible within reasonable rules and limits. As I said earlier, the student must feel their power, their ability to choose and direct their life so they can lead their life. We then follow success.

After much scaffolding and accommodation, you might wind up saying, "Teddy, you have not kept the past three commitments you made. I want you to have success here and need to see commitments kept to keep you in the program. I need to hear from you if you want to remain here, what you will commit to, and see those kept, or I need to hear from you that you really do not want to be here and help you in some other way. If you make new commitments and do not keep those, I will have to recommend another program to the court. What do you want to show about yourself from here on?" Now Teddy may say a bunch of wonderful things, but the bottom line is that his behavior is his answer. Is he keeping commitments, fulfilling agreements, bettering his situation? Scaffolding, but with limits in place. Follow their success at keeping their own word.

A common problem in classrooms is the student who does not sit for long and zooms around the room at best functioning only as a distraction. You may have to scaffold with short contracts and commitments to sit for thirty seconds or a minute then another thirty seconds—then another repeatedly before you get up to five minutes. "Herbert, will you help everyone at your table learn by sitting down. Can you sit for two minutes? Good let's thank Herbert for committing to sitting!" The important elements are that you are not just telling them to sit (behave), you are asking them to sit so they are upholding a class value, providing a lot of social reinforcement when they are spontaneously sitting, and having peers also socially reinforcing the student for sitting. "If Herbert helped you be a better learner or enjoy the video more by sitting, give him a thumbs-up. Thank you, Herbert!"

A district superintendent told me about a teacher upset with a defiant student who was often late for class. The teacher demanded the student be suspended for a day. The superintendent said he would do so, and he told the teacher he had a day off as well because he was late to his job on several occasions. "Well, that is different!" asserted the indignant teacher. Is late, late? Is a day off for lateness the rule for all lateness? Are there special circumstances to the rule? How many social and legal rules did you break today? (I usually exceed the speed limit no matter what it is.) The teacher wanted to hammer the rules but when it comes to those same rules judging him, he wanted the spirit of the law invoked. After hearing this account, I thought about asking the teacher why it was different, going for the spirit of the law, and asking the teacher for commitments to be on time. Then I would tell the teacher to do the same with the student so they could have a more understanding and forward moving relationship too.

The issue is not just the rules or consistency with the rules. The issue is whether you drive the values of the program and build up those values consistently and congruently in you and the students. I trained a middle school alternative program that clearly drives high values and this past year went to over ninety-four percent average daily attendance and an average gain of three years of academic progress per student in 7 months. There were no suspensions the first two months of school! Everyone is scanned for weapons every day. You are not to cuss, bully, fight, or yell. All the usual rules are in place. However, the teachers give the students great worth, dignity, and value. The teachers answer Essential Questions all day long, are strict to uphold the values of the school (kindness, patience, helpfulness, trustworthiness, and diligence), and filter all social behavior through those values. If you violate a value of the school, you make a contract, make a commitment, and do something to be contribution. The students are always moving forward and have all the responsibility for their actions. They keep showing up for more responsibility too! A few do not, but it is very few.

When you work from a value-based, rather than rule-based, lens on what is occurring in the classroom and school, life actually becomes more clear and simple. It is no longer that you hit someone. Instead, you created a situation where people feel unsafe and may be afraid to like and help you. It is no longer that you are suspended for hitting someone; it is what you can do to restore feelings of safety so people will want to like you, trust you, and help you more. It is no longer that you have your head down and need to be paying attention, it is what can you commit to once you are ready. You can say, "This is when I am available to help you so if you need to sleep now, you will need to find a friend to help you get the instructions." You can say, "Who is willing to help Teddy get the assignment once he is fully back?" You can say, "Before you sleep, will you show me you're committed to learning by first finding someone who will help you get caught up by tomorrow?" Would you rather go after a student for sleeping or go after a commitment from them to learn when they are willing to be alert? If I insist on sleeping, are you able to let me—kindly and patiently—experience missing out or will you insist on me experiencing your attempts at power over my sleeping?

THE REAL WORLD?

What is that? It is the chorus of, "That's not the real world! We have to prepare them for the *real* world!" This is especially popular in high school settings. Sure, if you fall asleep in the job, you will probably be let go—unless you have a really good reason, a strong union, an understanding boss, you don't get caught, you manage your sleepiness really well so your job duties are not compromised, you suddenly take a sick day, you are a convincing liar, other people lie for you, no one cares, they are glad you are asleep, people laugh it off, or they let this one go but tell you next time there will be hell to pay, or… Which is the real world? The teacher who wanted a student suspended for lateness thought the student needed a real-world lesson. However, the same teacher recoiled at the idea of suspension for their own lateness. There may be an ideal world, but you and I have gotten away with all sorts of things. I think it is hard to find a "real" world just as there is no clear answer for what is "fair." What is real love? What is real justice? What is a real friend? What is a real Christian, Democrat, or Republican? What is a really good joke? What is really smart? Who is the real you? Opinions abound and what is real appears different under changing circumstances. It is a quantum physics world after all.

Has anyone ever tried to kill you, force you into a gang, threatened your family, or tried to sexually violate you? Do you take different routes home because the bigger kids will beat you up if they find you? Do you go to bed hungry and afraid? Do your parents hate you? Do you keep a secret so you will not be put in foster care? Do you wonder what it would be like to have a furnace instead of kerosene heaters at home? Do you only get one pair of new shoes a year? What is real life if any of these are occurring? What if you suddenly had money, and were safe, and free of secrets? What would real life be then? Is one of them unreal?

What if your parents destined you for Yale, Harvard, or MIT and shuttled your six-year-old self from one lesson and club after another, as soon as school was over? What if your parents only smile and like you when you get good grades? Do you have the best and latest of everything, but your parents are too busy to play any games with you? Do you have a parent popular and powerful in the community yet is a moody alcoholic at home? Do your peers make fun of you because got a few zits and will not sit with you at lunch because you are a dweeby brainiac? What is real life to you? Across the country, there are new standards for classroom evaluation, principal evaluation, and movements to base teacher pay upon test scores. Is that real life now? Which is real - optimism or pessimism in facing these changes in education?

If a student really wants to sleep, can you really prevent it? Why do they want to sleep? Maybe they were guarding their little brother from a raging adult. Maybe they partied their brains out all night. Why are you so sleepy? Does it matter? Yes, it does, yet what will matter most is the direction you take it and the values you uphold in the long run. Several years ago, a tall student fresh from an alternative program tossed his heavy book bag across the room at his eighth hour teacher. It just missed her. Why? He said he asked her for three days to call on him so he could show his peers he was smart. He asked her again at the start of class, she said she would (again), but did not after he had repeatedly raised his hand to be called on. WHAM went the book bag by her head at the end of class. He violated a rule and needed to be taught a lesson! What lesson will serve him and the school best? What lesson will give him a better future?

What lesson does the teacher need to learn? From his perspective, she did not keep one agreement with him in three days. How could she blank on his big voice or miss his large hand for three classes? What could be going on with her? What lesson will help her and this student have a better future relationship? What was the plan for this student to re-enter the school successfully anyway? Was it a team effort with clear goals and steps to greater success or was the student on their own? Who really wanted him to succeed and made no secret of it? Who was answering his Essential Questions gladly and with intentionality? *It was not just a broken rule; it was a broken climate and culture at the whole school level.* If you make it all about rules, your climate and culture will degrade to highly dramatic striving, defending, and rigidity (rigid rules or rigid chaos).

To keep the school, classrooms, and everyone in the school moving forward, you want to be value-driven. Filter everything through the best values you can imagine, and uphold them in all processes. What Essential Questions and values are in play if you really need to sleep? If you toss a book bag or yell at someone? If you are hung up on the rules or blurt out right answers before anyone else has a chance to be recognized? Or are as obnoxious as can be? Or cry because you earned a B, not an A, or want that late student suspended? **The health of the school climate and culture is reflected not in how well rules are enforced or how many rules are followed. It is reflected in how few rules and tools are needed because there is an abundance of great values regulating the system.**

I listened to a middle school student haughtily arguing with the student teacher about how she was sure the "real" teacher would give her full points on her point chart for speaking respectfully in class. She definitely was not respectful at that moment, yet the focus was not on that. It was on the points and playing the student teacher against the primary teacher. The student got full points from the teacher, because the teacher deemed the student "better than yesterday." The student gave the student teacher a smug "Told ya!" There was no consequence, no clear line drawn around her snide and demeaning attitude and words. No clear values were upheld or committed to. A business model was in place and the student was definitely giving staff the business. This student needed to hear a clear personal message of stop with the truth in love. Maybe something like, "When I hear you speak like this, I feel you are talking down to me. Whether you get points or not, I would like you to rephrase what you are saying so your words and tone sound kind and respectful. I'll be back in one minute to see if you have found a way to do that." Giving her a minute is kind and respectful. I want to be the model of what I want her to be and do. I want her to stop, reflect, and plan her words and attitude carefully. So, I literally show her how — not tell her. I want to totally sidestep the power battle over points and make it personal. I want it to be value driven and about who we are being. That is how you can be the advocate in consequencing. She may turn around and be respectful and kind or she may continue to be contentious and snide. That is when I then move through my decision tree of cheering on or going for another contract with a limit attached. "Since I am not hearing you rephrase in a kind respectful way, I am going to speak to (main teacher) about your choice. Tomorrow, for me to make a positive recommendation, I need to have at least three kind and respectful interactions with you." With this response, I am keeping it personal, setting clear pathways, speaking the truth in love, staying focused on values, and moving forward. Even if she turns around and says," I don't care if you think I'm anything!" I will have moved on and am looking forward to tomorrow. My mood and direction are no longer devoted to her so she is being technically "ignored." At most, I might say, "OK." I will still be modeling and giving her experiences of kindness and respect. I will still be keeping my mood and direction, still be attuned and intentional, and not socially reinforcing more contentious, snide commentary from her. I will have a clear limit and pathway lined out for her that I am committed to. More importantly, I am keeping my dignity and hers so she has a model for the future. The second I step into the quicksand of her attitude, I will have shown her my dignity is somehow in her hands, plus reinforced her for her effort to tempt me into handing it over. I find it ironic that someone invented a "game" for this girl to learn how to be kinder when a "real" personal relationship with her would be much more immediate, powerful, and kind. She was given a game and played it well to "win". Should we expect anything else?

RESTORING

So let's say you have done all the above and the inept girl continues to be just as proudly disruptive with her incompetency as ever, the contentious student is still rude and snide, and there are two guys bordering on safety issues with their out of seat behavior. Failed contracts and commitments litter the floor. After your observation, the consensus is you are not socially reinforcing the problems, or if you are, they are small. Further, the observation affirms the positive reinforcements, Essential Questions, and values are all at a high level thus offsetting any of the negative social reinforcements. It has been a couple of weeks of no stabile progress in any of the four ways. Now comes surgery. The patient is a mess. We must act carefully and calmly to rearrange, remove, or replace something in order for healing to begin. Just as you do not want to be admitted to the operating room and find no one really has a plan (Holy cow, Dr. Best! We better Google this one fast!"), you do not want to be on your heels when problems occur. You need to be on your toes and moving through a series of planned steps. This I refer to as triage. If this: then that, and so on through a decision tree of steps. Afterwards, the healing begins, but for the moment, we just do not want continued suffering or death. For this level, think remove, replace, rearrange.

A persistent tattletale exemplifies a simple example of remove, replace, or rearrange. He would not stop reporting every small infraction, so he attained few academic accomplishments while being reviled by his peers. We made him the teacher's assistant for finding good things. Periodically in class, the teacher asked him to report on his peers who were exhibiting the class values—being their best, being kind, building stamina, and so on. He was soon befriended and enjoyed by all. The inept girl could be given the job of helping students in earlier grades, the contentious student a job helping in the office greeting people, or the out of seat tag team become crossing guards. Students who insult and bully others can help with the disabled or impaired students. We take the student's gift and replace its direction with something useful and positive.

With more serious behaviors, you can follow the school discipline code. The key is to follow the procedures with the calm, careful demeanor of emergency room staff. Usually the code can be followed and acts of restoration and contribution added on. Thus a student, sent to in-school suspension and yet to re-enter regular class, would need to commit to two or three things that repair and contribute to the well-being of the class. In addition, you can possibly identify the student's gift and give it a useful direction. The kindergartner who steals could be assigned the duty of keeping track of a few things in the classroom that other students check in and out from him.

An example of removal that has proven an extremely effective intervention for some incredibly obnoxious students of all ages has been short-term removal outside class. The teacher buzzes the office when the student is grinding away on everyone's nerves, whining incessantly, yelling and running around, dominating the ability of you to be heard by the class. Someone, anyone, then comes by and escorts the student out of class for five minutes. There is no talking between the student and adult as they spend time in some bland area or room. After five minutes, the person returns the student to class. The teacher gives the student a few minutes to show some desired behavior or attitude and then celebrates how the student has brought (class value) back to the room. Sometimes peers are asked to voice their appreciation too so the student can be reinforced for desirable social actions and attitudes by peers as well. As soon as they revert to being obnoxious, they are out again. The keys to this are to keep time-out short and find reasons to celebrate them BEFORE they are out or obnoxious. This is to prevent them from having to act out to get their Essential Question answered through negative social reinforcement. Research done decades ago showed anything more than five minutes of time-out will likely beget revenge, and that one minute is actually most effective even for teens. The common idea of a minute for each year of age has no basis.

To make the above plan even more powerful, the student is out of the room and sitting in a socially bland room except for one thing. When they return to the class, they need to have a plan to contribute to the value set of the class. A particularly disruptive fifth grader began his school year after two arrests during summer. During his fourth grade year, he was terribly obnoxious and disruptive, gross and vulgar. He was often on the streets at night and defiant at home too. Less than one week into his fifth grade year, he was sitting in the AP's office for disruptive behavior about forty-five minutes into the school day. The AP calmly told the student how he had influenced the class by taking away learning time, making himself unhelpful to the future of the other students, and being unkind. At no time was this shaming or intended to shame. It was all truth in love fact with respect to the values of the class and school. The student was told he had to apologize to the class. He had taken away from the class in front of everyone, and now he needed to put good messages back in to the class in front of everyone. Not only that, he had to come up with three things he would do to help the class learn and see him as kind. He began crying. "How am I going to do that?" Notice, he was not arguing with the assignment, only wondering how to do it. After about thirty minutes of patient waiting by the AP (setting a clear mood and direction), the student was ready. He apologized to the class, the class told him they were happy and would help him too! Kindness flowed back and forth. After four years, someone really held this student accountable at the level of social values, instead of trying to deal with his behavior.

More than this though, this process told him clearly he was a person of value, powerful, impactful, and needed in the school community. He had overtly humiliated his own dignity and value for years in awful ways. Through the process with the AP, he may have felt shame over his behavior, but no one tried to make him ashamed. The effort was to make him more clearly valued and connected to the class than ever. He was striving and defensive for years, until he had an opportunity to answer his Essential Questions in an uplifting way within his community. He is doing remarkably better in academics and socially connected to the class and teacher in far better ways. His teacher is clearly enjoying him and values him, and he does the same back to her.

Generally, just depriving a student or class of recess or lunch means you become their entertainment. It works sometimes, but when these removals do not work, you want to move to acts of restoration and restitution. Serving time in the office or suspension room is usually nonproductive and often reinforcing. Having the student think of something they can do to repair and restore relationships in the school is far more productive and gives everyone dignity. Keep it personal and moving forward.

There may be times where you rearrange by having all the desks facing you. We rearranged a class of extremely off-task socializing first graders so all the desks faced the teacher. They had been in circles so when they looked up, they saw peers. In a middle school class where students almost constantly were out of their seats and wandering, we made rows of desks that began at the back wall. Now there was only one way in and out of rows and the wandering decreased significantly. We have used rearrangement by having all the rest of the students leave the room because someone is unsafe or having major tantrum. Once safety is restored with the student, the student then needs to do some actions to help the rest of the class and the teacher feel safe. If a small group is really off track and off task, I have had teachers split the classroom in half. Those that act motivated and ready to learn sit on one side and the teacher teaches to them. Those disruptive and not ready, sit on the other side. It is actually effective and short-lived as you divide and conquer by welcoming some back after showing signs of motivation and readiness. Soon the last holdout is all alone and usually begins to show signs of readiness and cooperation. Do not just recognize them for their behavior. Recognize them for excellent values as people. "Gabe, I see you have chosen to invest in your future and help us all prepare for a better future. Come on over, please join us." Oh, happy day, the truth in love, holding forth high values, and answering Essential Questions all in two sentences. Bam!

I usually do not recommend rearranging students who are not getting along if the teacher thinks they are capable of working it out. To rearrange them would be management, not resolution. Go for resolution and reinforce them for being open-minded, problem solving, respecting dignity, and other values citizens need. You may have to scaffold and structure a lot, but in the end, you have a better climate and culture. One creative teacher took two boys that were in constant competition for her attention and made them a team with many helper duties.

I urge you to read Diane Gossen's work about restitution and what others have written on Restorative Justice. They offer clear frameworks that cover most situations from minor home and school problems to multiple felonies. The main themes are the person who broke the rule must do something to restore emotional and physical safety to the people affected by his or her actions. Yet the main goal is that the spirit, dignity, and hope of everyone is repaired as best as possible. They may read like procedures or steps, but the purpose is to answer all the Essential Questions and values to all involved. Years ago, when I worked with victims of abuse, I used a model of repair and restoration Cloé Madanes (1990) designed. The child victims were put in the driver seat of a lengthy process whereby the offender offered full acknowledgement, full responsibility, and committed to doing whatever the victims saw as necessary for healing to begin and a better future to occur. This was always an amazing and fulfilling process for the families, the offender, and my own spirit. I was there to guard the truth, to prevent the offender from evading or escaping anything and to empower the victims so they could be fearless in dealing with the offender. The process was revelatory in power for everyone concerned. When students act out, do serious emotional damage to others, and create great uncertainty in the future as far as the possibility of further emotional injury, they are also harmed. Their Essential Questions are in jeopardy just as those of the other people involved. Can I trust myself, am I safe, am I good, am I wanted, can I hope just to name a few. The main outcome is not that there is a price paid, a problem fixed. The main outcome I am after is that of the student contributing to the well-being of others and upholding excellent values within the community over time.

Story Time: Vile

A group of 5 fifth graders were sitting in the office area to see the assistant principal for disciplinary action. A parent was visiting the school and these five boys began to speak and act very gross and vile to her. The parent made a negative comment about the school and left. The wonderful secretaries were appalled, embarrassed, and angry. This was a very good school, yet continually struggled to get beyond its bad reputation. Now bad news would likely spread. Less than 5 percent of the student body had any office referrals, yet now the entire school was likely to be cast negatively again. What restoration could happen with these students? What did they need to restore?

They needed to restore the secretaries, the parent, and the reputation of the school. How? I made a list of about 25 ways. This included the following: becoming school greeters, singing the secretaries favorite songs to cheer them up, writing news letters about the school, being escorts for visitors, improving the school grounds and décor, apologizing to the parent, inviting the parent back to have a positive experience they planned in advance, complimenting peers during passing periods, becoming mentors, making positive comments during morning announcements to the entire school, and giving mini presentations on the values in the school pledge. They could also use their own brains to think of ways to restore the school image and culture.

Story Time: Insults

By December, one of two teachers had quit as this particular first grade class was so out of control. All the students knew each other intimately as they all lived close together. There were six incredible, defiant, insulting, volatile boys and some very in-your-face- girls. By March the class had significantly improved and my visits spaced out. When I returned after two weeks, the class was boiling over with insults and harassment. The teacher was back to drill instructor. What had happened was two boys got into a big fight the day before over name calling. Now the class was name calling. It was a giant hot potato everyone was passing at lightning speed.

I asked the teacher to begin speaking very calmly, soothingly, and find all she could to love and enjoy about them. In 15 minutes the class was calm, seated, working. DANGER WILL ROGERS!! This is when teachers are tempted to stop and she did. She began telling students when they were done, they could go over to the library area of the room which meant they were separated from her! Sure enough two boys began insulting two girls and had them in tears, while two other boys swapped insults and were shoving each other. The teacher hit the office button.

An adult came in and wanted to take the two crying girls. I asked them to take the four boys and bring them back when they were calm. While they were gone, the class began a discussion of what can you do when you hurt someone's feelings. The teacher began a list on the board. When the four boys returned, they were asked the question, but had no idea. They were sincere. Peers began to help them think of ideas and one volunteered he could let someone have his turn at kickball! That seemed to spark more ideas and soon there was a list of around 12 ways to restore others. The four boys were then charged to pick one idea each and bring kindness back to the class sometime that day.

All of a sudden the teacher realized it was past lunch time and scrambled to get everyone out. During that, the most challenging of the boys came up to hug her, but she bluntly said, "Not now." He sulked off to a corner of the room. With all but us three gone, I asked the teacher, "Why do you suppose Jamar wanted to hug you?" She said,"I don't know because I've been on him for two days." She walked over and said, "Why did you want to hug me?" He shrugged. She is a bright person and came back with an answer to an Essential Question. "I have lots of hugs for you Jamar if you still need some." He jumped up and squeezed her tightly, then zoomed out to lunch. The teacher was moved and said, "I didn't know he cared." She restored the class, then him to the class, then him to her, and lastly, he restored her. I see this pattern over and over. The most challenging student in the class answered her Essential Questions after she had spoken to his. He became a positive leader, a guardian of the teacher and the class culture.

Remember that the more something repeats in the brain, the more easily and likely it will repeat. When something traumatic occurs, you want to jump in there and create new pathways as soon as possible. You want repair. I am against students being sent home for days before any repair efforts are made. The entire school loops on the trauma for days before any efforts to heal are made. I want that conversation that same day or the next day. It may be too soon for a solution. But it is never too soon for the message that everyone involved will be repaired, restored, and efforts to do that begin.

The student who threw the book bag needed restored and the relationships repaired to mutual support and respect. The student that throws a desk, cusses out the teacher, teases the hearing-impaired student, punches a big dent in a locker, or punches someone out, has just severely thrown their Essential Questions into greater jeopardy and brought alienation and more shame upon themselves. To do those things, they did not have good answers in the first place. Sitting at home separated from the people who are perhaps the best equipped and most needed for a good future will not do much to reduce the shame or fear. We have to teach everything. To me, teaching how to come back, repair, and rebuild a path to greater love is essential. It cannot just be a "try again" or some lecture about "don't do it again." **If the adults of the school are indeed the best equipped and most needed for success then they need to act like it. They need to provide the best they can to redeem, heal, and propel that student back into successfully contributing to their own future and the future of the school.**

Imagine that you are that student, and you just blew it. You just did something you will regret forever. What would you want people to understand about you? What would you want them to see in your heart and spirit as the true you? How would you want to be treated? What would you hope they would let you say and do? Now consider that you already have vastly more positive answers to your Essential Questions than that student has to theirs. Where will better answers come from? We must be a source and answer. What is the value of school if we are not a source of good answers? Where will my fulfilling education of heart and spirit going to come from when every other area of my life is failing me? Can I count on you? I hope so. **You hold the yearnings and hopes of many souls in your hand day after day. You matter immensely. So does that student.**

In the spirit of triage, list some common occurrences at your school and create some ideas for acts of restitution and restoration. Have some plans and ideas ahead of time so when repair is needed, you have some possibilities. One hilarious event (OK, not for some) occurred when I visited a school with an amazing person, Gabrielli LaChiara. Four kindergartners pulled down their pants in front of everyone in the cafeteria. We arrived at the idea of having them draw pictures of themselves with their pants up to show they would keep them up. This could have been taken another step and the boys could have shown the pictures to the people in the cafeteria so everyone would know they would not drop their trousers again. Sometimes it is just that simple. Of course parents were notified and all the other conscientious steps taken, but the restorative act was sufficient and no further incidents occurred.

Once you have established that you are after their best and want them in school by restoring them, you will automatically be infusing the climate and culture of the school with many positive values. We have been discussing how to drive values through consequencing, let us look next at driving the school with values when things are going well.

CHAPTER NINE
Building A Reflective, Conscious Mind

As you begin to drive the classroom and school with values, you are automatically building reflective and conscious minds. If school is to prepare students who can wisely manage the freedoms of living, school needs to take direct aim at building minds capable of being wise. When school aims at creating followers, carrot chasers, and incentive deals, then school is directly opposed to building wise, reflective, conscious minds. To develop self-control and emotional maturity, to sustain fulfilling answers, people need to have the ability to accurately assess, reflect, summarize, and plan. If not, then people are primarily reactive, or floating through experiences. Typically, I observe many students (and schools) operating moment by moment.

These moment to moment students and schools are not adding up experience, reflecting on what just happened, wondering what might happen, or even connecting to what they see everyone else doing. Students watch others in the class go to the carpet and do not think, "Oh, I should too." You can say to them, "What do you see the class doing?" They will likely tell you what the class is doing but it will still not cross their awareness they should too. When you ask them, "What should you be doing?" Often they reply, "I don't know." Most likely, you will need to give them a personal invitation. Some schools may hear of more successful, joyous schools yet not reflect or connect either.

At the same time they do not read social cues well, they often do not consciously process what is getting in to them or happening within them. Something pops into their awareness and they act it out. You talk about a horse and they act like a horse. You talk about being itchy and they scratch. They are reacting or acting upon something—rarely observing, studying, reflecting, deducting, inducting, making associations, or even creating many cause and effect connections. In essence, they have no internal guidance system that is modulating, governing, growing within them. They are constantly in direct experience and at the mercy of whatever comes their way. Whenever they cannot have something, it is the end of the world because that is the only moment that exists for them; or they may just go to the next thing as if nothing happened. When they get what they want, they lose interest in it within seconds because something else has crossed their path of experience. You can talk to them about the expectations until you die and they still will turn around and act as if expectations never existed.

"Didn't we just talk about...?"

As you might have already deduced, "management" does not help these students at all. You have to scaffold these students into adding up experience. You have to build an aware, reflective mindset within them and help them add time and experience up. Academically, these students usually have poor verbal comprehension. They may hear or read correctly (accurately perceive), yet not have acquired the ability to sum up, form a conceptual framework, or draw a deduction or inference.

Some students are very accurate at assessing, brilliant academically, and yet poor at discerning social meaning, weak in divergent thinking, and are so used to being externally managed that they have little idea how to handle any freedom. They may be very poor problems solvers, overly dependent of others for guidance, and not even see freedoms fully available to them. They may see the freedoms and become overwhelmed. Their thinking is bound by the situation they are in such that they have problems transposing, synthesizing, and summarizing experiences. By driving values, you will be developing these abilities.

In my experience, school does a poor job of teaching verbal comprehension because school rarely requires and rarely teaches students to develop conceptual frameworks for the life they are actually living. Not only do many students have difficulty summarizing stories in books, they usually have difficulty describing, summarizing, and postulating about what they are actually experiencing in their immediate life. Why? I say it is because there is a huge emphasis on following expectations and behaving with little emphasis on the spirit of the rules. Not taught values and the benefits of values for everyone, many students instead learn to act right, follow rules, meet expectations, and not to think and reason in the moment. The other factor is students often get pitiful feedback on what they are doing. Stop, do, now, good, right, nice job, smart, good, I like that, awesome, you are following expectations, or good choice. What kind of vocabulary is that building? What cause and effect, relationship benefits, or citizenship is articulated in these? None. If discussing social values, they are usually mentioned in the abstract, secondhand, and as something to remember. I cannot count the number of times I have watched a teacher discuss how everyone needs to behave at some upcoming event without ever bringing to awareness how the students are actually being successful at that right now. The students are not filled with the confidence that they have already mastered the upcoming event. Countless times I have listened to classes discuss the meaning of some desired value without anyone ever noting how the class was actually living that value out in the present. It remained an abstract, distant discussion where no one was reinforced, nor overtly made aware they are already in full and delightful possession of the desired values.

To build reflective, aware minds you have to ask many questions so their brain begins to get in the habit of stopping to reflect and then add up experience. How can just doing that impact your teaching? How would that improve test scores?

Again, think scaffolding. First, you want to know if their perceptions are accurate. Can they correctly report what is going on external to them? Ask many questions. What are your feet doing? What do you see Chris doing? What did you hear Nashawn say? Is your body facing forward or not? Does my face look happy or do I look confused? You want to know if it is getting in with accuracy. You especially want to know if they can perceive their body position and actions. What do your eyes see? Where are your hands? What is in your hand? Are your feet on the floor or swinging?

Secondly, you want to help them tune in to what is happening in them. What do you feel like doing? Which emotion are you feeling? Is your mind calm? Do your feet feel calm? Are you breathing fast or slow?

Thirdly, you want to help them discern what is significant out of all that they are experiencing. What is the most important aspect or the most important meaning they need to form? Are you looking out the door or at the board? Are you growing your brain by looking out the door? You go even farther by asking them how they are or are not growing their brain by looking out the door. They need to figure it out, not be told. They can see the rest of the class on the carpet. Now ask what that means to them. Do not tell them to come to the carpet or they simply obey without much reasoning. Literally, say something that they need to think. You become their metacognition. "What does that mean if we are all on the carpet and you are part of our class?" They can tell that they knocked over another students pencil box. What could they do to make that student feel they will take care of their pencil box? When you help people feel better, you are kind.

You can reverse this by presenting them with the significance and asking them to fill the details of what they are experiencing. "You are being really kind right now. What are you doing that shows you are a kind person?" This is a potent way to build the student's reflective mind because you have found them obviously doing something positive. This relaxes their brain and opens it for learning and thinking.

Fourthly, you can push their deduction and induction farther by asking other types of questions. I have watched teachers only ask questions. They give no directives or orders. "Based on what we learned yesterday, what do you think we will be learning about today?" "What do you think I am about to say?" "Are you being your best right now?" "If you were going to be helpful, what sort of response could be made?" "Although Antonio has hurt your feelings, can this be a chance for you to show your integrity?" "Why wait to play the guitars and not just begin strumming as soon as I hand you one?" "How does waiting to play help me as your teacher?" You want to expand the possibilities and help them reflect, summarize, and plan in to the future. This helps children to trust their intuition, which is often what life experiences have scrambled. They have lost their lighthouse and we need to help them find it—if not build it- again.

Here is an example of why being positive is not enough, and checking to make sure the student has accurately perceived. A teacher came up to a low-achieving student who is a frequent behavior problem and said, "When you helped Teagan, it made him want to help you too." This is certainly wonderful and it was true. It is a great example for reinforcing success while it was actually occurring. However, when I checked for understanding, the student did not get all the steps involved. How did he help Teagan? Did he know it was helpful? How did Teagan help back? Did our student take what Teagan did as something helpful? Could he tell that Teagan liked the help? Did he like Teagan's help? Once accurately perceived, the student can get the social meaning and impact of what is going on.

Usually students with the most intense needs have the most transitions, variety of situations, and people to contend with on a daily basis. They have help poured on them here and there by this and that person. We overload their ability to develop a reflective, aware mind. We give them too much to take in and, by making the help task oriented rather than aimed at the life they are living at that very moment.

This sounds like a lot but if you are not checking for understanding in real life and building their mind up to socially comprehend what is transpiring, you may not have much success on less salient, compelling tasks like books and tests. In addition, you will have felt you were being positive but the student just cannot get it. With proper scaffolding and a clear direction, the student above can learn the value of helpfulness and the reciprocity of helpfulness. This is a value-driven classroom of conscientious students in the making.

Many students need the above positive interaction with you over and over as they are so used being questioned only when they are in trouble. They are already a challenging child and have likely been interrogated, quizzed down, and investigated numerous times with heavy negative emotions. You will get poor results trying to get them to reflect when you are unhappy with them, when they are in trouble, and under pressure to come up with answers (that will most likely only dig a deeper hole for themselves). They need to learn you have their best interest in mind, are helping them in a loving way to be more competent, and that will take repeated experiences. This goes back to the foundation of consequencing discussed earlier. Do not expect to build an aware, conscious, reflective mind in a day. It takes weeks, but it is doable. After considerable scaffolding of their awareness you will be able to ask them how they are being kind, how someone else in the room is being kind, how can they be kind on the field trip, how their quiet helps others learn, and they will have detailed, cogent, congruent insights and summaries. They will be able to plan, guide, and choose wisely, all in real life in real time. Then their verbal comprehension of academics goes up. They know what is going on, and exhibit comforting confidence and trust within themselves. Scores go up and behavior improves in cycles of co-regulation.

CHAPTER TEN
The Value-Driven Classroom

As I entered the class, students were sitting all around the room and had just finished their tasks. The teacher began asking students "Who did you see being their best the entire time?" Hands shot up around the room and students began talking about who they saw being their best. Then, to some of the students not yet named, the teacher asked, "How were you being your best?" The students gave clear details describing exactly how they or their peers were being their best. Henry did not stop reading, Jefferson let Achton go first, Pouja finished but did not bother anyone still working, and on and on. This was kindergarten. This happened many times a day and was the center of the wheel connected to all aspects of the class.

In another room, the teacher had a class discussion about what integrity and dignity mean. As students shared ideas, they identified ways in which they thought the teacher and their peers manifest these values. They discussed how they might show more integrity as individuals and as a class. They discussed how to uphold the dignity of others during different difficult situations they had experienced at school. This was third grade. They were planning how to face life with consciousness and conscientiousness.

A story earlier in this book concerned a principal having to substitute in the self-contained BD/ED room. A student, who had earned computer time, was on his way to the computer but another student cut him off, and sat defiantly in the seat. Rather than fuss, the student turned and headed for a computer across the hall. The principal praised the student for making a good choice and not getting upset. However, the cut off student began trashing the room across the hall and threatened that on the bus ride home he would tear up the peer who had cut him off. The principal was trying to stop the threats and aggression, when I asked her if the cut off was right or wrong. Being very insightful, the principal began telling this wild student she was sorry, that it was not right his classmate cut him off, and she should have made the other student move because he was not being kind. The wild student stopped, quickly calmed, and announced he was OK to ride the bus and would not harm the other student who had cut him off. The principal switched from a behavior-driven room to a value-driven room. She upheld the dignity of the student. The student immediately regained his values of kindness and dignity, too.

Then the principal got both students together and told the guy who had jumped on the computer that he was not being kind and, he needed to do something to show kindness to the person he had cut off. He apologized and gave up some of his free time for his classmate to use. Now everyone had some dignity and kindness flowing again. Upholding the values changed everything for everyone.

In one class, it was time to line up. The teacher told the students she was going to close her eyes and count the seconds to see how efficiently and safely they could line up. She closed her eyes and said, "Go," and in seconds, there was a well-ordered and quiet line. She celebrated their efficiency and consideration for the safety of others. Then she announced that she believed the class to be so trustworthy and considerate of others, that they no longer needed to have a bubble in their mouths while walking in the hallway. "You can, if you feel you need it." Her efficient, considerate class walked safely, efficiently, and quietly down the hall. The teacher was scaffolding efficiency and consideration big time! Why have behavior crutches when you can have value-driven citizens?

A school spent two weeks downloading and celebrating the integrity of students, staff, and parents. I walked in and they acknowledged my integrity. Students had pieces of paper they carried all day to jot down their thoughts and observations about integrity, who they saw manifesting integrity and how, and where during the day did they see it in action. Many of these notes went up on a long wall and classes read and studied them to learn what integrity could be, looked like, and felt like. Then the school picked another value and then another. The discussions were deep and inspired. Integrity, trustworthiness, consideration, and other values grew and grew as the social reinforcement and the high bar set by the values wove and drove through the culture of the school.

In a high school chemistry class and a culinary arts class, the values of kindness, safety, and respect for others were the center of all class process. Anything less than full kindness, safety, and respect were consequenced at a high bar. When you mess with knives, fire, chemicals, and tempting colorful hot stuff in close quarters, it helps to have internally guided students. You can build students who become self-guiding and reliably handle the freedom, or you can try to guide everyone every day the rest of the year.

I was sitting in a third grade class when the neighboring fourth grade class asked to enter the room. The entire fourth grade class came in and apologized to the third graders for not being respectful and kind when the third grade class was working to improve their reading. The fourth grade class had been too noisy in the hall earlier that day. The fourth grade class arrived at this course of action by consensus after the teacher had them reflect on how they had been doing at upholding their class values that day.

At the end of every PE class, the teacher groups the students for five minutes for them to point out peers who had been kind, safe, responsible, honest, and fun to play with during the class. They are not just to say their peer was honest or safe, but also to identify how they were safe or honest. It is February and the teacher has written one office referral so far. Last year, by February he had written close to a hundred. He is having a great time teaching students to be conscious and conscientious value-driven citizens.

When three students were suddenly are silly and loudly disruptive, the teacher turned to them and told them they needed to show their dedication and kindness to others before coming to the carpet. Small limits like that are usually quite effective in helping students focus. The teacher did not tell them to be quiet, remember expectations, or behave. She told them to show up with their values again. They did. She celebrated them for dedication and kindness.

Each morning in an elementary school, students recite the school pledge. Each morning the students commit to be kind, be peace builders, be helpful, and do their best work. It did not matter what class they are in, teachers look for anyone keeping their commitment to any part of the pledge. On occasion, teachers ask students to explain how they as the teacher are keeping commitment to the values of the pledge. This is amazingly powerful as it emphasizes the social responsibility and importance everyone has to the climate and culture of the school. It makes the teacher an excellent model of how to be accountable, honest, accept feedback, and grow as a person with the help of others. It lets students learn how to speak the truth in love, help others, be a citizen of school, and to feel valuable within that community. It is powerful social reinforcement, attunement, intentionality, and precision. It feels wonderful.

A fifth grade class spent weeks on friendship. When the students ran into problems, the teacher asked them how they could solve their problems as friends. It could be academic or social.

"What do you think it will look like for you to work through this like friends?"

"Mi'Chelle is struggling with this part of the lesson. How can we help her as a friend?"

"Even if you do not particularly like someone you get paired up with, how can you still respect each other and work together in a friendly way?"

The class processed these common events through the value and standard of friendship. With a clearly defined class culture and climate, everything moved in that direction.

Many schools have trouble with students on the bus. We created "bus school". Students on the bus come together and are involved in a discussion of how they can help each other feel safe, help the driver do their best driving, and be kind. Students and drivers learn each other's names so they can connect with each other when boarding and departing. When problems occur, they are brought together to resolve it. The drivers were valued, as we made clear to students that school begins when they board the bus and does not end until they depart at the end of the day. They became a small value-driven community.

A fifth grade room has a line of value words going across the lower level of the board. Each student has a magnetized nametag that they thoughtfully place under the value they wish to be seen for that day. As the lesson is taught, the teacher will pose a challenging question to the class and say, "Who are my risk-takers today? Ah! Charles and Evita. What do you think?" He will pause class to have peers comment about each other and how they have shown their value of choice. Even the most challenged or challenging students put their name up to be recognized for positive values.

In a second grade room that blew two teachers out by Christmas, it is now April. The students also have values on small posters around the room, which they get to sign as they show the values. The recognition may come from a peer, a class discussion, and any person in the school. There are no points, no prizes, only the warm and fulfilling appreciation of others for you as a person and citizen. The third teacher began in January with TESC blazing. She is ending the year tired, yet with a classroom of students eager to learn, to be their best, and in touch with their power to extend the limits of both.

A first grader began to act out more and more over the course of 3 days. He told the teacher he was going to have to move to a foster home. He wanted to tell the class because that meant leaving them. When he did tell the class, student after student spontaneously told him about his values that he would take with him and how they would remember him for his kindness, being a good friend, trustworthy, helpful, principled, thoughtful, and more. His sadness and anguish turned to a confidence he would be ok. He had something more than whatever the future might bring, something more long lasting.

By driving values through the classroom (and the bus), you can focus your direction on continuous improvement, on getting better and better, and on how good can it get. Once this direction clearly drives everyone in the class as a community, all connections and attachments become more secure. Growth in social and academic learning takes off for the sky! I have watched many classrooms where the class is extremely patient and helpful to a teacher as that teacher sets out to redeem students other staff and peers had given up on.

By knowing what we value and how these values look like in operation, we will have a well-defined path and direction. We can take aim at broadening and deepening them in everyone and every process or event in the school. The voice of the school—through you—will be able to articulate, congruently demonstrate, and pursue a climate and culture that has a clear trajectory for deeper answers, deeper restoration, and deeper values.

The more you drive values, the more order appears. The more you drive for order, the harder it is for values to be experienced. Too many schools are procedural. One procedure after another occurs with how to behave drilled repeatedly. Stop, go, do, don't, now, not now, one day after another. That is uninspiring school when that is all there is. Moreover, I think heavily procedural management often treats students as if they are incompetent and they then act that way. Chicken or egg? I say we should assume the highest level of competency we can imagine and hold tight to it. Remember that our expectations are likely to come true because we are in the dance of the Essential Questions where we co-regulate each other's Essential Questions and expectations. It only took a few minutes for the inept girl to convince the student teacher they were both inept. It only took a few minutes for the mean kindergartner to ask for a letter home to tell her mother she was good. It is just that fast!

Why and how do we treat them as if they are incompetent? We do excessive thinking and cuing for them. When we have to scaffold a lot, we do it too long and remind the students: listen, remember the expectations, if you hear my voice clap twice, get a bubble before you go into the hallway, are you getting this, shouldn't you be…, didn't I just tell you to? And there are countless other ways in which we assume the students will not remember, won't listen to us when we speak, will talk in the hall unless they have their mouth preoccupied with a bubble, don't know when to pay attention, cannot handle anything but assigned seating at lunch, and cannot learn. We often handicap our students and ourselves with tricks and treats that become chains and boulders, and not stepping-stones to magnificent socialization and school culture. I know several teachers who routinely ask the class to consider how they could be doing better, be more independent, and be more like their career dream.

These tricks and treats are totally unrealistic and useless in their adult life. I wonder why teachers walk in the hallway with a bubble in their mouth when they could be modeling true self-control and adult behavior. I wonder why teachers clap for attention all year and never get to the real useful lesson of teaching students to be alert for the teacher's voice and respectfully listening when they hear the teacher's voice. We can easily become slaves to a procedure—like the science teacher running around helping students who had their station light on—and never get to living in freedom. By driving values and going for the highest bar you can imagine, you can bust free. You may have to scaffold to arrive at that high bar of students as inspiring citizens, just like math and science and reading. The goal is the same: learners who can learn on their own and guide their lives.

There are schools that run like well-oiled machines where the worst thing that happens is someone tells another student to shut-up or calls someone a bad name. Every day is a happy day and students are well-behaved learners. Despite being a happy safe place to be and learn, there is still the temptation just to let the machine run day after day. The bar can be raised and an exciting drama begun through the social curriculum toward greater peace, joy, freedom, and citizenship.

As an example, after a test was distributed, Josh mentioned he had not received it. Debbie piped up she had an extra and Josh could have it. The teacher said, "That's OK he can use this one." Although the problem is solved quickly, Debbie could be celebrated for contributing to the class values of kindness, efficiency, and awareness.

At circle time, a teacher asks questions and, as she began to ask another, hands shot up. The teacher responded with "Not now." She could have celebrated their enthusiasm, courage, and passion for learning, then asked them to save all that eagerness and shoot up those hands as soon as she got to the end of the question. Reinforcing the zeal and passion students bring and not thinking so much about procedure and getting something done, we can accomplish more.

In a kindergarten class, the teacher was doing guided reading while the rest of the class was at centers. She looked up and found a focused student. She then asks the class to point to someone they noticed being focused. Many point.

"Who can commit to being a focused student for five more minutes so every time I look up I see your focus?"

Many hands.

"You are so exciting!" said the teacher. "OK, here we go—begin!"

She reinforced the class value of sustaining focus and, rather than assigning a task to do, brewed excitement.

Students finished a test and the teacher celebrated how quietly they worked and, by being quiet, helped each other to do their best. "Hi-five your quiet neighbors for helping you do your best." Joyful hands. The students were so much more than doing a test. They were helping others do their best. In terms of content and process, the above examples illustrate how you can use the "what we are doing" (content) and the "how are we doing it" (process) to create a more value-driven classroom full of learners who want more.

Mr. Allen literally had 2 boards, one with the lesson, one with the class commitments and values, right next to each other. As the lesson progressed, he stopped and had the class self assess how they were doing (upholding commitments and values) as they went through the lesson. "We've been doing some really hard math! How have you been keeping your first commitment up here?" How they approached and learned subjects was just as important as the subject itself. In this way, he was able to engage a distracting student that had been bugging him to no end and scaffold him into a serious, eager learner.

As we raise that bar, we want to know exactly what to keep, stop, and grow along the way as we build a classroom driven by values. This takes having a *big* picture (values) and clarity of all the *specific* details and steps that will eventually bring it fully forth. We give those details while answering Essential Questions, restoring people, being congruent, and skillfully using social reinforcement and consequences. The climate and culture of your class and school manifests from what you truly value and the Essential Questions. To be answering Essential Questions and avidly engaging in restoring students and staff requires you to sustain certain values. The bottom line is, the greater the clarity you have about what you value, and congruently live them out, the better everyone's life will be! Get out there and co-regulate!

All day, every day, as we go through the sending and answering of the Essential Questions, we are given a multitude of choices—opportunities to go in many directions with our emotions, thoughts, words, and actions. Without a big picture, we will be all over the place and, most importantly a moving target to others. This will vastly increase striving and defending in ourselves and others. We need to stay focused on our number one priorities. We also have to know exactly what these priorities look like so we can reinforce and scaffold them in others and ourselves. Without this *big* picture of *specific* details, you are headed for stormy waters and, when they come and they will, you will have no compass or rudder to help anyone, even yourself, make it through turbulent seas. However, it is not just being ready for turbulent seas. It is about raising the bar higher and higher on ourselves and guiding the culture of school toward greater peace, joy, and citizenship.

For those schools or classrooms where the Essential Questions are not answered well, or answered in negative ways, defending and striving prevail. As a result, little growth in the climate and culture occurs because values in which people thrive do not develop within the culture of the class or school. There is a climate and culture—there cannot *not* be one—under such circumstances, but it is stagnant. No one can go anywhere socially or emotionally because of all the defending and striving over every little thing. Uncertainty prevails. You will not get patience from the class as you go about redeeming the most challenging students because the class will not experience you as doing it for their well-being as a community. Think of a good marriage or friendship where the value of commitment is assured, even through thick and thin. In some marriages, any day it could be over and thus there is striving and defending. Where the commitment is assured, many storms and challenges are met with hope and surmounted. Think of relationships where there is some addiction or severe toxic qualities that make others emotionally unsafe. The values that manifest in those conditions usually reflect fear, suspicion, incongruent personalities, enabling, and the effects of intense competition such as lose-lose dynamics.

In lose-lose dynamics I "win" if you lose more than me—even though we both lose. Never-ending control or power plays occur as people defend and strive against real or perceived danger to their Essential Questions—or even physical safety. Further, there will be a growing disconnect between what people internally value and the outward appearance of those values. The values will become hard to see and experience in others and in ourselves. We may end up appearing harsh, punitive, and devaluing as we tell another how kind they should be! Why? We are so defended and striving for kindness that we are no longer kind. At that point, no one can help anyone, as everyone has become the same. We need to know what we really value, and how the values look in action so they can plainly be seen in us. If they are seen plainly, then they can be clearly experienced and well taught. Nothing confusing is in the way of the learning, because the total experience adds up.

Consider this example: Students rush into their fourth grade class announcing they had earned "compliment" rewards for good behavior from two other teachers while at art and in the hallway. These add up toward a party. While announcing they earned good behavior rewards, they were being disrespectful to the teacher and running around the class horse-playing. The teacher and students were soon in an argument that ended with the teacher telling them to get to work and she would see if they earned the compliments or not. If the class culture focused on values, rather than some reward scheme, the teacher would immediately have recognized that the students were not being people she could compliment, and set some limits on the students to show kindness. The values of the class would be driving every second of class process. Earning a party would not be the goal. Upholding the values of the pledge and/or class values would be.

As I wrote earlier, research over the years shows teachers have significant differences in their use of positive reinforcement the academic and social curriculum. The studies show teacher responses to be about eighty percent positive when speaking to academics, and about eighty percent negative when speaking to social behavior! While students are positively responded to and reinforced at a high level for academic success, they receive little positive reinforcement and positive interaction for social success. Why do we have so many social problems in classrooms and schools? We are literally growing more problems via social reinforcement. No one would dream of being negative to students for eighty percent of their interactions regarding academics, yet research says that is the case socially. Would you ever expect to grow someone's math skills or language comprehension skills with eighty percent negative responses? Heck, no! You would literally grow more incompetence in students over time and grow more unmotivated students. It is the same with social behavior. For the most part, when teachers are saying they are positive, they are. Yet it is primarily in the academic curriculum. It is the social curriculum where there is generally inadequate positive reinforcement.

What I did not write earlier was that Beaman and Wheldall (2000) found even the twenty percent positive responses had little predictability. What teachers were positive about in the academic curriculum was fairly stable and predictable. Concerning social action or qualities, what teachers were positive about was practically random. Again, no one would teach an academic subject area like this, but we apparently are teaching like this in the social area. No one would hire a coach with an approach like that. However, there is more to this than just being positive. Even if you are more positive in the social curriculum, it has to be precise, attuned, and intentionally going somewhere. I have watched teachers give out many positive compliments that added up to very little.

YOU GOT SKILLS

Good news! You have great skills already in the academic curriculum that are highly effective in the social curriculum! Think how attuned and intentional you are with your academic curriculum. You are *very* attuned and intentional. **You may not realize it, but this attunement and intentionality is the most important aspect of your reaching achievement! It is also the most important factor in building citizens of excellence who are self-driven socially.** You got skills! Once you fire up your attunement and intentionality in the social curriculum, the academic and social curriculum become congruent in *you*, and there will be nothing in the way of learning. Once you apply these skills with zeal and direction, you will definitely achieve great climate and culture. Have a clear vision of what you value socially, give those values all the positive reinforcement you can, and have a clear—a super clear direction—in responding **with** those values **to** those values.

DRIVING VALUES OR CHASING RABBITS?

The values have to be built. If I value just behavior and following rules, if all I am after is a field of planted crops soaking up the sunshine of my lesson, then I am quite limited in building up anything in my climate and culture. Every student knows the teacher is married to the lesson, but it is up for grabs if the teacher wants to get married to the students. Some teachers run classrooms as if the dating will continue only if you behave and do not cause any trouble.

"Thank you for following our class rules, Tom."

All that tells me is I followed a rule, you know it, and appreciate it. I am seen and heard for following a rule. Many view this as reinforcing, and it is, but it is not enough. What is your intention? What is your *big* picture that, as a student, I will certainly and eventually discern? My very being will drive me to discern a story about our dance of the Essential Questions. Where is the story headed? How attuned are you to me as a person? I will download those meta-messages, and that will provide the full context and meaning to the praise. Do you have me on a trajectory building and deepening me as a person, or do you just want me to be no trouble to you? Are you invested in everyone in the class, or do you pass out praise to shame those who are having problems? Are you there to show me goodness and gifts I did not know I had, or does the room revolve around what you like or dislike?

I might get to stay on green, get a slip of paper, get to sign a chart, or earn a field trip or party. I might even get to have my name in the school lottery for a special prize. Perhaps I will hear how you like this and that about what I am doing. Maybe I will feel lucky, glad, happy, proud, better than some others because of my special status in the community. However, still I will not be on a real trajectory where there is a building up of powerful lifelong values and love. However, if you explicitly show me how I am being some value, such as conscientious, and holding the bar higher and higher on what being conscientious is all about, then you are engaging me in learning something new, deepening my conscientiousness, building me up as a person, and building up my internal guidance system. Now you have me on a journey of discovery and are teaching me something new!

If we are just telling students what they already know and valuing them only for good behavior, we are going to bore them to death and/or mostly anger them. Try having a marriage like that, and a spouse will get angry and resentful.

"Honey, you cooked dinner tonight just like you should have! Good job. I am going to put another marble in the jar so you can earn that vacation trip to Indianapolis!"

Why do we think children deserve that? I think children are far more aware and sensitive to the quality, attunement, intentionality, and integrity of their relationships than that. I think we all deserve far more than that.

I know schools where few rules are broken, where there is no tall pile of discipline reports, or students lined up in the office. They have incentive programs and prizes for good behavior, for following expectations, for achievements, and plenty of excitement over who will be the winner. I can see how they work and, yet to me, they are chasing the latest rabbit. The hook is that of excitement, being lucky, maybe next time, try harder, and, if you do, you get something a select crew of other lucky people get. A new round starts, and, if you did not win, you try to win in the new round. Try and try again. It is intermittent reinforcement, just like shopping and slot machines. Research shows that buying new things and winning does give our brain a good kick, but it is short-lived. Carefully crafted commercials make us want the next best thing. We are certainly made with a bent to covet and get a thrill from obtaining what we crave. If you convince the school to chase a rabbit you succeed at reducing some behavior problems, yet at what cost? What is the lesson to those not beguiled into chasing a rabbit?

You may get perseverance, but it is at running around the same track over and over. It may seem like change, yet it is only shopping in different places for different things, or still gambling but at different games, and ultimately still chasing a rabbit, which is a Type One change, not Type Two. Schools and classrooms reinvent new prizes, places, games, or charts as they reinvent the rabbit.

It is not a tally of points that matter, nor even the scores on the tests. It is the inner-life stories we carry about our courage, our ability to reach deep inside ourselves to be someone better, our boldness to openly love and be loved, our determination to have a meaningful life (not just a successful one), and our stories of redemption that really matter. Remember that our brain has to make stories. Those stories are the story of our life and profoundly affect our ability to cope, love, learn, and even physically heal. Educational culture that teaches students to be rabbit chasers cannot lead to courage, love, or meaningful life in any part of the school culture. When the rabbit dies, no one knows what to do and those who relied on it become afraid. What to chase now?

How does chasing a rabbit build up values and dignity? How does that promote every student as valuable, answer Essential Questions, create a community of caring and empathetic citizens, refine internal guidance systems, or deepen social wisdom? How does that truly value the voice and relationship of the adults in the school? How can that feel like love? I think such plans are demeaning of dignity and ultimately stunt personal growth. The system depends on students wanting the rabbit and chasing it. If I do, I am "good." Advertisers prey upon us constantly to chase their products so we can believe we are good or even special people. It is a total fabrication to trick us into surrendering our value as people for some moment of possible glory. Some students see right through these fabricated games and reject them. Not everyone goes for, or is ready for, intermittent reinforcement. Some cannot handle waiting until the drawing or do not want the prize. Guess what tier of RTI they fall into? Rather than build up intrinsic motivation and empathetic concern for the community, some programs want students to chase a rabbit repeatedly. Why not just build love in a real and dignified way?

With the value-driven classroom, answering the Essential Questions, and strictly upholding strong values, motivation is placed fully within the student. The student gets to show up and develop stronger, deeper values within the community. Everyone will understand the values, how they mutually benefit us, but more importantly, the values will be congruently experienced and acted upon. If someone hurts another, the value of kindness is up-held, and good feelings are restored or moved closer toward feeling safe again. Fantastic stories then occur. I can make a socially reinforcing huge deal about someone's hurtful actions or a hurtful person, or I can make a huge deal out of how people are restoring kindness and safety, thus opening the doors for more growth in our community. I can make a huge deal out of bullying, or out of healing, empathy, and pride in good things that better us all. I could punish a disrespectful and defiant student, I could entice them to behave so they can win a prize, or I could provide direct answers to their Essential Questions, get commitments from them to be their best, and then cheer on their success so they feel they are valuable as a person in a community of other valuable people. As they succeed at keeping commitments, I can entice them with their own successes. I can go further and link that student to peers who are also persistently and intentionally being their best. Then I have a building and growing culture and wonderful stories developing in the hearts and minds of the school.

As said earlier, I have observed teachers talking to the classes about some value, how the class needs to be more (value), and even identify ways to be more (value). Yet they never actually find that value in action before their eyes, or at any time in the past. It remains an abstract discussion and not a successful event for reinforcement. Remember, you want to follow the actual success with reinforcement. **By the logic of social reinforcement, if you only talk about the value, you are just reinforcing the talk!** It becomes head knowledge and something to remember on a quiz, not something occurring right before your eyes or an actual part of you. I watched several middle school classrooms discuss ten qualities of good students. Some even had students write about why these qualities were important. Only one room discussed how the students had shown any of these qualities during the lesson itself! In the other rooms, these qualities remained external and not reinforced in any students. When you are driving values, they are the center of all activities and, because they are so important, reinforced with great intentionality and consistent direction.

In a middle school one year, there was too much horseplay in the passing periods, which produced many angry, tardy, upset students in their next classes. Messages to not horseplay came from teachers as they watched from their doors during passing periods and repeating:

"Remember—no horseplay."

"Stop that! Get to class."

"Don't do that! Stop that horseplay!"

By the laws of social reinforcement, horseplay increased, as it should. Staff then switched to cheering efficiency, kindness, determination, being worthy of not being tardy, and going for every minute of education one deserves. Horseplay literally vanished. Visitors to this school are amazed by the calm, orderly transitions where students actually get to talk. Being efficient and kind and having a few moments to speak to a friend or teacher in the halls helps everyone in the school be more successful. Helping and cheering on others to be more successful became reinforced and instilled as a value evident throughout the school culture.

Many students and spouses pay us back for turning them in to just a job well done or just a winner by driving us nuts, as if they were mosquitos of bad behavior. They know in their hearts that such ploys devalue them. If you are a rabbit chaser, you still have to affirm your Essential Questions and a life to prepare for! Even if you win the rabbit, you need to know who you are in this world, and if you will chase prizes or rewards forever. **Students want to be a people who are valued, loved, wanted, and needed on a deepening journey with someone else.** Abstract discussions of values will just reinforce more abstract discussions. Most of the time, the students behaving the worst know all about the values the teacher discusses. There is an old axiom. The more you are discussing your relationship, the less you are actually having one. Stop discussing one and have one with your students.

They want you. These students, who know what to do but rarely do those things, usually get more from the teacher than anyone else in the class because the teacher is more mentally and emotionally attached to them. Their string is always taut. The teacher works hard to arrive at a coherent attunement with the student and signals it with, "If you know what to do, why don't you do it?" **If the student knows what you want them to do and does not do it, the answer to "then why don't they do it?" is they *are* doing what they *need* to do. They are getting you more deeply attached to them.** By not doing, they are more deeply attached to you than by doing. They need to do it because that is the only door you left, or they perceive left, open for them. The problem is that it is attachment through striving and defending. Driving values and the Essential Questions lets them attach through actual success where you define the direction.

What are the things that endure and thrive beyond rich or poor, beyond today or even lifetimes? I would be hard-pressed to find any educator who does not want to create lifelong learners. What a stupendous value and goal! How will this happen socially in schools? How can we create scholars of living? Is not wisdom of greater value than intelligence? Is not the act of being a teacher a greater lesson than the subject being taught? If I want to build lifelong learners, is not the desire and resourcefulness of learning more important than the amount learned? I think so. Watch the YouTube videos of Sir Ken Robinson. He thinks so, and has compelling data on how the prevalent model of education greatly decreases divergent thinking. I need to know what desire, resourcefulness, and perseverance look like in me and in students so I can build those values congruently, positively, and deeply.

I meet many teachers with excellent values that are treading water, hoping no problems will pop up, and trying to get through the day moment by moment. They say," behave, behave," daily from August through March. They are kind, patient, thoughtful, and dedicated people. Yet, the teachers arrive at April still trying to get students to follow the most basic rules, and, by May, are exhausted.

"Remember to raise your hand!"

"Don't interrupt!"

"Walk!"

They are not headed anywhere with their social curriculum. They are just getting to tomorrow. They are generally trying to advance the academic curriculum and not advancing any social curriculum, other than wanting no problems to interfere with academics. It is easy to feel this way and grind the day out, saying:

"Well, at least Tommy didn't yell too much, I think he was feeling a little sick."

"The good news is its Friday."

"I'm trying to make it to break."

For whatever reasons, they are not on a mission, a journey, a deepening of their social curriculum, or building better upon better. They would love to be teaching with their whole heart, yet find themselves retelling the same story daily rather than finding the success to scaffold into a new one. In systems terminology, the students and the teacher lock into a highly repetitive process with no new information entering the system to change it. The teacher will say, "Those students!" And the students will say, "That teacher!" The teacher and the students show up with the same old attitude. Chicken or egg? The systemic answer is "Yes." It's eggs making chickens and chickens making eggs.

THE CONGRUENT MANIFESTATION THROUGH LEVELS OF SCHOOL RELATIONSHIPS

Values of merit keep these teachers going day after day, but may not easily show though the way they respond to all the invitations and events of the day. This is why the values need to manifest congruently across school process. For example, I listened as two fourth graders argued with the assistant principal about who started the name-calling and shoving. They each argued they were not as bad as the other whose words and actions were far worse. As the other student was *so* much worse, what could he do but to come back stronger? Makes sense to me. It is lose-lose time. Then the AP pulls out the lecture, the phone home, the warnings, and starts in on the boys with messages they are in deep trouble, punishments are coming, and be afraid and regretful. Of course, these students are there almost every day. The AP is coming back stronger with the *same* emotions and threats and misery-inducing punishments the boys were passing back and forth. We typically believe this should teach them to stop, and because the AP is the authority figure, it seems it should.

However, at the social curriculum level, there is little difference between the boys' actions and what the AP is doing. It is just more of the same. The two students are not learning anything new that they did not already know to do. Do you think they will pay the AP back? They have repeatedly shown the AP that no matter how many times they are threatened and punished, they will always come back with more. See you tomorrow!

It is more of the same all over again—the hallmark of Type One change. This leads to greater, bigger, longer punishments, more inventing new rabbits, and more unwanted behaviors. Who will teach something new? What? How? They play biggest loser with each other and with the AP in this case. It devolves into power and control. No one talks or behaves kindly or with dignity and the true positive values of all participants become hard to see. No paving a path to success occurs. The biggest loser dynamic may soon jump to the adult-adult level where the administration and the teacher threaten and retaliate with each other.

"You better shape them up!"

"But what can I do? They are so bad I had to (act badly but not as bad)."

"You need to show them who is boss!"

In essence, the administration is telling the teacher to be more like the students. This is how small problems escalate into system wide problems. The same solutions propagate and actually expand the problems while adding more rigidity to the system.

Could we teach these two students to contribute goodness and kindness to their welfare and future, and the welfare and future of the class and school? If not, they are not at their best. What about acts of restoration to show themselves at their best and bring good feelings back to the class and teacher? If the AP had discussion focused on those consequences, what values would they experience from the AP then? What new learning and pathway would open up for everyone? Graciously, this is what happened. The lose-lose argument was cut short by the AP as he focused the students on a simple standard of values. He focused on the fact that what they did was not kind, not helpful, and not building a better future for the climate and culture of the school. It did not matter who was worse, only that something happened that was not sustaining important values. Now, they needed to put those values back into action in the school climate and culture.

What Essential Questions of the teacher or the AP in the situation above need fulfilling answers? If those fulfilling answers came repeatedly, what would the social curriculum from that teacher look and sound like then? Would those values then shine clearly and congruently through all aspects of the teacher's emotions, attitudes, actions, choices, words? Most likely! Our students have values, and when we can give fulfilling answers to their Essential Questions, they will shine through more clearly too. They make even arrive at new values because we have shown them something new. When we know exactly what values we want, *and* we know just what they will look like, *then* we can grow and deepen them like an Olympic coach who builds champions. We will be able to take the class/the school to new levels of social scholarship in action. Therefore, we need not only to be clear what we cherish and find inspiring, we need to have ways to enact those values in a congruent way.

Story Time: Congruent Values, Congruent Experience

There was preschooler who was violent to peers and staff almost daily. His well-known home life, which also involved social services, was unsafe, dangerous, and violent. One day this student smashed a peer between two cabinet doors. The teacher gracefully zoomed over and removed the peer from between the doors. She began to patiently, soothingly talk to him, check him to see if he was OK physically and emotionally, and comfort him. He settled down, said he was OK, and the teacher released him to another part of the room.

What did the violent student experience? What did he need in his life that he was not getting? He watched, transfixed on what was transpiring between the teacher and his peer. He was vicariously experiencing being cared for, protected, soothed, and loved by an adult. He was learning something new! If the teacher had gone over to the aggressive student and started in on him, what do you think he would have learned? What would the peer who was being smashed have learned? The aggressive student would have learned that school is a lot like home and—get this—the hurt peer would have had the same problem passed to him! His hurt emotions and body would have been second or maybe even ignored! Anger would have ruled the climate and direction of the relationships, and any grudge, lingering anger, or fear in the teacher would remain the primary emotions of the class. Soothing and hope would be dwindling away with each new outburst of aggression. More and more hurt would build in those aggressed upon. The aggressive student would induce his emotional issues deeper and deeper into the climate and culture of the people in the class and the school! This is how problems are passed like hot potatoes when we respond to them with incongruent values. It is co-regulation.

The story continues, but let us pause. Are you thinking, "I would never have let him get away with that?" Perhaps you think he needs a hang-'em-high lesson about aggression. Maybe there are thoughts this young man needs punishment or he is never going to learn better behavior. He might need a safety aid, removed from school for a few days, and/or put in a school for disturbed children. After all, the caregivers in his life are not going to be much help, are they? Well he already was in a school for students needing early intervention, was in a room of three adults, and had already been missing too much school.

What are the values we want this young man to learn? What does he need more of that will guide him to be a safe and loving friend? Don't aggressive people loaded with striving and defending already mark his life? So far, life has taught this four-year-old person that aggression is your best option. He is overloaded with it, applying it too broadly, randomly, harshly. He has already been hung higher and harder than you can legally do, and he has met far more scary people than you. Getting tough would teach nothing new, not create pathways of kindness and empathy for others, nor make school staff any different from the harsh people he has already met. Type One all the way.

To continue: after caring for the hurt student, the aggressive student was told to take a time-out and think of a kind thing to do. He did. He stood alone a moment and found a person to play kindly with. He was recognized for being kind. Just ten minutes later, the teacher called the class to carpet circle and our aggressive student was waving a sharp pointy-edged plastic square in the air near his peers. The teacher moved each student away from him, telling each one as she went "Now you are safe." The boy threw the card across the room and then he heard "Now you are safe." The teacher congruently lived out the value of caring and safety. The student and the entire class experienced it as they witnessed the teacher. They learned something new that will hopefully be a lifelong learning. The aggressive student joined in the singing and mirrored the teachers' movements. **He had someone to BE like, a new way of being that he was learning firsthand, and changing his values in the process.** All the way a Type Two. The teacher was installing the experiences of love and kindness he needed into his brain and emotions.

He can pick the card up later and might do it on his own or with a simple request. For some, throwing the card would have begun a power show and maybe become a rodeo barrel race. "You pick that up now." "You shouldn't do that. That's dangerous!" Will the student learn anything new about being aggressive and intimidating others from the adult display? **It is dangerous not to teach new values to someone who is already aggressive and doing things they should not.** If our personal example is not doing the teaching in a congruent way, we are making the lesson confusing. Remember the substitute loudly saying "Why! Why does it always have to be a big deal with you, Romero?" Not congruent. Nothing new. The student and teacher have the same problems. My deal is bigger than yours is, so quit. I can make you more miserable than you make me, so quit. What values are there in those personal examples? They are there for sure, but are hard to experience.

Remember the fussy class in which the student told the frustrated teacher she was getting what she was giving? There was congruency between the class and teacher in their fussiness and frustration. The student brought the value back into focus for the teacher and she began to drive the mood and direction of the room in a new, more grateful, kinder way. That moment really helped her see her authority. **The student was actually telling the teacher she still was the authority in the class!** There just needed to be a better direction and intention to it. She actually would be helping you be the best teacher possible.

How do you expect me to behave when you do not really treat me as a wanted, valued, sought after, inspiring person? I think few students would voluntarily show up to school to learn under the current paradigm of school. **They always show up to be seen, heard, loved, valued, needed, enjoyed, and boldly hope. I have never seen this fail in any setting!** When we do not address these issues or fight against them, we struggle to get the academics because we are at cross-purposes with human need. It is the science of attachment. The values we hold dear will align closely or in opposition to the students. When our values and actions are congruent in everything we do, we can actually teach them. They are taught by the student actually experiencing them in us.

Many of us achieved success because we did the right thing, we did not fight the system, we accepted chastisements, and learned to avoid intense punishments. In fact, we have a good life because we valued knowledge and went for all we could get. A lot of us have a large amount of self-esteem connected to the fact we know so much. We may think if kids would just learn how knowledge could provide them with so much, they would behave. Ipso facto, if I can just get them to behave long enough, they will see the value of what I and school offers them, feel the joy of learning, and then end all their silly, unwanted antics.

Of course, it is sad and aggravating to see a child wasting their education when we know so well its benefits. *However, the social curriculum first needs to benefit them.* The challenge to success is often two fold. One is our methodology with the social curriculum is often so ineffective, we inadvertently grow more problems. The second is we may communicate negative answers to their Essential Questions by whom and what we value in the class. If you are all about valuing your lesson over valuing the students, they will make you pay. Your lesson will be stuck at the launching pad and only your frustration will have liftoff. Most students have to know they are more valuable to you than the lesson, and unfortunately test this by frustrating the lesson. Your response to this will clearly let them know your values.

OUR PROCESSES AND INTENTIONS WILL MANIFEST AS OUR VALUES

There are unlimited social relationship possibilities that could manifest in a room of twenty-plus people across a building of hundreds (or thousands) of people. They will be loaded with sending and seeking around the Essential Questions. What values will you uphold by your sending and seeking? How your words, thoughts, actions, attitudes, reactions, postures, all line up (or not) will determine those values. Do you even think you should teach values? In the same way we cannot not have a social curriculum we will indeed teach our values whether we want to or not. Our actions are our morality, our values on display for all to see and experience every second of every day.

How do you want to respond to the fact that you will be teaching an unavoidable social curriculum where your values are on display and being taught nonstop? I hope with powerful resolve to teach the best values you can by being those values.

You would not begin the school year without a clear academic subject to teach, a clear academic curriculum to teach with, a multitude of options to reach each student with, and a clear outcome in mind for even the first week let alone the year. There is a popular book written about just setting up the first day of school. Would you attempt to teach without prior training and some mentoring? Heck, no! You prepare! We need to be just as prepared and goal driven with our social curriculum too. Sometimes, an academic curriculum can be sprung on a teacher at the last minute, or they are assigned to a new grade level, or a new building and room, or…who knows what! What will carry you through these changes? Your Essential Questions and values will.

PLANNING THE SOCIAL LESSONS

Do you have a high level of clarity, planning, scaffolding, and training with the unavoidable social curriculum as you do with your academic curriculum? Do you really know what you will be "teaching" via all the tones, words, gestures, choices, responses, reactions, movement, time you devote to certain social events and not others in the room? Here are just a few major aspects of your social curriculum to sort out:

What will help look like and what will trigger me to help? If I give help, what is my ultimate goal?

When and why will I choose not to directly help?
Will I be the answer machine or will I teach them how to think, to learn, to reflect?
Will I value answers or learning, effort, and zeal?
When students make fun of others, what do I want as my goal for the class?
What do I really value concerning talking in class?
If I do not teach love, what will I be teaching?
Do I want my power to maintain order or let them experience and grow their power to direct them self?
What lesson will my responses to unexpected change actually teach the class?
If I am not having a great day emotionally, what do I want my students to learn from my example of how I handle that?
How can I teach and grow kindness among students?
What do I consider kind and unkind?
When there is bickering and fussing between students, how can my response be an example of assertiveness and contracting?
Am I predisposed to seek out, go to, see, hear, or speak to someone often? Who am I the least predisposed to?
Do I want to have people pay for problems or to strengthen them so they have a pathway to success? Can I do both?
What am I already concluding about my job, my students, my peers, the administration, and myself?
What else could be possible for me to think, begin upholding, seek, and find?
When students act as if they do not care about education, how can I care about them?
What feelings and thoughts do I want to build every day in my students as to what life is all about?
What are three things I want each student to know about himself or herself by October?
What will my mood, direction, and values teach them about life?
What will I want to intentionally socially reinforce?
What is my plan, my options for moments when big trouble comes?
What can I easily take as personal that would be far better left as impersonal?

Without this level of clear *big* picture of *specific* details in the social curriculum—what you teach them about life, and what life is about—will not be goal driven nor have intentionality. It will more than likely be mood driven, procedural or want driven. We are on a cattle drive to college as a nation aren't we? When you are having a bad day, when you feel lousy and anxious, what do you want your students and the rest of the school to learn about handling these tough times? It will be a teaching moment no matter what since the social curriculum is always active and messaging overtly and covertly. What do you really, really want your social curriculum to teach? Mr. Tom was having a bad day and he…. He showed me to be fearful, invisible and stay as far off his radar as possible. Or he showed me how to focus on many good things going on. He showed me how to: be hopeful, to know we have great help in times of need, to be patient, to be kind (even if you feel as grouchy as can be), to apologize and uphold the dignity of others I have been mean to, to know it is *his* bad day and not my fault?

BE YOUR OWN COACH FIRST

Once I know what I really want to reinforce, celebrate, affirm, and devote myself to, I will more clearly be aware of what I do not want to reinforce. I will be clearer on what interferes, detracts, and fights against what I am going for. I can glue myself to moment after moment of sending and seeking what I want more of and be less set off course by anything else. Having what I want firmly and clearly in mind will help me keep authority over myself and my direction or goals for the social curriculum. Thus, I will appear and be congruent in my sending and seeking, I will be a lighthouse and not a moving target, a guide rather than an explorer, a coach on a mission instead of an enthusiastic audience, and a train on the tracks that not easily be derailed by any little tangent. One metaphor is that you are a ship setting sail for a specific destination. There will be those who love to be on board with you and those in the water kicking the hull and rudder trying to sink you or divert you off course—maybe to sail nowhere!

Your task is to keep sailing for your destination with both hands on the wheel! Keep going forward until, you are so far out to sea, those not on board decide to join you or give up. However, even though in the water, you are also continually answering their Essential Questions and hoping they will be joining you soon! This is the key to success and actually, a nonnegotiable on the list of things you really, really want. You have to want them all on board with you. Some teachers or administrators may be secretly hoping so and so will drown or at least stop beating against the ship.

This cannot be. If true, you will not be congruent in answering the Essential Questions and will not so secretly be communicating only some are worthy of the boat. This will throw everyone—even those on the boat—into questioning the safety of their existence and create tremendous striving and defending as they may be thrown off too. This is why prejudice and other forms of exclusion and devaluation are so bad. They devalue us. I was in one school where even if the students are not present, I could hear and feel how the staff did not want them. Visitors to the school made similar assessments about it after just an hour or so of being in the culture of the school. How do you think it felt to the students to be so unwanted, disliked, and thrown off the boat? They made the teachers miserable which reinforced the beliefs and attitudes of the teachers. Several times in this book, I asked "Chicken or egg?" The truth is, if we are really the authority, the teacher, the person to be respected, the most educated person in the room, then as adults, we have to break these cycles of mutual reinforcement. If not, we are just like the students, teaching lose-lose. We would not even be respecting our own gifts, talents, and the hope we have to offer others. We would not be respecting our life as still full of wonderful living. Like the students, we would be wasting our talents and withholding a treasure. What are students to think when the most educated, gifted, knowledgeable, entrusted person they know acts nearly helpless, dismayed, and unhappy with them and their chosen profession? What is the boat's destination and what will life on the boat be like? You are the captain.

THEY NEED TO BE CALLED THE NAME

Imagine you are hired as an Olympic coach. I go flying in a series of super twisty flips off the twenty-meter board and you say, "Good job, Tom—that was awesome!" I have learned zero about what to stop or grow to the next level of excellence. You are not building my skills. You do not have me on a path of greater success that I know of, nor are you talking to me as if I am or could be a champion. You liked my dive- it was awesome. I guess I will try again and maybe be more awesome in some way. Even if it was awesome, can I be a champion?

If you do not *really* think in your heart that I can be a champion, I will soon know it. Somewhere in you that belief, that vision of me, as a champion *has* to be there. If you do not believe, I need someone who does. Dr. Michael McFarland did his doctoral thesis on high achieving, high poverty, and high minority middle schools in Texas. It turned out that every school had a superb principal who built up leaders among staff, and a highly defined single focus for the culture of the school. One principal had all staff trained in teaching gifted students because all students were to be treated as gifted champions of learning. Scores shot through the roof! If you are my coach and all I ever hear from you is how well I dive, how my toes are just so, and my how straight my back is, you still have not called me a champion. I need to hear that I am. I need to hear that word. Call me the name.

You could hear about your excellent lesson plans all day but someone someday has to say, "Excellent teacher" to you. Remember the fourth grader who leaned in and asked, "Can I read?" He was not asking to read, he was asking if he was competent. He had been at the table for years but had not heard he was a reader! To his astonishment, the teacher told him he was an excellent reader and had some scores at a fifth grade level! She went on to describe his profile of strengths and relative weaknesses. He was so proud! He had been called the name: reader. He knew what to keep, stop, and grow now, but most of all, he knew he was a reader and in the game.

What effect do you imagine not knowing had on him? Now suppose his other Essential Questions were just as unanswered? What would you say to the fact he is a minority student? What would these factors likely do for him? Find someone to affirm today! Show them they are stepping closer and closer to being a champion, like a champion. Perfection is not obtainable as an end point, but students can near perfectly seek. "How are you being your best right now?" "What didn't you give up on today that you were tempted to give up on? How did you persevere?"

You actually are an excellent coach already with the academic curriculum. You know where your athletes are starting, where they need to be, what they need in the way of skills to get them there, and how to scaffold that success. You know to be encouraging, hopeful, specific, and you look for every teaching moment possible. You guard against anything that might interfere with the best growth possible. In fact, you purposefully build in teaching moments daily and have a schedule of goals to accomplish them by. You reinforce the daylights out of any success so they learn to persevere and believe as you do. I can make it, I can get it, I can have hope in me because every day my teacher says so, and smiles, and brags on me, and points to the math problem on my paper and says,

"You got it right!"

"You are learning to add and subtract!"

"Look at what you can do!"

Now I need also to hear I am a champion, your intentionality, the direction this is going. "You are a mathematician." In a classroom of EMH (Educable Mentally Handicapped) students, they are called thespians, mathematicians, writers, scientists, and good friends. "Look at how you knew what "half" was every time. You are such a mathematician!" This is not overstatement or fluff. You are not getting far in math if you do not know what half of something is. We have to be named. This level of clarity and opportunistic zeal for success is essential with the social curriculum too. As much as we think children and adolescents should already be champions at social behavior, should know what to do, or should at least want to be a champion, it is not always the case.

Academically, we build interest from next to nothing. Students learn the letter A and then, if we stick with them, support them emotionally and with the right steps of success, they will be able to write the best introductory paragraph ever about George Bernard Shaw, or a dissertation on string theory, or a love letter, or a eulogy for a lifelong friend. Would any of us really fuss at a child for not knowing the letter A? They bring what life has taught them so far academically and socially. Out of all the possibilities, students bring what life has taught them. It is their best choice so far. If something really better, dependable, and enriching had come before, they probably would have taken it. We are doing exactly the same thing. We bring them what we believe to be **our** best choices so far academically and socially. With our best choices, we hope and persevere.

I was training staff in a psychiatric school and asked the staff, "Where does hope in students begin?" They unanimously said, "In the student." Actually, it begins first in you. You are the teacher and you hold the vision firmly before them. If you are waiting on the student to believe or you stop believing, what lesson did you just teach? We have to hope first. Here are some other questions to specifically answer connected to you having hope. Will you be teaching to keep believing in other people no matter what? How will you keep good boundaries while you communicate hope to someone who has none? Are people really good and redeemable? If the student is going to a terrible home every night, can you make a difference every day? We have been answering these questions already as we teach daily. The goal is to be intentional, conscious of our answers and the impact of that on the class climate and culture. These questions and our responses to them are part of our social curriculum. Our responses will become part of the sending and receiving around the Essential Questions. What we get back will generally be what we sent. After many events of sending and receiving have occurred, patterns will emerge that begin to define the climate and culture. These defining patterns will translate as the values of the system. "Oh, that school. The teachers there are so _____ to the students." It is co-regulation and it is science. It can be an accidental process or an intentional one. This book is about being intentional.

DRIVING THE VALUES

In trainings, I have people identify the values they value the most. What values must their friend have, their children develop, and their life be a witness to? What do you stand for and what won't you back down from? People often list trustworthy, dependable, loving, kind, patient, persevering, forgiving, self-controlled, and integrity. Other values that educators commonly select are grateful, determined, just, respectful, hopeful, principled, honorable, upholding dignity, compassionate, creative, dedicated, being peaceable, and self-motivated. I like committed, being your best, conscientious, accountable, reflective, and keeping a big picture. We pick the values up front because whatever values you pick for your classroom or school will be the doorway that everything passes through, the standards by which everything is assessed.

You can pick a few to begin with, or as many as you can handle. Your values of choice will be your *big* picture. Now, how will these values appear in action in you, your classroom, in your students? Remember, we are after congruency. Understand they are rich concepts that will appear in many ways across many settings. (This is where divergent thinking is important and helpful.) You can gain a lot of insight into how the values appear across many settings by asking. I asked five preschoolers playing with a pile of LEGOS how they were being friendly and two immediately said, "We're not racing." To race creates competition and fears of abundance because you could eventually be running out of LEGOS. Have you ever thought of not racing as a moment to teach and build kindness in the class culture? What about finding "not racing" as values of "good friend," or some other value you have picked? Can you find it manifested in lining up, in lunchrooms, answering questions in a group, choosing activity centers, reading together? There are many other aspects of being a good friend and being kind. Finding students sharing, letting another go first, smiling at someone, welcoming someone, asking politely, are just a few things students do that we can use to teach them how they are a good friend and kind. By doing this focused teaching, you can reinforce and build up being a good friend, being kind, or some other value as part of your climate and culture. The more you find it, the more you reinforce it, the more it drives the climate and culture from within the students.

A kindergarten teacher held patience, focus, and being a scholar as primary values in her room. She taught what these concepts many times a day by finding students engaged in examples of them. She read books to them about these concepts, had students find her being patient, focused, and scholarly. She had students finding each other engaged in those values. When students got off track, she asked them to find their patience, focus, and/or scholarly determination again. She rarely spoke about how they needed to behave, as the focus was on the upholding of the values.

If you were off track, you brought yourself back in line with the value. This works excellently in high school too. Students have had years of "behave" and really go for being able to show up for values.

In a special high school class full of frequently truant students, most of whom had a juvenile record, some who had psychiatric hospitalizations, all of whom were way behind, I challenged myself to find "conscientious" as much as I could. I found it nine times in fifteen minutes in one student. I was attuned, intentional, stalking for conscientiousness. I found it when he went outside the door to take a test he missed yesterday. He had studied. I found it again when he was double checking his answers, when he came in the room and waited for the teacher to stop talking before he spoke, when he had sat down and began to interrupt the teacher but checked himself and then apologized. When he asked for clarification, when he wanted to make sure he was on the right question, when he told a peer to chill so the class could recover from a short flare-up, and when he politely asked who I was. Who in the school, anywhere, was looking for, finding, and building conscientiousness in to the consciousness of this young man on the edge of independent life? What conclusions did you jump to when I described special, truant, juvenile records, psychiatric, way behind? You made a story of some kind. I hope you use that ability to make new, amazing, loving, inspiring stories; not form conclusions. Make the story then set out to see, to hear, to feel it coming true before your eyes. It is all there waiting for you. Parents Are Teachers (1970) contains excellent examples of creating your own story.

You can have a wall loaded with student reports of outstanding values that can be meaningful and useful. Reading assignments, the school news, letters to parents, and guest speakers can be used to weave and drive the values into the daily life and conversation of the school. Reports from students all over the school can be used in class discussions to promote deeper comprehension of the value, serve as a visual of all the wonderful social interactions across the school, and give visitors a clear idea what the school is really teaching in the social curriculum. If someone is not showing much integrity, you can say you would like him or her to find integrity and do something you or someone else can write about. "Right now I could not say you are showing your integrity. Will you take a moment to plan how you could show your integrity in this situation?" Use the assertiveness steps if you need to. "When I see you texting under your desk, I cannot honor your integrity. Will you stop and show integrity I can honor the rest of the period by being engaged and asking questions that help us all learn?"

SHOW UP

I like to say we are asking students to "show up" when we approach the climate and culture through values. When you just tell students what to do, they either do or do not. They obey or not. When we ask students to be someone or something, they can show up. They can give us something from within them. A fourth grader was off track and wandering among peers. Ms. Patterson could have told her to sit down and finish her work, but instead said, "I am looking for you to be a problem solver right now." The girl "showed up" by getting back to her work and joined right in the class discussion that followed. A charming but frequently distressed Charley was melting down because Ms. Crull did not want to do Charley's preferred musical activity. "I am NOT doing this!" exclaimed Charley. Ms. Crull could have told Charley to take a time-out, to get over it, or that it is not such a big deal. Instead, Ms. Crull said, "I know you are disappointed (attuned) but I hope you know we will do it someday (abundance). I hope you will find your patience and join us." Charley did in about four minutes. She got to show up and did so with her best. What do they get to show up with? The class values.

I did not know his reputation at the time, but I was watching the most renowned and challenging student in the entire school doing his best to disrupt a music class. The teacher was exceptionally strong as she kept looking for kindness in the students and kept her direction flowing to the best students. After about fifteen minutes without success at derailing the mood and direction of the teacher, Mr. Renowned stopped all disruption, watched the class from a distance for about four minutes, and slowly wandered over to me. Before he could say a word to me, I knew I needed to model kindness as that was clearly the value driving the class. As he got close, I told him, "I know kindness is important in this class and you are being kind by letting everyone else enjoy the activity even though you don't seem interested in it. Note, I followed the success and telling him or reinforcing what to keep. He said, "I am. I could be doing this." He messes with a nearby peer for a second. I said, "You're right. You could." (He let me know he wants to be a difference that makes a difference and I validated that he had the power.) He sat by me at a computer station and did not disrupt the remaining twenty minutes of class. Was he truly in the lesson? No. Was he doing anything to further his reputation as number one trouble? No! Was he starting down a road of success? Yes! Was he open to having his Essential Questions answered? Yes! Was he living up to the value of kindness as defined to him? Yes! Can we grow and build more success from this point on? Yes! And we did, intentionally. You scaffold students all the time and this is an example of social scaffolding. He showed up.

In a whole school assembly of about 400 elementary students sitting on a wood gym floor, the principal was after them to quiet down. "Give me five," he said. No result. He then tried the hand clapping. "If you can hear my voice clap like this." Clap-clap…clap-clap-clap. No result. "We need to get quiet so our program can start" No luck there either. He repeated the give me five, did some more clapping, and the chattering continued. By now, teachers were trying to quiet their classes. Then the music teacher jumped up in front of everyone and announced she was looking for the quietest, most respectful students. She found a few, and then a few more. In less than a minute, the gym was quiet. She celebrated how everyone was polite and kind. The program began. Everyone got to show up and not just behave. First, someone had to be looking, have a clear mood and direction, find some success, and then follow the success to grow it. Students show up for that. They are glad to show us their dignity and power, if we let them. It is also social reinforcement and an example of following success with attunement and intentionality for the best.

Many Essential Questions are answered just by your direction and intention that students will show up. They will know almost immediately if you want them to show up and believe they will. Why would you do that? Because, you want to answer their Essential Questions to the best of your ability. You will model and transmit many outstanding values in that process. By so clearly pursuing and expecting students to show up, I transmit that students have outstanding values within them. Once students know you are really after them to show up, and do so lovingly and congruently, they will give you their best and respect you. **In other words, as you are helping them show up to be the best person possible, they help you show up to be the best person/teacher possible. They truly want you to be!** It is co-regulation at its best!

Students come to school and they want you to show them how to live and love by being alive and loved by you. They do not want a discussion, they need the experience. They want a social education in truth, life, living, and hope. Too many already know what those values are not. Once they know they are learning those, they show up for academics too. If you just sit back and watch students interact, even in the gifted classes, it is all about life and love. How do I get my Essential Questions answered? What does a person look and sound and act like who has them answered really well? What do the words sound like that answer the questions? Who will teach me I exist, I belong, I am good, I am competent at something, I can believe and trust in myself, I make a good difference, I can hope? Who will restore me when I mess up? Who will look beyond the need or desire to behave and see real values in me? I have them, who will notice? Who will hold a high bar for me so I know I am a champion of living and learning on my way to being an even greater champion? Who will show me new possibilities and build me up rather than tear me down or break me? Who will know I am the way I am because I need to know I am lovable, can give love, and need to experience it? Who can see through my striving and defending and provide?

Love is all about provision. My wife loves me and she provides, anticipates, and plans for me in many ways. School is to provide an education and cannot provide just half (academics) because the great need is not for more smart people. I do not need a smarter wife. I do not need smarter people in the grocery store or the hospital or the city council meetings. We need smart people, but foremost need kind, eager, willing, creative, joyous, wise, loving, and grateful people to show up. Most any doctor is smart. Whom do you pick to heal your inner most issues and concerns? What is that something they must have?

Authority is a word I hear a lot in schools. "Show them you mean business. Show them you are the boss. If you do not start out hard, they will have no respect for you. Don't let them get away with that." Those seem popular and are as empty as can be to me. They have no information about what to really stop, keep, grow, or head for. They just tell you to cop an attitude bigger than the one those students have. Lose-lose game on! That is what is being modeled. Expect to lose in the BIG picture.

Think about this scenario. A student suddenly kicks another and it is a hard kick that hurts. What "authority" shall you show? You could show authority by jumping all over the kicker and sternly ream them out so there is no question what they did was wrong and bad. We could guilt them and possibly shame them for being unkind and not having self-control. You could wield authority over them and punish them good. Or, you could show "authority" in a different way by first caring for the hurting student (assuming the aggression has stopped). You could express compassion, caring, soothing, hope to the victim and make sure they are restored or on their way to restoration and good feelings. Then you could address the aggressor and set limits about how they need to show up with kindness and compassion for restoring of peace and joy. You assert your authority over the values, and most importantly, are a personal example of those values in action.

What we want is for the unkind and hurtful student to experience kindness and compassion. Our actions would not only model kindness and compassion, but give the aggressor the experience of them too. We can directly install those experiences through the modeling. The aggressor was unable to contain strong feelings so we also want to model self-control over strong feelings. If we jump all over the aggressor for jumping all over someone else, what do they really learn from us? If they hurt others physically and we hurt them emotionally, what do they really learn from us about kindness and compassion? **You may think this is a hard task, and it is, but it is exactly what we are expecting the hurtful student to do. You are the change you want to see in the world.**

Your true authority in the Essential Social Curriculum certainly comes from your ability to maintain your mood and direction, but one more thing as well. It is that no matter what is happening, you can always set a higher bar for students as a person. You always have this card to play, and you are always playing it. You are never out of moves with it. This is why you restore, redeem, and never stop. They may stop but they cannot stop you.

My friend Trudy was principal of an alternative school and she would not visit students if they went to jail or juvenile detention. She told them up front. She told them she did not want to see them in those settings and only wanted images of them in school with her. One day a student was arrested at school and Trudy told him she wanted him back at school as soon as possible. He never came back. About seven years later, she orders from the drive-through window for some fast food and the voice in the box says, "Is that you, Ms. Walters?" It was that student. Trudy recognized his voice too. He met her at the window and told her how much her words meant to him that day and how he wanted to come back. "I remember everything you told me, Ms. Walters." He thanked her for the things she had told him.

What did school teach him? He was showing competency with a lesson taught seven years ago. He showed up. He was grateful. He redeemed Trudy! He told another person they were still valued and living inside of him. He had not given up. He was not ashamed. The joy he felt overshadowed everything in the past. He had joy with her. After seven years, he was the one saying, "Yea! You're back!"

You hold the authority, the last card, the final judgment, the ultimate consequence, the last move. It is always there and you can play it a hundred times and always have more. It is the message you are loved, worthy, and boldly hoped in. It cannot be taken away, it cannot be defeated, and it cannot be undone. Once you really hold this about another, it lasts a lifetime. Science and life have shown one person is all it takes to change a story, to change a life. That person is **you**.

No matter how you feel about yourself right now, go and teach your students they are loved, worthy, and boldly hoped in and inspiring to you. Do not back down or back off. They will be grateful and joyful. They will make certain you get the lesson too. They will love you back, help you feel valuable and worthy to be a teacher, and love you as a person. Say words they can always cherish, treat them in ways they will always want to repeat with others, and especially let them know they are wonderful answers to the Essential Questions of others. Tell them many times a day. Do not settle for good behavior. Build values so they have something to live by and pass on by their example. Build values so they know they have value to others and belonging in a community of people. Do not let them think for a second they are just something that needs to behave and learn like a well-oiled machine, or that just needs to sit and be a follower of rules and expectations. Build up leaders of self, conscious and conscientious thinkers and doers.

Some students have had their intuitive truths scrambled and mangled. When students experience you respecting and valuing their dignity, letting them have their power, and believing they will show up with the best of both, they might test you and see if you can be broken by what has broken them. Do not take that personally. They need someone to show them how to survive assaults on dignity and deal with twisted power. They want you to want to help them even if you do not know exactly how. They do not need you to be perfect. They need your devotion. They want someone to believe in them even if you do not know exactly why. They need your hope. They want someone to give them power so they can begin to own their life and actually be someone, even if you are afraid of letting some go. They need your courage. They want someone to show them they are lovable even if you are feeling not so lovable. They need your boldness to love. They need your vision to see beyond their current state of striving and defending. They need your compassion. They need someone to help them see they are more than their successes and more than their failures and are part a community of value, dignity, and restoration. Even if you are all about scores, data, and behavior, they need your human kindness. All day, every day of school you will be teaching your levels of devotion, courage, love, hope, faith, belonging, forgiveness, values, respect for the dignity of others, and kindness. You do not even need to say a word to clearly teach them, but it is a thousand times more powerful when you do name it. Imagine going to buy a marriage certificate without ever having to declare your love, commitment, or even that you are actually married. Name it. Declare it! Celebrate it!

A middle school teacher spoke up in front of ninety others and said, "My students asked me last week, 'Who is that man is that comes into our classrooms? (That would be me.) The students wanted to know because they said all their teachers are so much nicer to them when he is in the room." I rarely speak to the students but they know I am there to help school be a better place. They are always kind and respectful, and some quite helpful. Yet I rarely speak. What can you say to students without words? I smile. I might up pick something they drop. I let them go first. I give them space. I always respect their teacher. I never glare, stare, or single out. If they are kind to me, I thank them. I always smile back. I hold doors for them. I can answer Essential Questions and impart significance with almost no words. So can you. You already are. Do so on purpose with intentionality.

In return, students are very kind to me. Even in alternative high schools, they are kind. Students want me to read to them, hug me, hold doors for me, show me work they are proud of, and want me to be their dad, just sit next to them, and read to me. Even if they are throwing a gigantic tantrum, they never run in to me or put me in harm's way. There is nothing special about me, and they know I have no power in the school over them or their teacher. Yet you and I do have a special power; the power to impart dignity, significance and love to others with or without words.

Another teacher said she felt badly because she wanted to do so much for her students but never got to it all. You may never get to it all, but the students know you want to, are not defeated by not getting to it all, and as such there is abundance of love and devotion toward them. *That* is what they really need. *That* is the wonderful lesson they will pay you back with. Some voice, maybe from a squeaky drive up box, maybe from a surgical mask, maybe from a podium, maybe from a crowded aisle, or maybe from the across a table will joyfully and eagerly say, "Is that you…? I still remember what you said to me." They will do so because of the many messages you sent without a lot of words through the climate and culture, your mood and direction, the congruency of your answers to their Essential Questions, and how you loved them by showing them they were a treasure of values that they can use to live by and love others with.

I spoke with a young man who had caused havoc for one and one-half years before getting a teacher who wanted and loved him. He knew she was not going to let him go and he fought it. After a while, he calmed and seemed to be trying out this new idea he might be good after all. After a few weeks of that, he had an explosion before fully accepting he was a good and valuable person. He expressed great remorse over the explosion and cleaned everything up. He was right back where he needed to be in his class with a teacher who was playing her card on him higher and higher. Two months down the road from that, I asked him what he had learned from his teacher. He said she taught him he was kind, a good friend, trustworthy, respectful, and responsible. He could tell me exactly how he was too. Then he told me how he learned some academics: how to draw, how to read, and how to do math. That teacher taught him he had a future as a person in a community where he could love and be loved. She had unrelenting hope in him and made it plain. After our talk, we were back in the classroom and the best student in the class asked this guy over to his house for a sleepover! The joy on this young man's face was like the sun! He told the class he had never been invited over to anyone's house. Not once. Now he was treasured. He existed. He was seen, heard, and good. He belonged and made a difference to others. He was lovable, competent, and safe. He could be his best self and could hope. What values did he live by? He was kind, trustworthy, a good friend, respectful, and responsible. School taught him that. His success and the love of the teacher changed all his classmates too. Everyone learned something about the value of others, what values really look and sound like in action, how to handle problems, how to keep ones' dignity, how to not diminish the dignity of others, how to love, how to find the good in another, patience, redemption, restoration, and joy. I call that essential curriculum. The Essential Social Curriculum. Joy and peace to you!

References And Resources

Alliance for Excellent Education. 2005. "Teacher Attrition: A Costly Loss to the Nation and to the States." Washington, DC: Alliance for Excellent Education. http://www.all4ed.org/files/archive/publications/teacherattrition.pdf.

Ariely, Dan. 2010. *Predictably Irrational: The Hidden Forces that Shape Our Decisions*. New York: HarperCollins Publishers.

Beaman, Robyn, and Kevin Wheldall. 2000. "Teachers' Use of Approval and Disapproval in the Classroom." *Educational Psychology* 20 (4): 431–46.

Becker, Wesley C. 1971. *Parents Are Teachers: A Child Management Program*. Champaign, IL: Research Press.

Becker, Wesley C., Charles H. Madsen, Carole R. Arnold, and D. R. Thomas. 1967. "Contingent Use of Teacher Attention and Praise in Reducing Classroom Problems." *The Journal of Special Education*, 1 (3): 287–307.

Berne, Eric. 1996. *Games People Play- The Basic Handbook of Transactional Analysis*. Ballantine Books.

Blackwell, Lisa S., Trzesniewski, Kali, and Carol Dweck. 2007. "Implicit theories of intelligence Predict Achievement Across Adolescent Transition: A Longitudinal Study and an Intervention." *Child Development* 78(1): 246-263.

Cameron, Lisa, and Margaret Thorsborne. (2001). "Restorative Justice and School Discipline: Mutually Exclusive?" In *Restorative Justice and Civil Society*, edited by Heather Strang and John Braithwaite, 180–94. Cambridge, UK: Cambridge University Press.

Dickson, Carolyn Bacon. (presentation at the 2006 US Department of Education No Child Left Behind Summit, Philadelphia, PA).

Espelage, Dorothy L., and Susan M. Swearer S. 2011. Bullying in North American Schools. New York: Routledge

Espelage, D, and Swearer, S. 2003 *Bullying In American Schools: A Social-Ecological Perspective on Prevention and Intervention*. New York: Routledge.

Fabelo, Tony, Michael D. Thompson, Martha Plotkin, Dottie Carmichael, Miner P. Marchbanks III, and Eric A. Booth. 2011. *Breaking Schools' Rules: A Statewide Study of How School Discipline Relates to Students' Success and Juvenile Justice Involvement*. New York: The Council of State Governments Justice Center.

Fredrickson, Barbara L. 2001. "The Role of Positive Emotions in Positive Psychology: The Broaden and Build Theory of Positive Emotions." *American Psychologist*. 56 (3): 218–26.

Glasser, William. 1969. *Schools Without Failure*. New York: Harper and Row.

Gossen, Diane C. 1996. *Restitution: Restructuring School Discipline*. Chapel Hill, NC: New View Publications.

Grove, Tom, Howard Glasser, and Melissa Lynn Block. 2007. *The Inner Wealth Initiative: The Nurtured Heart Approach for Educators*. Tucson, AZ: Nurtured Heart Publications.

Hamre, Bridget K., and Robert C. Pianta. 2001. "Early Teacher-Child Relationships and the Trajectory of Children's School Outcomes through the Eighth Grade." *Child Development*. 72 (2): 625–38.

———. 2005. "Can Instructional and Emotional Support in the First Grade Classroom Make a Difference for at Risk of School Failure?" *Child Development*. 76 (5): 949-67.

Hester, Peggy P., Jo M. Hendrickson, and Robert A. Gable, R. 2009. "Forty Years Later—The Value of Praise, Ignoring, and Rules for Preschoolers at Risk for Behavior Disorders." *Education and Treatment of Children*. 32 (4): 513-35.

Hughes, Jan, and Oi-mon Kwok. 2007. "Influence of Student-Teacher and Parent-Teacher Relationships on Lower Achieving Readers' Engagement and Achievement in the Primary Grades." *Journal of Educational Psychology*. 99 (1): 39-51.

Kohn, Alfie. 2001. "Five Reasons to Stop Saying 'Good Job!'" *Young Children*. http://www.alfiekohn.org/parenting/gj.htm

Lewin, Kurt. 1951 *Field Theory in Social Science; Selected Theoretical Papers.* edited by Cartwright, D. Oxford England: Harpers.

Lounsbury, John. 1991. *As I See It.* Westerville, OH: National Middle School Association Press

Lyubomirski, Sonja, Laura King, and Ed Diener. 2005. "The Benefits of Frequent Positive Affect: Does Happiness Lead to Success?" *Psychological Bulletin*. 131(6): 803-55.

Madanes, Cloe. 1990. *Sex, Love, and Violence.* New York: Norton and Co.

Morrison, Brenda. 2006. School Bullying and Restorative Justice: Toward a Theoretical Understanding of the Role of Respect, Pride, and Shame. *Journal of Social Issues*. 62 (2): 371-92.

Novotney, Amy. 2009. "Resilient Kids Learn Better." *Monitor on Psychology*. 40 (9): 32-3.

Perry, Bruce D. 2006. "Keeping the Cool in School: Promoting Non-Violent Behavior in Children." *Early Childhood Today*. http://www.teacher.scholastic.com/professional/bruceperry/cool.htm

Shores, Richard E., Susan L. Jack, Philip L. Gunter, David N. Ellis, Terry J. DeBriere, and Joseph H. Wehby. 1993. "Classroom Interactions of Children with Behavior Disorders." *Journal of Emotional and Behavioral Disorders*. 1 (1): 27-39.

Siegel, Daniel J. 1999. *The Developing Mind: Toward a Neurobiology of Interpersonal Experience.* New York: Guilford Press.

Skinner, B.F. 1974. *About Behaviorism.* New York: Random House.

Skinner, B.F. 1968. *The Technology of Teaching.* Des Moines, IA: Meredith.

Skinner, Ellen, and Michael J. Belmont. 1993. "Motivation in the Classroom: Reciprocal Effects of Teacher Engagement and Student Engagement across the School Year." *Journal of Educational Psychology*. 85 (4): 571-81.

Slee, Roger. 1995. *Changing Theories and Practices of Discipline.* Oxon, UK: Routledge.

Sutherland, Kevin S., Joseph H. Wehby, and Paul J. Yoder. 2002. "Examination of the Relationship Between Teacher Praise and Opportunities for Students with EBD to Respond to Academic Requests." *Journal of Emotional and Behavioral Disorders*. 10 (1): 5-13.

Twemlow, Stuart W., and Frank C. Sacco. 2008. *Why School Anti-Bullying Programs Don't Work.* Lanham, MD: Rowman & Littlefield.

Watzlawick, Paul, John Weakland, Richard Fisch, and Milton Erickson. 2011. *Change: Principles of Problem Formation and Problem Resolution.* N.Y.: Norton

Willis, Judy. 2007. "The Neuroscience of Joyful Education." *Engaging the Whole Child*. 64 (9). Alexandria, VA: ACSD. http://www.ascd.org/publications/educational-leadership/summer07/vol64/num09/The-Neuroscience-of-Joyful-Education.aspx Summer 2007, V64. www.essentialsocialcurriculum.com

www.ingramcontent.com/pod-product-compliance
Lightning Source LLC
Chambersburg PA
CBHW080548170426
43195CB00016B/2718